PROFESSORS, PATRONAGE AND POLITICS
The Aberdeen Universities in the Eighteenth Century

Quincentennial Studies Series

THE STUDENT COMMUNITY AT ABERDEEN 1860–1939 (1988)
R D Anderson

ABERDEEN UNIVERSITY 1945–1981: REGIONAL ROLES AND NATIONAL NEEDS (1989)
edited by John D Hargreaves with Angela Forbes

KING'S COLLEGE, ABERDEEN 1560–1641: FROM PROTESTANT REFORMATION TO COVENANTING REVOLUTION (1990)
David Stevenson

BAJANELLAS AND SEMILINAS: ABERDEEN UNIVERSITY AND THE EDUCATION OF WOMEN 1860–1920 (1991)
Lindy Moore

Forthcoming titles include:

THE ABERDEEN ENLIGHTENMENT: THE ARTS CURRICULUM IN THE ABERDEEN UNIVERSITIES 1717–1800
Paul B Wood

THE STUDENT COMMUNITY AT ABERDEEN BEFORE 1860
Colin A McLaren

THE UNIVERSITY AND THE STATE IN THE TWENTIETH CENTURY: THE EXAMPLE OF ABERDEEN
Iain G C Hutchison

QUINCENTENNIAL STUDIES
in the history of
THE UNIVERSITY OF ABERDEEN

PROFESSORS, PATRONAGE AND POLITICS
The Aberdeen Universities in the Eighteenth Century

Roger L Emerson

Published for the University of Aberdeen by
ABERDEEN UNIVERSITY PRESS

First published 1992
Aberdeen University Press

© University of Aberdeen 1992

All Rights Reserved. No part of this publication may be reproduced, stored in a retrieval system or transmitted in any form or by any means: electronic, electrostatic, magnetic tape, mechanical, photocopying, recording or otherwise, without permission in writing from the copyright holders.

British Library Cataloguing in Publication Data

A catalogue record for this book is available from the British Library

ISBN 0 08 040916 4

Typeset and printed by AUP Glasgow/Aberdeen—a member of BPCC Ltd.

For my mother
Doris Sanders Emerson

Foreword

In 1995 the University of Aberdeen celebrates five hundred years of continuous existence. Some eighty other European universities had been established before 1500, of which about fifty have survived to the later twentieth century, though not all of those with an uninterrupted history. At Aberdeen, King's College and University was founded in 1495, and Marischal College in 1593, the two combining to form a single university in 1860. Such a long institutional life invites close historical study, as well as celebration; but the 1980s were not an easy time for British universities, and it is therefore the more striking that in 1984 the governing body of the University of Aberdeen decided to commission a series of historical studies in honour of the quincentenary. The decision to commit funds to this project, and to give the Editorial Board such a free hand as we have had, makes the University Court's decision the braver and more honourable.

This fifth volume in our Quincentennial series, together with the sixth which will shortly follow it, deals with the eighteenth century—academically one of the most distinguished periods in the university's history. Both volumes are by Canadian scholars who have specialised in the Scottish Enlightenment. Professor Roger L Emerson here studies the professoriate of the two Aberdeen colleges, while Dr Paul B Wood in the next volume to be published will deal with the university's curriculum.

Professors, Patronage and Politics is an exceptionally thorough study of the men who held appointments at King's and Marischal in the period between Britain's Glorious Revolution and the French Revolution. Only by a long familiarity with the academic and political worlds of that time could justice be done to the complexities here revealed. The intricate stories of academic and national patronage and politics are firmly placed in the context of British and European attempts during the eighteenth century to assimilate separate regions and cultures. The political element in university appointments is overwhelmingly clearly documented—but the author recognises equally clearly, and explains, why these appointments were usually given to able scholars, rather than to mere party adherents. In some ways, Marischal College, which was more open to political intervention in its appointments, especially after 1715, fared better than did King's, which remained more of a closed community, though not one wholly immune to outside influences.

The general editor is grateful to a number of people who have been particularly helpful at different stages in the production of this volume. Dr Nicholas Fisher was the original commissioning editor, and editorial advice was also given by Dr David Stevenson and Mr Donald Withrington. Assistance in locating illustrations was given by Mr Colin McLaren (University Archivist), Mr Iain Beavan and Miss Myrtle Anderson-Smith (Special Collections, University Library), Mr Charles Hunt (Curator of the Marischal Museum), and by the staff of the Scottish National Portrait Gallery. Professor Carol Gibson-Wood identified the Blackwell portrait in the Pierpont Morgan Library. The owners and keepers generously gave permission for these illustrations to be used in this volume. At Aberdeen University Press Miss Marjorie Leith, herself a graduate of the University of Aberdeen, has given the present book, as also the earlier volumes in this series, her devoted and meticulous attention.

JENNIFER CARTER
General Editor

Contents

FOREWORD		vii
LIST OF ILLUSTRATIONS		xi
AUTHOR'S PREFACE		xiii

CHAPTER 1   Contexts

I	The Political Contexts	1
II	Aberdeen and British Politics, 1690–1800	9
III	The Universities and Colleges	14

CHAPTER 2   The Jacobite Colleges, 1690–1717

I	King's College and University	18
II	Marischal College and University	26
III	1715 and the Purging of the Colleges	32

CHAPTER 3   The Squadrone and the Argathelians, 1717–1730

I	The Squadrone Years at Marischal College, 1717–24	35
II	King's College and University, 1717–25	38
III	The Growth of an Argathelian Interest	45

CHAPTER 4   The Argathelians, 1730–1761

I	Marischal College, 1730–42	59
II	King's College, 1730–41	59
III	Family and Party Contests at King's and Marischal Colleges, 1741–5	63
IV	Argyll's Second Period of Power, 1746–61: Marischal College	70
V	Argyll's Second Period of Power, 1746–61: King's College	74

CHAPTER 5   The Universities and Colleges, 1761–1800

I	King's College With and Without the Tutelage of Outsiders, 1745–85	78
II	Marischal College and the 3rd Earl of Bute, 1761–85	87

    III   The Union Crisis and the Consolidation of Henry
           Dundas's Regime, 1785–1800   93

CONCLUSION   102

ABBREVIATIONS   107
NOTES   108
APPENDICES   131
BIBLIOGRAPHICAL NOTE   174
INDEX OF NAMES   175

List of Illustrations

1	G & W Paterson, *A Survey of Old and New Aberdeen*, 1746	15
2	George Keith, 10th Earl Marischal	16
3	Front view of old Marischal College	27
4	Thomas Blackwell II	33
5	John Ker, 5th Earl and 1st Duke of Roxburghe	37
6	Archibald Campbell, 3rd Duke of Argyll	44
7	Patrick Duff	46
8	Lord Milton	49
9	Thomas Reid	68
10	James Beattie	71
11	James Hay Beattie	71
12	George Campbell	73
13	John Chalmers	75
14	South-east view of King's College	79
15	James Deskford, 4th Earl of Seafield	85
16	John Stuart, 3rd Earl of Bute	88
17	Henry Dundas	94
18	The 'Seven Wise Men'	98

Author's Preface

This monograph on Aberdeen's universities is related to a longer on-going study of the Scottish professoriate 1690–1800. Visitation commissions left 24 regents and professors in place in 1690, and 330 or so other men were appointed to chairs in the Scottish universities before 1800. Of the over 450 appointments which these men received, something is known about 80 per cent. There is quite a lot of information on about 65 per cent of the cases, and it is possible to be reasonably certain about the circumstances surrounding 41 per cent of the appointments. The sources of information pertaining to the Universities of Glasgow and Edinburgh are the best and fullest. They are poorest for St Andrews, with the Aberdeen institutions falling in between. These sources and a host of others have been used to compile the materials on the professoriate which appear in the appendices. It is from this wider study that I have come to the views of the Aberdeen colleges expressed here.

    The institutions of Old and New Aberdeen in most respects resembled the other Scottish colleges and universities. King's was more family-dominated, more nepotistic and more faction-ridden. Marischal after 1715 was a place in which the recruitment of teachers was handled by the crown's Scottish political managers. King's remained a largely closed corporation; Marischal was much more responsive to outside influences. It offers a good example of what local interests and Scottish politicians expected a university or college to be and do. My perspective on the Aberdeen institutions is one which is national and British, not one which is local and provincial. The sources for it have been found in Edinburgh and Glasgow nearly as often as in Aberdeen. In this respect this monograph breaks, as do others in this series, with the tradition of writing about the colleges largely from sources in Aberdeen.

    Until quite recently eighteenth-century Aberdeen has been rather ignored by students of Scottish culture and politics, although its Jacobites have received more attention than they probably deserve. The tendency has been for historians to see the North East and its capital in a provincial perspective which emphasised its remoteness and isolation from the concerns of other Scots. There is, of course, something in that. Years of economic decline had perhaps made the region more conservative by 1700 than was the case elsewhere. A distinctive and religiously based high culture, so nicely studied by G D Henderson, seemed to set Aberdeen and its region apart from other areas in Scotland. Aberdonians often seemed to share neither the values, economic vicissitudes nor the piety of other Scots. Aberdeen's universities have also not drawn the attention which has been lavished on those in Glasgow and Edinburgh. Small, poor, neglected and seemingly unimportant, the northern colleges have escaped much scrutiny. This study seeks to address some of the shortcomings of such views. It does so by concentrating upon the political contexts in which university appointments were made. These appointments may have been local affairs, but they often involved Scottish politicians in Edinburgh and London, and they point to Aberdeen's place in a national political system. Affected by ideology, by the patronage practices accepted by all during the eighteenth century and by the needs of the state to control and order life throughout Britain, Aberdeen's political values and experiences during the eighteenth century had more in common with those of other Britons than is often realised. The best way to show this is through prosopographical techniques.

Aberdeen university and college appointments during the eighteenth century had a double political context. On the one hand they related to the interests of local men—professors, noblemen, town councillors, clerics—who expected their protégés to be loyal and to support within the educational corporations the values and beliefs which they themselves held. On the other hand there was an extra-regional component to nearly every professorial appointment. This came from the fact that patronage networks extended outside the city and region and were controlled and manipulated by politicians in Edinburgh, London and, with Jacobites, perhaps even Europe. Many outside the North East felt they had a stake in appointments and sought to influence them. To do so was the objective of the visitation commissions in the 1690s and in 1716–17. It was the objective of the Kirk and a concern of political factions active throughout the century. To show how these various politicians worked and how successful they were is one of the aims of this study. Another is to provide information on as many appointments as possible. Many of the sources relevant to this contain further information about the professors, some of it unknown and hitherto unused.

My work on this project has been aided by many people who deserve

AUTHOR'S PREFACE

thanks. Dr Dorothy Johnson, Mr Colin McLaren, Dr Andrew Cunningham, Dr Gordon DesBrisay, Miss Judith Cripps, Mr Jack Baldwin, Dr Douglas Duncan and the late Mr C P Finlayson have all supplied me with information which I would never have found by myself. I am grateful to the Keepers of Manuscripts at the Scottish Record Office, the National Library of Scotland, the Universities of Edinburgh, Glasgow, St Andrews and Aberdeen, and to Miss Joan Ferguson, Librarian of the Royal College of Physicians of Edinburgh, for permission to cite manuscripts. To Paul Wood of the University of Victoria and to my colleagues in the Interdisciplinary Seminar on the Eighteenth Century at the University of Western Ontario, in particular to Professors I K Steele and F A Dreyer, I am also indebted for criticism and advice. To Laura MacFadden who typed this manuscript, to my wife, Jean Dalgleish, and to my editors, Dr Jennifer Carter and Dr Nicholas Fisher, I owe a special debt.

Chapter 1

Contexts

I The Political Contexts

British politics from the Glorious Revolution to the French Revolution can be characterised in many different ways. Each of those which follow bore upon the history of the Scottish universities and affected what happened in both Old and New Aberdeen and in their colleges.

At one level, British political history resembles that of every other sizeable European state in which stable, centralised and national government emerged in the seventeenth and eighteenth centuries. That story is one of the integration of culturally distinct regions, possessing particular and unique institutions, into larger units governed in a more uniform manner from one centre by figures whose outlook was increasingly national rather than regional, provincial or local. Understandably, these national politicians tended to come from the largest and most populous regions. From this perspective, British politics in the period 1688–1800 saw the partial assimilation of Highland and Lowland Scotland, of Wales and Ireland, but also of the English regions and counties, into one governmental system run from London and from regional, but no longer autonomous, administrative centres such as Dublin and Edinburgh. Nowhere in Europe was this transition easy or one which progressed steadily and without violence. Opposition from many groups with vested interests in the maintenance of an older order was intense and often successful. In Scotland the processes of integration had long been operating; they had even produced a union of England and Scotland during the Commonwealth of the 1650s. That had dissolved at the Restoration when legislation obnoxious to the restored king and his friends was repealed. Among those laws were the ones enforcing the union of King's and Marischal College into one Caroline University (1641, 1654).[1] But the process of integration did not stop. It can be charted in a series of steps during the eighteenth century of which the following were perhaps the most important: the establishment of the Hanoverian succession (1704); the abolition of the Scottish army and navy and of the Scottish parliament (1707); the abolition of a Scottish executive body, the Privy Council (1708); the imposition, despite the Act of Union's reservations concerning the Scottish law and courts, of a British supreme court which could overrule the sovereign courts of Edinburgh (1710); the curbing of the pretensions to independence in the Kirk (1690, 1712, 1784); the gradual alignment of the administrative and fiscal systems of the two kingdoms (*c*.1708–*c*.1780s); the disarming of Highlanders (1716, 1746); the abolition of feudal tenures and heritable legal jurisdictions (1747); the effort to 'civilise' the Highlands through military and economic means (from the 1690s onwards); the efforts to apply the same laws, particularly those concerning treason, in both England and Scotland (1709–1790s). Not to be divorced from these political events and trends were those which opened English markets to Scots and which by 1800 had produced a British economy showing a high degree of integration.[2]

British political and economic integration was brought about by secular means. King William might rule his kingdoms by the grace of God, but he and his successors did so equally by the acts of very human conventions and parliaments. Hereditary, divine-right monarchy, along with its implicitly absolutist pretensions, had been mortally wounded in 1688–9 although its complete overthrow would take much longer.[3] After 1689 it was difficult to defend religiously based monarchical political theories; few who did so were likely to be given patronage by those actively engaged in British politics. The political theories which justified the rule of Dutch and German kings in Britain looked back to the 'ancient constitution', to natural law and contract theories, to Machiavelli, Hobbes and Harrington, or to utility. In no case did they provide a large role for religion in the affairs of state. Indeed, they demanded that the pretensions of established churches be curbed as the price of their protection and support. Religion was not divorced from politics but it was expected that religious belief, behaviour and religious institutions would in some ways conform to what politicians found reasonable.

The restored Presbyterian Kirk of the 1690s could not thoroughly reform and purge Scotland as many of its ministers wished to do. The king and many in the social *élite* would not have that.[4] The Kirk could try to police the universities and it did so from the 1690s to the 1740s at Glasgow, Edinburgh and St Andrews. In Aberdeen, the local gentry protected religious deviants whose ecclesiology and piety were not those of the south, and bigoted Presbyterians (like those who hanged Thomas Aikenhead in 1697) found no place in Aberdeen.[5] By 1712 the Kirk had been forced to tolerate worship using the Anglican service book, and the gentry were again free to choose their parish ministers—a right which in the end worked for moderation in the Kirk and against Evangelicals.[6] By the 1740s it had become impossible to place the latter in the professorial chairs of Scottish colleges.

As late as 1745 the Kirk could block David Hume's appointment to the chair of moral philosophy at Edinburgh. Technically it everywhere retained its right to consent to university appointments, but this right was not used in the second half of the eighteenth century and went by the board in 1806 in the famous case involving John Leslie at Edinburgh University. Leslie was allowed to subscribe to the Confession of Faith even though he was a sceptic or fideist. By the 1780s, Scotland's best systematic theologian, George Hill of St Andrews, had reached an ecclesiastical position which was little better than Erastian. As a Church politician he found it easy to work with Henry Dundas, the political manager of the kingdom from c.1780 to 1806. Professors should and would conform to the established Kirk when appointed, but there was far less serious inquiry into their religious views after about 1750 than there had been in the thirty years after the 1690s. One reason for this was the convergence of the theological views of Calvinists like Hill and those Anglicans who chiefly supplied the materials for his sermons and theology.[7] Scottish Moderatism which set the tone for the established Church in the latter half of the eighteenth century was reasonable, tolerant and able to allow a larger role to the state than had the men who guided the General Assemblies of the early years of the century.

Secularity of outlook did not bring indifference to religion but it put a different value upon faith and upon the expressions of it. Religion came to deal more with this world, with morality and reasonable behaviour and less with a transcendant God faced by the individual in prayer, communion and public worship. At the same time the function of the universities changed partly as a reflection of these trends. The colleges shifted from providing a fairly narrow scholastic training, which had often culminated in the education of ministers, to offering a far more liberal, polite, useful and scientific education. This was largely designed for men who expected to be employed in a competitive world in which useful knowledge was a necessary asset. Useful now referred to the understanding of the natural and social worlds, not to the way to find happiness here and hereafter.[8] As the ideological orientation of the colleges shifted, there was a decline in the importance and presence of the religious within their walls. This went a long way towards opening the universities to the new sciences, to their methods and to new moral and political theories based on these. It was equally important in the inculcation of the values of politeness and utility which in Scotland as elsewhere were among the hallmarks of the Enlightenment. These changes came earliest to Glasgow and Edinburgh, but Marischal College was not far behind. The regents at King's seem to have been later in accepting them.

Alongside assimilation and secularisation, a third characteristic of British politics during the eighteenth century was its pursuit by groups which were usually as devoted to the economic and power interests of the men and families which composed them as to any ideological principles or ends. Power was sought for gains measured in terms of places of profit and honour, places useful for the garnering of more of the same. Great men sought great offices for themselves. For their kinsmen, dependants, servants and followers, they sought to obtain every place and office they could get. Obtaining such posts maximised their power. In a university context it also meant shifting obligations to chaplains, tutors, governors and friends on to others; and the patron's prestige went up and his expenses went down when his protégés got academic jobs.

The lust for patronage and position extended far beyond the offices of state. Church livings, university chairs, municipal offices, posts in corporations of every sort, as well as places in the households of the great and well-to-do tended to form a single system in the minds of those who administered patronage. For a Duke of Argyll there was no clearly defined line between what he did as a private person bestowing a job and what he granted as a political figure. In each case he expected loyalty from the recipient and a willingness to support the Argathelian interest. Recruitment in most institutions was political. This was as true of the universities as of any other corporations having livings of some value.[9]

From 1689 to 1800 the political groups which mattered in Scotland centred on the great noblemen without whom the government could not control the country: Marchmont, Roxburghe, Queensberry, Tweeddale, Buccleuch, Hamilton, Douglas, Montrose, Stair, Atholl, Gordon, Argyll and the representatives of other families whose titles had been lost through political miscalculation or misfortune—Mackenzie, Stewart, Drummond, Keith and perhaps a few others. Dependent on those grandees were lesser noblemen and lairds whose ranks supplied the professional classes. From those were drawn the political managers of the great houses and of the unstable groups which their leaders formed. Thus, we find men like Sir John Clerk of Penicuik, Mungo Graham of Gorthy, Andrew Fletcher of Saltoun, Thomas Hay of Huntington and Henry Dundas closely associated with and acting for the 1st Duke of Queensberry, the 1st Duke of Montrose, the 2nd and 3rd Dukes of Argyll, the 4th Marquis of Tweeddale and the 3rd Duke of Buccleuch when these magnates were among the most prominent supporters of parties which sought power in the government of Scotland both before and after the Union. How they organised their activities is of some interest.

From 1689 to about 1708 patronage in Scotland, particularly that of the universities, seems to have been relatively uncontrolled by a central office. That of the crown went through the hands of the secretaries and chancellor.

Divinity posts usually involved Edinburgh clerics like Principal William Carstares (d. 1715) or Glasgow's Principal John Stirling (d. 1727). Other places were secured from their legal patrons by a variety of people seemingly unconnected with one another or with the government. By 1708 greater order had come into the awarding of places. This was partly a consequence of William Carstares's ability to keep his eye on affairs at Glasgow and St Andrews. He was related to Principal Drew at St Leonard's College and to professors at Glasgow. Carstares was an efficient man who seems to have worked well with Lords Seafield and Mar; from around 1706 to 1714 they were the crown officials most involved with university patronage. Also important to Carstares's effectiveness were correspondents whom he could trust at the universities. In King's College he found one in George Gordon the elder, and later in David Anderson. At Marischal he seems to have had none until 1711 when Thomas Blackwell became professor of divinity.[10] By that time Principals Carstares of Edinburgh, Stirling of Glasgow, Drew and Hadow of St Andrews and Dr Blackwell of Aberdeen were all actively and jointly involved in Church affairs and eager to see the colleges guided in the 'right' direction through the recruitment of sound men. They also all had ties of one sort or another to leading members of the Squadrone faction in politics which replaced Mar and his friends as Scottish managers after the death of Queen Anne in 1714.

The Squadrone was a Whig faction led in 1714 by the 1st Duke of Montrose, a chancellor and benefactor of Glasgow University. He was given the office of secretary of state for Scotland, a position which he surrendered in 1715 to the 1st Duke of Roxburghe who kept it until 1725. Under the Squadrone lords Carstares kept his power and may have improved the system for the administration of patronage—his fragmentary correspondence suggests that he did. The Squadrone's system is nicely described in a letter of 1742 from James Erskine, Lord Grange, to the Marquis of Tweeddale. Grange recollected that the Squadrone had had regular correspondents in the principal burghs and corporations. These had written to an Edinburgh manager or *sous-ministre* who had forwarded their information, along with his own recommendations, to London, where a committee of five or six Scots from this faction had made decisions which were then given to Roxburghe or to others who might be involved in implementing them. This scheme Grange wanted revived in 1742.[11] Tweeddale did then produce a variant of it. Thomas Hay became his chief Edinburgh agent with ecclesiastical matters handled by Robert Wallace and by Thomas Tullideph, principal of St Leonard's College. Hay was advised in Edinburgh by Robert Dundas and Alexander Arbuthnot, but it was Hay's letters which went to Tweeddale in London.

When the Squadrone lords lost power in 1725 they were replaced by a faction led by the 2nd Duke of Argyll and managed by his younger brother, Archibald Campbell, 1st Earl of Ilay and, after 1743, the 3rd Duke of Argyll. The Argathelians used a system similar to that which Grange described. Correspondents sent their information and requests to Andrew Fletcher, Lord Milton, in Edinburgh. He sorted these, commented on them and sent recommendations to Ilay in London. There Ilay came to decisions, took the appropriate actions and eventually sent back to Scotland his judgements, crown warrants and whatever. Just as we know that Tweeddale in 1742 found correspondents at Glasgow, Edinburgh, St Andrews and Aberdeen (Thomas Blackwell the younger), we also know that by 1728 Ilay had reliable informants in every university. From the 1720s until they lost power in 1742 at Walpole's fall, Ilay and Milton operated their system. They revived it in 1746 when they again managed Scottish affairs for the British government. Their system lasted until about 1765 when ministerial instability in London made it difficult to maintain a coherent patronage organisation. When politicians were out of power, they and their friends concerted opposition measures through their old channels.

From 1766 to about 1778 no one faction held a dominant position in Scottish affairs. Crown patronage was influenced by many people and groups.[12] The most organised political force in Scotland was probably the Moderate Party in the Scottish Kirk. While it meddled little with parliamentary politics or with patronage outside the Kirk and universities, it did influence appointments in most of the colleges. Its effectiveness was increased by the fact that its leaders generally supported the government and were supported by it.[13] By 1778 or so, Henry Dundas had begun to put together a party which would remain the dominant Scottish political faction until the reforms of the 1830s. By 1784 Dundas had beaten back the attacks of the Foxite Whigs, led in Scotland by the Erskine brothers— Henry and David, 11th Earl of Buchan. Just as the rebellions of 1715 and 1745 helped the Squadrone and the Argathelians to consolidate their power, the Scottish reactions to the American and French Revolutions helped Dundas to do so. By the early 1790s he deserved his nickname, 'Harry the 9th'.

The universities were clearly part of the patronage system which all political leaders aspired to control, and it was not just regius chairs or the sensitive ones in the divinity halls which they wished to fill. Correspondence concerning virtually every post occurs in the papers of the managers. Carstares worried about regents and professors of Greek. Montrose kept a sharp eye on Glasgow. The papers of Lord Milton or Henry and Robert Dundas contain letters on nearly every chair. If there is an exception to those statements it is offered by King's College which was so structured as to make the interference of outsiders difficult.

In part the concerns of politicians were ideological. No Jacobites were to be appointed and probably none were at Edinburgh and Glasgow after 1690. After the rebellion of 1715 that would have been impossible anywhere. The major reason why the politicians were interested is that these university places provided good livings and appropriate rewards for some of the people who served them and whom they had to serve. Appointees in a general way reflected their patrons' ideological values and interests. Since loyalty was a reciprocal relation for clients and patrons, this kept the professors unalienated from the political nation from which, in any case, many of them also came. Identity or similarity of outlook was an important condition for sponsorship and generally meant that candidates for university jobs shared their patrons' increasing interests in polite, useful and novel subjects and in improvements of every kind. Since most candidates resembled each other in these respects and were about equally well recommended, it was often easiest for politicians to pick the most talented men. Talent in this part of the patronage system certainly counted.

Dullards could not be appointed because they would not attract students to the institutions where the masters lived by fees as well as salaries. Moreover, to give a post to a poor teacher would be doing him no favour. Colleagues who found their fees diminished by the poor teaching of one of their number could be expected to harass such a man. There were unwritten minimal standards of competence which were almost always observed. Similarly, there were standards of morality, conduct and manners which were seldom breached. Scandalous professors no one wanted. Scotland was also very fortunate that, until the Dundas era, the principal political managers were themselves men of intellect and improvers who tended to pick the bright and the best when they felt they could do so. Carstares, Roxburghe, Ilay, Bute, and the Moderates gave the kingdom its most impressive intellectuals, doctors and scientists and very much helped to create the Scottish Enlightenment.

British politics was only partly a search for patronage and office. Because it was assimilationist it also had to be ideological. Nowhere was it more so than in Scotland. From Scots, not Englishmen, changes were required, many of them dictated in London. Jacobitism in Scotland was one reaction to all that.[14] It drew upon traditional loyalties to the Scottish royal family and upon long-held religious and political beliefs. It also expressed the dislike which many Scots felt between about 1710 and the 1740s when they surveyed changes which produced few if any obvious advantages for them. The mere existence of Jacobitism placed a premium upon ideas which could counter its effects. Jacobite-inspired rebellions, scares and rumours of subversive activities agitated Scotland for years after 1688 but notably in 1689–90, 1708, 1715–18, 1722–3, 1745–6, and even as late as

1759. Most of these years were followed by an increased interest in political and religious conformity. Purges of university professors took place in 1690 and 1717. Throughout the 1690s, indeed until 1702, visitation commissions laboured to reform the colleges and to give them a set of standardised and safe textbooks. The Union was followed by threats of visitation at St Andrews[15] and by increased concerns over the orthodoxy of candidates for regencies and chairs. The 1720s saw efforts by both the Squadrone and the Argathelians to tighten control over the universities through a variety of means. Visitations, financial pressures, the creation of new chairs and appointments were all used to ensure that corporations remained loyal, conformist and reflective of the views of the dominant political *élite*. In 1746 and 1748 it was important for the successful candidates seeking principalships in Aberdeen to point out their loyalty to the crown. At the end of the century something of this mood was restored when revolutionary ideas flooded Europe. Englishmen feared that Scots would not only read the pernicious writings of Thomas Paine but that they would use a Convention to organise a reform movement that would result in rebellion.[16] United Scots, like United Irishmen, had to be repressed. No sympathy could be shown to the French, to the Irish, to the native Painites, or to those who might foment republican rebellion in Scotland. Implicit in the demands of some of these radicals were calls for an independent Scotland. The century ended as it began with an ideological reaction to subversion which touched the universities.

Jacobitism, the religious views which accompanied it, and the Whiggish rejoinders to both, were not the only ideological issues of importance to Scots in this period. Others, centred on patriotism and perceived economic backwardness and decline, were also important. Scots by the 1690s believed they were less well off than they had been. Relative to their southern and continental neighbours they seemed socially, economically and intellectually backward. The parliaments of Charles II, James VII and II, and William and Mary had all concerned themselves with remedies for that condition. The issues with which they wrestled persisted throughout much of the eighteenth century. The remedies generally proposed were mercantilist improvement schemes, greater economic integration with England and educational developments which would give Scots a more practical, useful and professional education. Medical, legal and a more science-oriented educational pattern developed in Scotland at least partly in response to the demands for educational reform, demands which had been clearly articulated by 1700. Patriotic reform proposals had their ironies. Economic improvements seemed incompatible with the preservation of a Scottish state. The assertion of patriotic pride often took the form of glorifying the past but being shamefaced about the present. The past, treasured by patriotic writers early in the century, was not one which could easily accommodate the values and ideas of polite, modern-thinking Whigs. These perplexities were thoroughly canvassed during the eighteenth century and provided the themes for many enlightened works.[17] Similar soul-searching characterised much of provincial Europe, and was there also related to political changes. Scots, however, found their debates complicated by the existence of Highlanders, so culturally different from most Lowland intellectuals. The debates about patriotism, nationhood, improvement and backwardness necessarily concerned Highland policies. That these touched Aberdeen in a real way can be easily seen by any reader of John Ker's *Doniades* (1724) or James Dunbar's *Essays on the History of Mankind* (1780).

II Aberdeen and British Politics, 1690–1800

The North East during the eighteenth century continued to be somewhat distinctive demographically, economically, socially, linguistically and religiously, but it lacked institutions by means of which it could assert a real provincial identity. Its great noblemen had been reduced from overmighty subjects to magnates operating in the context of a British spoils system. Aberdeen, while it was a chartered and privileged burgh, was more significant as an economic centre than as the administrative capital of a province. In 1688 its most important civil courts were those of the sheriff, the burgh (where the provost and baillies acted as justices of the peace) and of corporations whose officials and magistrates were dependent upon or answerable to those Aberdeen courts or to Edinburgh judges. Since 1672 the jurisdictions of Edinburgh judges had clearly extended to the area's civil and criminal cases. The ecclesiastical courts of the bishop of Aberdeen and his commissary had recently been secularised when episcopacy was abolished in Scotland by a 1689 act of parliament. This was only one sign of the local changes brought about by the Revolution. A new sheriff-depute was appointed in July 1691, coming to office after the city had been visited by a parliamentary commission. This commission had faced hostile mobs but it had nevertheless disciplined the provost and had sought to ensure both political and religious conformity to the regime mandated by the Revolution Parliament. That was no easy task.

The crown could change legal officers and temporarily overawe the town council but it was harder to change the character of the Church in this region. King William was himself unwilling to force matters to bloody conclusions. Somewhat reluctantly, he had consented to the reimposition of Presbyterianism in Scotland. He was not prepared to countenance a persecuting Kirk especially in areas where there was overwhelming popular resistance to these changes. That there was such resistance became apparent to the visitors of 1691 as they were beset by rioters. They discovered that 'the most powerful people of the town and district [had] leagued together by subscription to a bond, in which they obliged themselves not to suffer their ministers to be ejected'.[18] Presbyterianism might be established but men committed to episcopacy retained the church livings and consequently would control the judicatories of the Kirk—the church sessions, presbyteries and synod—for some time to come. In the late 1690s this would make the choice of a professor of divinity at King's almost impossible. In the short run it also complicated the purging of the two universities of Jacobites and religious non-conformists.

The visitation commissioners who went to Glasgow, Edinburgh and St Andrews in 1690 expelled from those universities twenty-one regents and professors, sixteen of whom came from St Andrews. In Aberdeen no one was removed. Here the local notables on the visitation commission shared the outlook of those whom they were sent to investigate. But we should remember 'Ther [was] no Information of Accusatione exhibited against any of the forementioned persons', namely the professors at both universities.[19] The professors in Old and New Aberdeen subscribed to the Confession of Faith and took the oath to 'be faithful and bear true allegiance to their majesties King William and Queen Mary'; whatever mental reservations they had, they kept to themselves. That some had reservations is suggested by their conduct in 1715 when many who took these oaths broke them. In 1690 the occupation of Aberdeen by General Mackay's troops offered arguments for conforming and made the resistance which was offered even more remarkable. In 1695 the Act in Favour of Episcopalian Clergy, another testimonial to King William's leniency, gave many ministers in the North East a chance to legalise their position without giving up their religious beliefs or preference for episcopacy. This did nothing for those who had been deprived but it did help to retain a distinctive religious spirit in the churches of the North East, one that persisted into the mid century and one which was encouraged by the incomplete purge of the Aberdeen universities.

The abolition of episcopacy in 1689 deprived King's College and University of its chancellor, the bishop of Aberdeen. It also made conflicts between local Church courts and the General Assembly virtually inevitable since the latter could not be sympathetic to the ecclesiology, piety and theological leanings of Aberdeen's most eminent divines. These men, and deprived ministers from other parts of Scotland, contributed to the works both literary and practical which kept Jacobitism alive until the mid century.[20] Aberdeen, and the North East generally, did not find it easy to accept outside interference or other peoples' standards and beliefs. After 1689 there were years of constant friction and skirmishing between the Presbyterians and the remnant Episcopalians both in and outside the established church. The issues over which they fought sometimes divided families but more often religious and political factions formed along family lines.

Between 1695 and 1715 Aberdeen and the North East experienced much the same turmoil and distress as afflicted the rest of Scotland. The late 1690s were starving years. Scots who had invested so much money and hope in the Darien Company counted their losses by 1700. English trade policy before the Union was threatening. After 1707 it was negligent of Scottish interests and indifferent to the kingdom's needs. The Union did not even produce in the short run the economic benefits which had been expected to come from it. The political fevers of these years ran high and were not cooled by the Act of Union in 1707. This was as unpopular in the North East as elsewhere. It was followed in parliament by repeated slights to Scots and by legislation which they believed infringed the Act of Union. It was a northern peer, the 4th Earl of Findlater and 1st Earl of Seafield, who on 2 June 1713 moved the repeal of the Act of Union in the House of Lords. He was supported in both houses by Scots representing every political faction—old *politiques* and courtiers like himself, Argathelians, Squadrone men, Jacobites— all had had enough of Union and nearly carried a vote against it in the Lords. Political dissatisfactions were particularly rife in the North East. When rebellion came two years later it was an Aberdonian, the Earl of Mar, who first raised the standard of James VIII. It was Aberdeenshire which contributed proportionately the largest number of men to this rising and Aberdeen which for some weeks supplied a base to the rebels.

Aberdeen's experiences in the uprising of 1715 were unlike those of any other university town. There was genuine and widespread approval of the rebellion. Local noblemen—the Marquis of Huntly (heir to the Duke of Gordon), the Earl Marischal, the Earl of Mar (the Pretender's commander-in-chief), the Earls of Erroll and Kintore, Lords Forbes of Pitsligo and Fraser—and a host of lesser lairds went out for the Pretender. New Aberdeen elected a Jacobite provost and council. Taxes were levied throughout the county for the Stuarts. In all this the rebels were aided by the prayers of leading Aberdonian clergymen. Among them were Professor James Garden of King's and his brother George, Dr Andrew Burnett and William Blair.[21] Burnett had been a one-time candidate for bishop of Aberdeen; Blair was the rector of Marischal College 1688–90. These men were responsible for an address to James made at Fetteresso on 22 December 1715. Professors and regents at both Aberdeen universities were equally committed and addressed 'King' James in the name of their corporations. It is not surprising that in the aftermath of the rebellion repression should have borne heavily on the region, town and colleges. Some lords were forfeited including the Earl Marischal whose patronage rights in Marischal College and University reverted to the crown. The burgh had a new provost and council forced upon it. Ministers were deposed while some, including the Gardens, fled the country as did two or three of the college masters. By continental standards this was all quite mild, even when the executions of those who were caught, tried and hanged are considered. That was also true of the disciplining of the universities undertaken by a new visitation commission in 1716.

Between the end of the purge of Aberdeen Jacobites in 1717–18 and the next rising in 1745 political and religious disagreements remained an ever-present reality in the North East. They affected parliamentary and burgh elections, the politics of the presbytery and synod, university recruitment and the manifold activities of everyday life. This uneasiness was complicated by trials of strength between the Squadrone and the Argathelians and between their allies in the various corporations of the region. In the 1720s, when he was in opposition, Argyll seems to have found friends among some Jacobites or former Jacobites. In 1725 he and his friends came to power. When the Duke of Argyll broke with Walpole in 1737 his younger brother, Lord Ilay, remained as the ministry's administrator of Scottish patronage. The two brothers now worked at cross-purposes, one to overturn the ministry, the other to uphold it. Ilay lost much of his authority in Scotland and went out of power when Walpole fell in 1742.[22] He was replaced by the Marquis of Tweeddale, then the leader of the Squadrone. Tweeddale and his party never consolidated their power in Scotland and were particularly inept in handling Aberdeen. Their ineptitude contributed to the Jacobite rebellion of 1745.

In 1745 many people in Aberdeen were still sympathetic to the Stuarts, but this time they were far less supportive of the Pretender. He was joined by few noblemen and lairds. The burghs remained loyal to George II as did the universities. Indeed, King's sent into the field as volunteers Professors Thomas and George Gordon and John Chalmers. At Marischal, Thomas Blackwell the younger and David Verner did enough to ask later for favours justified by their actions and sufferings. The ministers of Old and New Aberdeen prayed for the English and not the Scottish king. Aberdeen was occupied, but Prince Charles seems to have been less warmly welcomed than was Cumberland as he passed through town on his way to Culloden. By 1750 Jacobitism and all it represented had been largely abandoned by Aberdonians. Like many of their compatriots to the south, some were soon to call themselves North Britons. There were no Aberdeen stirrings in 1759 when in Paris plans were made for another rising. It never took place.

From 1750 to 1780 Aberdeen's political history was largely devoid of incidents other than those concerned with parliamentary, burgh and clerical elections. Aberdonian politics centred on the spoils of office but ideology was not without significance. Aberdonians showed little sympathy for Wilkes, condemned the Americans and generally supported the government. Increasing numbers of local men drifted south to pursue careers in business, the services of the crown and the East India Company, or in medicine, publishing and a widening array of other occupations. Throughout most of these years, but especially after about 1763, there was no one dominant political interest in Scotland. Patronage, including that of the universities, was influenced by many men. In New Aberdeen the most important of these were the 3rd Earl of Bute and the professors themselves. At King's Lord Deskford and the professors ran things with little outside interference. That situation began to change in the late 1770s as Henry Dundas created his political party. As his interest grew so did the government's involvement with the universities. In Aberdeen this was first seen in the outcome of the attempts to unify the universities in the mid-1780s. This followed the election of 1784 in which Dundas and his friends had done well in the North East. By the end of 1793 the Dundas party included most of the notables of the Aberdeen area, most of the burgh councillors and the chancellors of both universities. These men were prepared to intervene in civic and university affairs to prevent the heresies and abominations of the French from corrupting the North East. The Dundas regime lasted well beyond the years dealt with here.

Politics and politicians played very differently upon the universities and colleges in New and Old Aberdeen. New Aberdeen was by far the more important economic centre; Old Aberdeen was its poor relation. The New Town flourished after the early years of the eighteenth century while the Old Town remained somnolent, although the outlying portions of the parish—Old Machar—saw new industry and people. New Aberdeen experienced substantial population growth and expansion while the Old Town kept pretty much to its limits and did not expand far beyond the long street stretching from the cathedral to the Spital. The old burgh had a town council but in many things it was subject to the rule of the provost, four baillies and council of New Aberdeen whose magistrates exercised the power of sheriffs and JPs over a portion of the county surrounding the two burghs. King's College professors were sometimes patrons of the Merchants and Trades Society of Old Aberdeen and even served as baillies and magistrates in the burgh. In New Aberdeen the city fathers gave patronage to the town's college, in which many of them had been educated and to whose endowments their families had sometimes contributed. In Marischal College the town council had legal rights, but it felt justified in meddling with matters which fell outside the sphere defined by those rights. Professorial recruitment was a matter which interested the council. The council could and did affect placements because it was politically important. New, not Old Aberdeen, was represented in the Scots parliament and after 1707 was the most important burgh in its electoral district. Marischal College reflected in many ways its urban setting and the desires of the merchants and tradesmen of Aberdeen. Technical and scientific education developed here and it was the Marischal College professor of oriental languages who in the 1790s was teaching Arabic and Persian to boys planning careers in the East India Company.[23] King's had a higher proportion of students from the Aberdeen hinterland, from the northern and western counties, and fewer from either of the Aberdeens.[24] It was more oriented towards the landed gentry and less concerned with the interests of merchants, artisans and the professional men who lived in greater numbers in New Aberdeen. In part this explains its Jacobitism, its financial troubles and its recruitment of teachers more often closely related to the landed gentry than were those of its nearby sister. It also shows why plans for union of the colleges in 1747, 1754, 1770–2, 1785–7 came to nothing. The more powerful town insisted that any united college or university had to be in New Aberdeen.

III The Universities and Colleges

Politics shaped the eighteenth-century educational institutions but these institutions also supplied structured contexts in which the political games had to be played. In Old and New Aberdeen, the constitutions of the two universities and colleges differed greatly. King's College and University and Marischal College and University had quite different eighteenth-century careers partly because their structures allowed politics to affect them in very different ways.

Both King's and Marischal had complex constitutions whose complexity was a boon to those who sought to manipulate university and college affairs. Both corporations' original charters had been amended, superseded, reimposed, added to, confirmed in slightly different ways and at different times by the Scots parliament. They had also been interpreted variously by visitation commissions, by local and Scottish courts and by the House of Lords. There was little that was absolutely incontestable about their constitutions if one wished to contest them. Many found reasons to do so. These included local gentlemen and clerics, town councillors, private patrons and those with rights connected with gifts held in trust, politicians and civil officials and, of course, the professors themselves. Ways in which these people could bring pressure to bear upon the universities will be discussed below. Here it suffices to note that in both institutions the crown made appointments, but that it filled only one at King's, as opposed to six at Marischal after 1715. At King's the synod of Aberdeen could elect the professor of divinity; at Marischal he was chosen

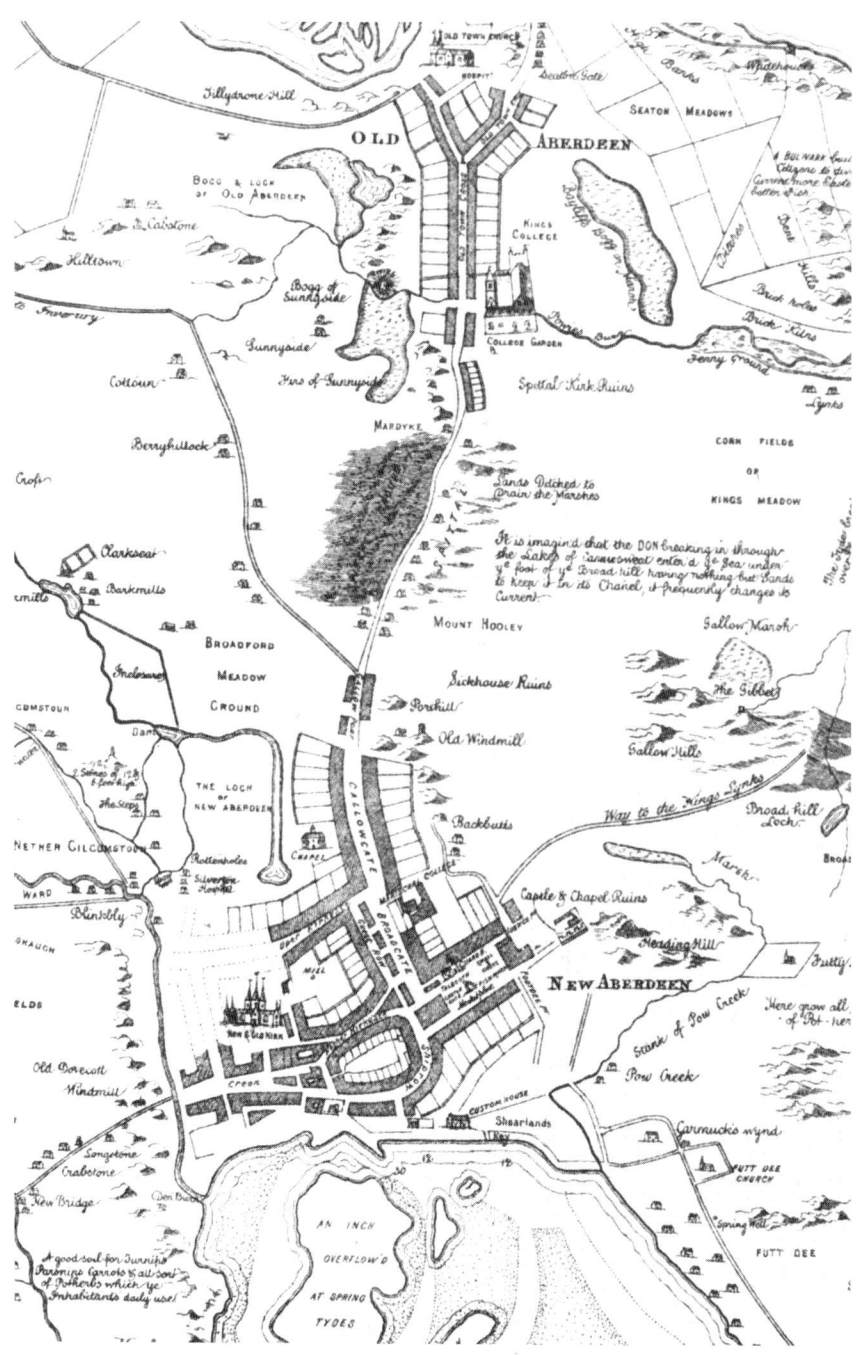

1   G & W Paterson, *A Survey of Old and New Aberdeen*, 1746 [detail].

2 George Keith, 10th Earl Marischal. Aberdeen University picture collection.

by the town, as was the professor of mathematics. The town usually gave a church living to the principal, whose salary was small. There were no private patrons at King's, but three families by the 1800s had some interest in how the chairs they had given were filled at Marischal. At King's the masters could virtually control the academic recruitment of a majority of the members of both the college and university. At Marischal they could legally fill only one honorary and stipendless chair of law set up in 1766 to facilitate the awarding of honorary degrees.

King's, as the larger establishment, might have had the more complex political history during the eighteenth century, but this was not so. Instead, the inbred professoriate of King's tended to monopolise power.

At Marischal College the lines of authority and power over appointments were clearer. Chancellors were more often present and the rector's chair was more often filled.[25] The political nature of the institution was patent. At Marischal interventions from outsiders were normal, expected and, sometimes, even buttressed the power professors could exert; at King's, there was a minimum of outside interference. Throughout the period King's tended to be a closed corporation and did not much benefit from openness to outside influences. The result was a brighter and less inbred group of teachers at Marischal, where there was also less bickering among the professors. At Marischal the prospects of professors were more clearly known to depend upon attention to the wishes of, first, the Earls Marischal and, then, the managers of the crown's interests. The constitutions of the two colleges thus affected their ideological orientation and the ways in which this was preserved and altered (see Appendix II, Tables 1 and 2).

In the period 1690 to 1715, this meant concerns to keep local institutions open to Jacobites and oriented towards the mystical and Episcopalian religious outlook which had tinged the views of the leading Aberdeen intellectuals between 1660 and 1690. The means of preserving Jacobitism becomes the first topic in the political history of the eighteenth-century Aberdeen universities. The game was the same in both Old and New Aberdeen, but the players and the strategies were different. In the long run the forces of assimilation and secularism would win, but until 1710 a Jacobite and Episcopalian interest was sustained in both colleges.

Chapter 2

The Jacobite Colleges, 1690–1717

I King's College and University

Before the Revolution of 1688–9 King's was an institution well integrated into the society of which it formed a part. Its chancellor was the bishop of Aberdeen whose cathedral was adjacent to the college properties. Bishop George Haliburton (1682–9) was a man who shared the mystical piety and religious outlook of his predecessor, Patrick Scougal (1664–82). After being deposed in 1689 Haliburton continued to ordain Episcopalian clerics for his old diocese.[1] The bishop, like his predecessors, had named the provosts and baillies of Old Aberdeen whose feudal superior he was. In the time during which Bishop Haliburton presided over the town, several King's College regents and professors had sat as baillies. In 1689 George Fraser and Patrick Gordon were still doing so.[2] Four of the nine professors at King's in 1690 were burgesses of Old Aberdeen and three others would become so by 1702. The commissary of Aberdeen, whom the bishops named, was also the vice-chancellor of the university. Throughout Haliburton's tenure this post belonged to James Scougal who was the son of a former bishop, the brother of Henry Scougal, professor of divinity 1672–8, and himself rector of King's 1683–5 and civilist 1684–7.[3] Principal Middleton and most of his colleagues were descended from or married into genteel local families connected with greater landed families—Leiths, Frasers, Gordons, Forbeses, Skenes, Muirs, and Ogilvies. As masters of the university and college properties they too were landlords, and patrons secure for life in the livings which they held. Collectively, the professors and their patrons and clients formed a tight-knit group. Episcopalian in ecclesiastical politics and conservative in outlook, they, like the majority of men in the North East, were not eager for change and certainly did not want it forced upon them. By 1718 that had happened. The great noble houses—Gordon, Marischal, Erroll, Mar—had been tamed or forfeited. The bishop of Aberdeen was gone. Church livings were now often filled with men who prayed sincerely for the Hanoverian who sat upon the throne which others still thought the rightful possession of a Stuart. The universities in Old and New Aberdeen had been purged of Jacobites. It is that transformation and the efforts made to resist it that we should now consider.

At King's the religious and political tone can easily be inferred from the views of the men who headed the university prior to 1715. Bishops and Chancellors Patrick Scougal and George Haliburton were members of the group of divines who encouraged the mystical piety of the North East which received its classic expression in *The Life of God in the Soul of Man* (1677) by Henry Scougal, the bishop's son. This book endorsed quietism, passivity and a withdrawal from the sinful world in which men were, nevertheless, still called to act and to act morally, charitably and with both the love and fear of the Lord before them. Scougal's ideas were kept alive in the university by his successor, James Garden, and by other masters who accepted them. In 1700 Garden's version of them was condemned by the General Assembly as heretical, an action which was echoed by later Assemblies.[4] In politics, Scougal's belief implied both a religious view of obligations and of the sources of political authority. They were consonant with Jacobite political theory and with the support of authority to discipline a sinful world. At the same time they justified charity and forbearance — qualities in short supply in late seventeenth- and early eighteenth-century Scotland. The piety of the North East was adopted by many Jacobites.

The chancellors could institutionalise their views by picking commissaries and professors who would not dispute them. Bishop Scougal appointed two of his sons to the former post: John (?–1681) and James (1681–98). James went on to a political career becoming MP for Kintore (1693–1702), commissary of Edinburgh (1693–6) and as Lord Whitehill, a lord of session (1696–1702). He voted with the Court party in the parliaments of 1698, 1700–1 and 1702.[5] He was followed in the Aberdeen commissary court in 1698 by Robert Paterson, the son of John, bishop of Ross.[6] Robert Paterson combined that post with the principalship of Marischal College which he held from 1678 until 1716. Like the bishops, these men had clear ties to local aristocrats upon whom they had depended for patronage and countenance. That was also true of the King's rector in 1688, Patrick Urquhart. Mediciner since 1672, Urquhart had been presented to his office by Bishop Scougal.[7]

It is equally certain that they were willing to see King's College filled with relatives. In 1690, King's was virtually two extended families. Principal George Middleton was the grandson of Thomas Gordon of Keithocks Mill and had married Janet, daughter of James Gordon of Seaton. Her nephew, John, was to become civilist in 1696. When he did so, he found already in the college Patrick Gordon, a son of Alexander of Keithocks Mill, and Patrick's son, George. Principal Middleton was also the relative by marriage of James Garden, the professor of divinity, whose brother, George had served earlier (1673–4) as a regent. Alexander Fraser (whose daughter was to marry Patrick Gordon's son George in 1705) was cousin to George Fraser and by marriage was probably related to John Moir, the second son of John of Stoneywood. Only three of the ten professors in 1690 could have lacked relatives in the college. It was this professoriate which the parliamentary visitation commission met in 1690 and in subsequent years. The visitors were not, however, able to change either the pattern of recruitment or the religious and political outlook of the college. All but one of the professors, James Garden, took the prescribed oaths to William and Mary and swore to uphold the Kirk established by law. That allowed nepotism to continue and ensured the appointment of Jacobites to university and college livings.

Appointments in 1693 and 1696 brought into the college two other sons of Patrick Gordon. Thomas Gordon, his fifth son, became conjoint humanist and successor to his father on 7 January 1693. Already in 1690 he had been dismissed from his office of regent at Glasgow University as a Jacobite.[8] Thomas Gordon seems to have demitted office by 2 March 1696, when another of Patrick's sons, Alexander, a former Episcopalian minister, became conjoint humanist. A third son, George Gordon, was made conjoint professor of oriental languages on 1 March 1693. John Gordon of Seaton, the commissary clerk, was elected to the civilist's chair in 1696. He was to be deposed from this sinecure in 1717 for his support of the Old Pretender. In 1696, Principal Middleton could find four Gordon relatives and James Garden in the university. Despite the visitations of 1690, there had been no change in the recruitment of men from mostly Jacobite families already represented in the college.

During the years 1690–8 King's lacked both a chancellor and a rector. In 1698 the masters chose as rector Sir Thomas Burnet of Leys, an opposition MP in the parliaments of 1698–1702 who later joined the Squadrone.[9] Burnet served in this office until 1705. In 1700 and in 1705, the professors chose as chancellors the 11th and 12th Earls of Erroll, men very like themselves in outlook.

John Hay, 11th Earl of Erroll was elected chancellor on 15 January 1700 and installed the following month. Erroll was sheriff of Aberdeenshire and a prominent local gentleman. In 1697, Erroll had been courted by the government with whom he voted in the following years, but he was also, or became, a Jacobite. He may have seemed to the masters like one who could help them find money or who could give other aid.[10] Money they sorely needed for a Greek chair which the visitation commission and the Kirk insisted that they establish.[11] The masters also needed assistance in sorting out the affairs of the divinity chair from which Professor James Garden had been deposed on 25 January 1697.[12] Erroll brought the college no new funds but he seems to have played an unanticipated role in the recruitment of teachers, one of whom brought with him new philosophical and medical ideas.

The Earl of Erroll was something of a *virtuoso* and friendly with Dr Archibald Pitcairne and his Edinburgh circle of iatro-mechanists. On 2 May 1703 Erroll nominated one of that group, Thomas Bower, for a mathematics chair at King's. This the masters duly created, but they found Bower no salary.[13]

Nothing seems to survive to shed light on Thomas Bower's early life. He first appears in the minutes of King's College for 3 May 1703. At that time Bower practised as a physician and surgeon but lacked an MD. King's made him more respectable, on 30 October 1704, when it gave him the degree of Doctor of Medicine. In July 1703, he went to Edinburgh to try to get a salary for his new chair (KCM, 5 July 1703). He seems not to have succeeded in this and was paid little, if anything, by the college. By 1706, Dr Archibald Pitcairne recommended him to the Earl of Mar as a suitable candidate for the Marischal College professorship of mathematics. He secured the post but the court of session found in 1707 that its previous incumbent, George Liddell, still possessed the chair. The town council of Aberdeen then settled upon Bower a pension of £40 a year which was irregularly paid. He was again in Edinburgh around 1707 where he was 'serviceable to the Scots Parliament in calculations relating to the equivalent'.

Accepting Pitcairne's iatro-mechanical and Newtonian views, Bower formed part of the remarkable circle of medical men influenced by that Jacobite physician and friend of Newton. Dr Bower seems to have expounded Pitcairne's theories in Aberdeen where he practised as a physician and where he probably also taught at least sporadically between 1709 and 1713. He is also said to have written all or part of *A Letter from Dr. James Walkinshaw to Sir Robert Sibbald* (London, 1709), an attack upon Sibbald which came from Pitcairne and his friends. In 1709, during the rectorship of Sir William Forbes, Bower mounted a campaign for funds with which to buy mathematical instruments. These were to become the property of the college, but were to be used by him and his successors 'for the many useful observations and experiments which may be dayly made by the Professors themselves for the Improvement of Learning, as for the instruction of the youth under their care'. His proposals certainly read as though he were teaching.[14] Later entries in the minutes (KCM, 11 July 1720) show that money was raised and spent on instruments. In 1710 Bower was also given a reversionary right to the principalship of Marischal College by the 9th Earl Marischal who would have been happy to see the new science cultivated in his college. Bower was certainly resident in 1710–11 when his right to vote in college meetings was questioned. He pursued the matter in the court of session until 1712, the year in which he is recorded as having assisted at a *post mortem* examination in Aberdeen. On 23 October 1712 he was elected a Fellow of the Royal Society of London at which time he also seems to have been on friendly terms with Sir Isaac Newton. He is said to have left Aberdeen around 1713 and demitted office in 1717, probably fearing that he would be ejected by the visitors along with most of his former colleagues. At that time, he was in London where he continued to be useful to former colleagues but also to their Whig replacements who sought favours from him. Bower died on 1 November 1723.

Dr Bower was almost certainly a Jacobite since he found patrons in men who were—Erroll, Mar, Marischal and Pitcairne—and had other friends who were in that camp. That made him acceptable to the masters at King's but his anomalous position as the holder of a new and unfunded chair made him less welcome. Excluding him from the college meeting and the corporation, as the masters tried to do, was probably meant to lessen the financial burden which his appointment had imposed upon the revenues. It is unlikely to have been, as was claimed by J M Bulloch, a move to exclude a Whig. Left to their own devices, the masters would doubtless have appointed no mathematician, or would have filled a new place with a Gordon or a Gregory, not an outsider who brought into the college novel ideas and methods as well as connections with the best Scottish and English minds of the time. Chancellors could, if they bothered, affect both the pace and direction of intellectual change in their universities.

Erroll's election as chancellor came in the midst of the protracted and complex efforts of the Kirk and visitation commission to oust James Garden from the chair of divinity. Initially in 1696–7 Garden had indicated his willingness to go quietly, but in 1703 he claimed that the Act of Indemnity applied to him and that he still held the chair since it had not been filled. The university had almost certainly obstructed efforts to fill the post in 1698, 1701 and 1703.[15] This is not surprising given the men whom the Kirk sought to impose. Those who rejected the post included Charles Gordon, a Whig who thought the Old Pretender illegitimate; Thomas Hogg, who like Gordon had been a Presbyterian minister in exile at Campvere; and Allan Logan, a prominent Ayrshire and Fifeshire witch persecutor. Finally, in 1704, Garden's brother-in-law, George Anderson, was chosen and admitted on 14 December. Anderson was an Episcopalian who had conformed to Presbyterianism in about 1694 and was a member of 'the family'. He preached at Tarves where the Earl of Aberdeen, a distant cousin of all the King's College Gordons, was the principal heritor.

It would have been strange if Erroll had not backed such a man; no better candidate could have been found.

Charles Hay, 12th Earl of Erroll, succeeded his father as chancellor on 2 December 1705. He too was a *virtuoso* who on 3 June 1707 was made an Honorary Fellow of the Royal College of Physicians of Edinburgh.[16] This earl sought to preserve the Jacobite character of King's by abetting those masters who elected Episcopalians loyal to the Stuarts. It is not surprising that Erroll was out in the 'Fifteen' or that he should have resigned the chancellorship on 14 May 1716 before the visitors could sack him.

King's also got a new rector in 1705, David Forbes of Leslie—a cadet of the Forbeses of Monymusk. Archibald Forbes of Puttachie (or Pitachy) was elected rector in 1708, followed in 1709 by Sir William Forbes of Craigievar. Leslie, Puttachie and Craigievar came from Presbyterian and Whig families.[17] It looks very much as if the masters were trimming a bit in the years around the Union. If they were, this may also represent a kind of compromise with a group in the college whose allegiances were shifting.

By the late 1690s Patrick and George Gordon seem to have accepted the Revolution Settlement. George by 1698 was even functioning as a government agent in the North, a role perhaps related to his regius chair established in 1695. George Gordon's politics may in part account for his admission to office in 1698 on an order of the chancellor of Scotland.[18] His appointment to the chair of oriental languages probably had involved William Carstares, King William's adviser on clerical politics and patronage, who usually had a finger in important ecclesiastical and university patronage throughout the period discussed here. By 1715 Gordon appears in Carstares's correspondence as one harassed by Principal Middleton and as a friend of Professor David Anderson, another sufferer.[19] By 1724–5 Gordon was amicably corresponding with that good Whig, the Rev. Mr Thomas Boston. Five years later Aberdeen Whigs were recommending his son George to Lord Ilay as his successor. In 1705 Gordon married the daughter of his colleague, Subprincipal George Fraser. Thereafter, Frasers and Gordons frequently voted together and pursued interests which sometimes diverged from those of their colleagues. Until 1708 this made little difference in a corporation making no appointments, but after that, appointments did divide the masters.

A rector was chosen in 1711, John Farquharson of Invercauld. He helped or at least did not prevent the Jacobite faction from retaining control over appointments until 1715.

In 1708, Dr Patrick Urquhart's son, James, was made conjoint mediciner with his father.[20] In the following year he sought and got a regency with the chancellor's aid. In 1709 Dr James Urquhart and John Gordon, the son of the Whig Presbyterian minister of Cluny, both sought the same vacant regency. A comparative trial was set to establish which was the better candidate. The trial was even held, despite John Gordon's bitter objection 'to his rival on the ground that Urquhart was "knowen to be of principalls and sentiments contrarie to the established government of the Church by his open and avowed dishanting the public ordinances thereof, and frequenting a form of worship disallowed by law"'. Gordon also charged that Urquhart was disqualified because he practised medicine contrary to the regulations governing the conduct of regents.[21] Because they had split along family lines, the masters did not proceed to an election although the men seeking the regency had been tried. George Gordon, professor of oriental languages and the Whig agent of Squadrone politicians, had been denied a vote in the meeting. Supporting his right to vote were his brother Alexander, George Fraser (his father-in-law), Alexander Fraser I (George's cousin), and Dr Thomas Bower whose rights had been equally slighted. Bower's and George Gordon's patents gave them all the privileges of founded members but the principal was determined that they should not vote. He probably assumed that the Gordon faction would vote for a Gordon. Doing so would give the Gordon family a near majority in the college meeting. In any event, the election was put off.

> Then when the Principal was gone to lay the Matter before the Chancellor, Mr. [George] Gordon procured a packed meeting, consisting of himself, his brother [Alexander], his good Father [i.e. father-in-law, George Fraser, the subprincipal who could call a meeting in Middleton's absence], and Wife's Cousin German [Alexander Fraser], where Dr. Bower was not present, and Mr. Gordon voted for himself, as the Man fittest to supply the Post.[22]

That election would have been carried against the votes of William Black, George Anderson, Patrick and James Urquhart—either by the vote of John Gordon or by the subprincipal's casting vote. The college was thus evenly divided between a Gordon family faction, and one centred on Principal Middleton and his relatives.

What happened next is unclear. Probably the rector, John Farquharson, or the chancellor disallowed Gordon's election. Since the thirty days in which the masters could fill the post had elapsed, the right to make the appointment reverted to the chancellor. Dr Urquhart, not Mr John Gordon, 'was put in by the Chancellor *jure devoluto*'.[23] Erroll had restored the principal's control of the college meeting, but he had not ended challenges to it.

In 1710 the balance was upset again by the election of David Anderson to the chair of divinity formerly held by the deceased George Anderson, who seems to have been no relation. David Anderson had been tutor to Sir William Anstruther's son John in the 1690s. By 1710, Sir William was a Squadrone Senator of the College of Justice with enough influence with William Carstares and other clerical politicians to secure this post for Anderson. Anderson's inaugural lecture was dedicated to John Anstruther, his former pupil.[24] After his election to the chair, David Anderson was immediately set upon by Dr James Garden, who wished to be reinstated, and who carried his case all the way to the House of Lords. Anderson's expenses were paid partly by the Kirk; Garden was supported by Lord Mar and by some of Aberdeen's Jacobite aristocrats. He lost by withdrawing his case but only in 1714, an act which left the legal questions undecided.[25]

Late in 1710, or in January 1711, Subprincipal George Fraser died. That opened another place and brought on another trial of strength between Jacobites and Whigs. This case again began with the exclusion from the election of both George Gordon and Thomas Bower. After that, the masters chose as the new regent William Smith, then teaching at Marischal College where the Keith family had placed him in 1693 (KCM, 5 February 1711). As an installed professor Smith could have been translated without a trial. Smith in 1715 was to address the Pretender as King James.[26] When Smith refused to serve, the place was opened to a competition which drew four candidates: John Gordon; Alexander Burnet, governor to the Laird of Drum's son (Alexander Irvine, who was 'out' in the 'Fifteen'); John Monro, 'governor to George Monro, the younger of Culrain' (a Squadrone Whig); and William Simpson, a Jacobite schoolmaster at Banff. These four drew lots for thesis topics on 12 March and were judged by the masters on 17 March. Simpson was elected by the casting vote of Principal Middleton who joined Professors Black, Patrick and James Urquhart. Middleton later claimed 'that Mr. *Simpson* had not only a great and distinguishing advantage of Mr. *Burnet* in all parts of learning but further, that Mr. Burnet so far acknowledged his own insufficiency, that he would not undertake the Reading and Exposition of one sentence of the Greek Tongue, tho' a competent knowledge of that Language hath ever been considered a necessary qualification for this office'.[27]

Burnet, who came to the election with friends and a notary to witness the affair, relied for his success on the votes of those who had been defeated in the Urquhart case two years earlier.[28] This time Gordon, Bower, Burnet and their friends would seek redress not in the university's courts but in the civil ones. The lords of session found on 21 December that Professors Gordon and Bower did have a right to vote in the college meeting and that Alexander Burnet had, indeed, been legally elected.[29] William Simpson moved on to Dalkeith where he ran a private school attended mainly by the sons of Jacobites and Episcopalians. Principal Middleton pursued his case to the House of Lords which gave him no satisfaction, although it did protract the period of uncertainty for the Presbyterian and Whig family faction now seemingly in control of the college meeting.[30]

Since this Gordon faction could probably not rely upon Dr Bower's vote once his personal interests were not at issue, the college remained unevenly divided into two family and political factions. In 1712 the Whigs had a majority if John Gordon the civilist voted with his Gordon cousins. If he and Bower voted with the principal, then the Jacobites would win.

In the summer of 1714 a vacancy was created when Subprincipal William Black died as a consequence of his imprisonment at Edinburgh for a riot he had led in Old Aberdeen. Black and his successor as subprincipal, Alexander Fraser, along with Principal Middleton and some of the other masters, had prevented the settlement at Old Machar of the Rev. Alexander Mitchell, a Whig Presbyterian.[31] Emboldened first by a High Church Tory government in London, and then by the prospects of a Jacobite succession, they had intruded John Sharp who 'performed the service of the Church of England untill after the battle of Sheriffmoor Feb'ry 1716'. The Gordon family faction might be Whiggish but most of its members seem to have preferred episcopacy to the Church polity settled in 1690. And the regent chosen in 1715 to replace Black was both a Jacobite and a Gordon, a judicious choice for masters who did not know how the political winds would blow. This regent, Richard Gordon, was son to John the civilist, and a relative of at least six of the institution's eleven other members.

By 1715, then, the Jacobites still had effective control of the university and King's College. Control had been sustained by the placement in 1709 of James Urquhart by Erroll and by the possession of the posts of chancellor, rector and principal. In 1714 it depended on the Gordons putting their family interests before their political and religious ones. However, what was equally clear was that the Jacobites had lost much ground since 1690. George Gordon's appointment to the new regius chair of oriental languages in 1695 had fixed his loyalty to the Whigs and the Revolution Settlement. Voting with him now were his brother, and usually their Fraser relatives. After 1710 they were joined by David Anderson. Whig governments after 1714 would not be without four or more friends at King's, even though they did little for them. That reluctance to act is understandable when one realises that King's College men did little in 1715–16 to repress 'the Disorders and Riots of the Students and Servants comitted during the late Rebellion', and that when later they did act to discipline those students, it was with considerable leniency.[32]

II Marischal College and University

At Marischal College no struggle was necessary to keep the institution loyal to Episcopalianism and the Jacobite cause, and there were no jurisdictional

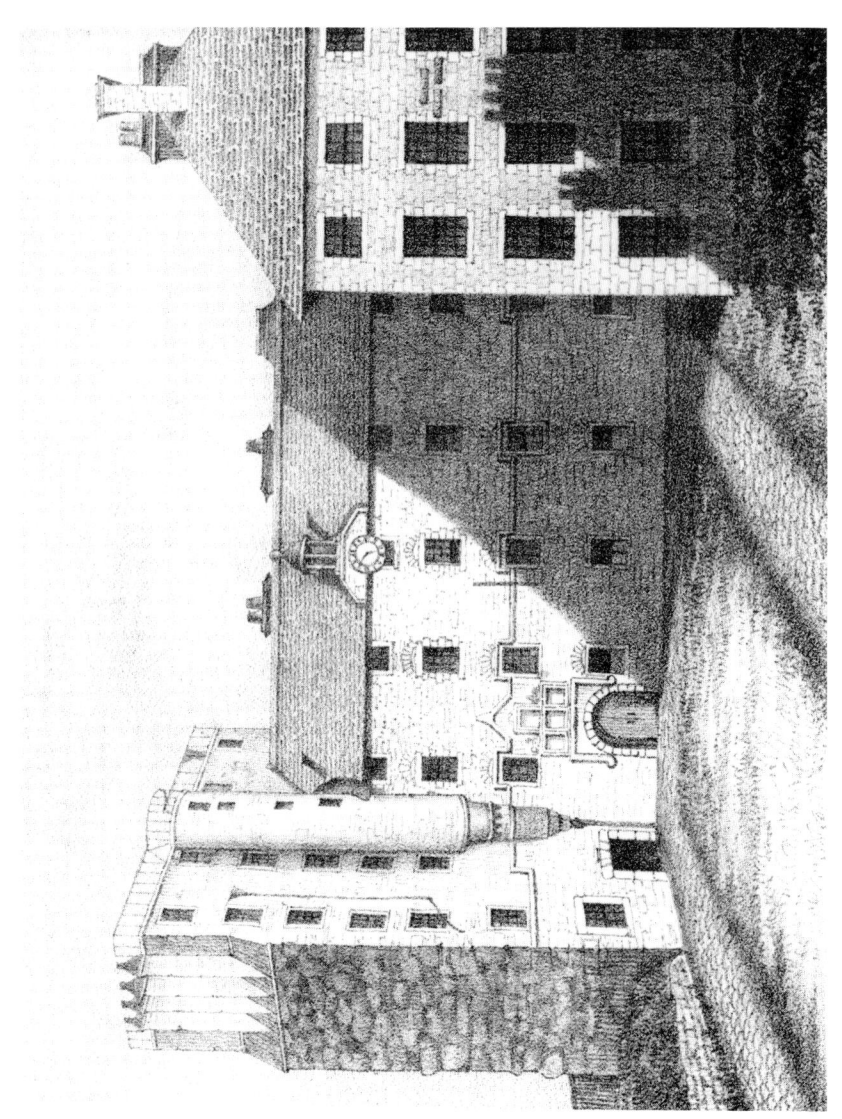

3 Front view of old Marischal College, AUL, LAE Stu e.

conflicts to complicate this endeavour. Five of the seven members of the university and college were appointees of the Earls Marischal. The other two men, the professors of divinity and mathematics, owed their posts to the town council which also usually gave a parish church to the principal, whose salary without this living would have been derisory. Provosts and councillors often found it in their interest to follow the earl's lead but professors here had no power to co-opt relatives. A family faction like that of the Gordons could not arise and change its loyalties as they had at King's. The Marischal College men had fewer ties to each other, more to their patrons, and in the end were better Episcopalians and Jacobites. The college and university in 1690 is worth a detailed look.

At its head in 1688 was Chancellor George Keith, 8th Earl Marischal, a direct descendant of the founder. He was followed in 1694 and 1712 by his son and grandson. Episcopalian in religion and Jacobite in politics, the latter earls were no friends to William and Mary although they were sometimes prepared to take their pensions and to accept office in their governments, as the 9th earl did in 1701.[33] Four years later he also accepted a Knighthood of the Order of the Thistle from James III. By blood and marriage, these latter earls were related to the Dukes of Perth, the Earls of Erroll, Kinnoull, Wigton, Galloway and Kintore, none of whose families was wholly loyal in 1715—the year in which the 10th Earl Marischal commanded the Pretender's cavalry. In 1719 he and his brother, James Keith, were among the prominent leaders of the Jacobite expedition mounted by the Spanish. The 9th earl was interested in mathematics and science but his politics were old-fashioned and his religious preferences those of the bishops of Aberdeen. His appointments also resembled theirs.

Robert Paterson, the fifth son of the bishop of Ross, had entered the college as a regent presented by the earl in 1667. In 1673 he had been given the well-paid post of librarian by the 8th earl, who in 1678 made him principal. Contemporaries believed that had he lived a few months longer he would have been deprived in 1717 for disloyalty to the crown.[34] A protégé of the Keith family, Paterson seems not to have been related to any of his staff in 1690. Others too had close ties to the Earls Marischal or to the Keith family. George Peacock, the eldest regent, was called upon to give the Latin funeral oration for the 8th earl in 1694. In 1717 he was one of four college men to address the 'king' at Fetteresso, the residence of the Earl of Erroll.[35] He was joined in that treasonous escapade by Alexander Moir, who in 1690 found in the college a distant cousin James. Both of these regents were the younger sons of Jacobite gentlemen and had relatives active in the Stuart cause from 1688 until after 1745. Subsequent to his deposition by the visitation commission in 1717, Alexander Moir kept a private academy in Edinburgh attended by the sons of Jacobite families.[36] The fourth regent was Alexander Litster, about whom nothing has been learned save that, like the Moirs, he had attended the divinity hall at Marischal.

The town council had been equally enthusiastic for men of similar persuasion. In 1684 it had appointed Patrick Sibbald professor of divinity. He had also taken 'the Test' that year, swearing to uphold Episcopalian Church order and the Confession of Faith of 1560, and had been readmitted to his Aberdeen church living. He is said to have shared the mystical religious outlook of Henry Scougal whose sister was his wife. The visitors in 1690 did not look kindly upon such men and efforts were made to remove him. Indeed, it has been claimed that Sibbald was deprived of his professorship in 1690. This is unlikely since he was calling himself professor and giving the town receipts for the payment of his salary 'for my service as professor of divinity from whitsunday [1696] to whitsunday [1697]'.[37] Sibbald served as rector of Marischal College from 1679 to 1688 and was clearly a man respected by the 8th earl, the professors and the town fathers.

Finally, the mathematics chair was held by George Liddell, the founder's great-nephew, who had come to it through the influence of the town council and his family, which had reserved some rights to its patronage. Liddell was deposed for disloyalty in 1716.[38] Such men clearly mirrored the outlook of their Episcopalian and Jacobite patrons. They were also more closely tied to the town's burgesses and professional men than to the local landed gentry from whom the King's professors were descended and into whose ranks they often married. Men such as these could also be expected to pick as rectors, assessors and deans of faculty individuals like themselves, and they could be expected to do so with little prompting from the college's patron.

In 1688 Professor Sibbald was succeeded as rector by the Rev. Mr William Blair, a man quite like the professor.[39] Associated with him as assessors in 1688–90 were three local ministers, one of whom had been tutor to the 9th Earl Marischal, and two Aberdeen advocates. One of the latter, Andrew Thomson, was son-in-law to Principal Paterson and had received offices from James VII. The other lawyer, George Keith, was the earl's distant relative, being a descendant of Keith of Auquhorsk.

The visitation commission of the 1690s did not much bother Marischal College; the 8th Earl Marischal was a member of it.[40] Since he was a prominent political figure, and later outshone by his son William, the 9th earl, Marischal College remained relatively free to go its own way until 1715 showed that way to be incompatible with the Revolution Settlement and Hanoverian rule. To see why that was, we need only to consider the appointments made at Marischal College between 1690 and 1715.

In 1693, the 8th earl gave a regent's place to William Smith who in time became son-in-law to Principal Paterson. Smith (he was Adam Smith's distant relative) had been tutor to the son of Sir Alexander Seton, Lord Pitmedden, a conscientious opposer of James VII but a man unwilling to take oaths to William III after 1688. Smith had also been governor to Lord Charles Hay, the Jacobite 12th Earl of Erroll and kinsman of the Earl Marischal. In 1711 Smith had been, as we have seen, the first choice of the Jacobite masters at King's for the regency then vacant. He too greeted 'the King' at Fetteresso in 1715 and was deprived of his post two years later.[41] In 1700 the 9th earl appointed to his newly created chair of medicine Patrick Chalmers of Fedrett, MD. An Episcopalian and Jacobite, Chalmers was deprived of office in 1717.[42] In 1710 the earl seems to have given Thomas Bower, even though he was no cleric, a commission to be principal should Robert Paterson die.[43] Bower, as we have seen, was in these years friendly with Erroll, Mar and Dr Pitcairne. Finally, the 10th earl made two regents in 1713 and 1715. The first was George Keith, the younger son of Sir William Keith of Ludquhairn, an impecunious relative.[44] The other was William Meston, the Jacobite poet who had been tutor to the earl's younger brother, James.[45] Both men were 'out' in the 'Fifteen' during which Meston was for a short time governor of Dunnottar Castle. Both fled to the continent in 1716. The earls sustained their cause partly through the university patronage of men connected with them and their friends rather than with sitting professors. The town council was more cautious in its nominations of mathematicians and divines.

In 1704 the town council tried to expel for immoralities the professor of mathematics, George Liddell. In 1706–7 it took as its nominee for the mathematics chair Thomas Bower, whose candidacy was pressed upon them by the Earl of Mar and Dr Archibald Pitcairne. Bower was doubtless a good man but the town council made this appointment without consulting the Liddell family and without holding a comparative trial as was required by the foundation. The councillors seem to have been interested only in pleasing the men in power, the Earl of Mar and perhaps the Earl Marischal. In any case, Dr Bower was not to get the mathematics chair; George Liddell was restored to office by a court of session decree in 1707.[46]

In 1693, and again in 1710, the council filled the divinity chair but not with Episcopalians or Jacobites. The first of these appointments went to James Osborne, who in the 1680s had been a preacher to conventicles and, somewhat earlier, had been outlawed by a bishop.[47] Osborne, a west of Scotland man, had come to Aberdeen from Kilmarnock in 1695 and had enough standing prior to his appointment in the university to be put on the visitation commission of 1697. Clearly pressure from the South had brought about this appointment of a man whom Robert Wodrow, a Whiggish 'high-Flyer', was to praise as 'extremely useful in that country'. Indeed, Wodrow went on to say that 'the Jacobites and Malignant party

[Episcopalian Tories] in and about Aberdeen, designed to put Dr. [Andrew] Burnet in his room'.[48] To avoid that choice being forced upon a divided council by the Trades, who were more Jacobite than the merchants and more easily influenced, the Aberdeen magistrates had written to the Lord Justice Clerk for support for the Whig Presbyterian professor whom they imported from Kilmarnock.[49] Osborne became an agent for William Carstares of Edinburgh and John Stirling of Glasgow.[50] In 1711 the town council again picked an outsider to fill this chair. Thomas Blackwell was a Glaswegian who had formerly held a Paisley living, but who by this time had been resident in Aberdeen since 1700. He too was a friend of Principals Stirling and Carstares and an active leader among the Presbyterians. Blackwell was on good enough terms with the city fathers by 1710 to dedicate to them a volume of polemical theology: *Ratio Sacra or an Appeal unto the Rational World about the Reasonableness of Revealed Religion . . . against Atheism, Deism and Bourignonism*.[51] Blackwell's title is significant because it shows him to have been an opponent of the heresies of the south and of the 'mystics of the North-East'. It was a defence of the order established by London and Edinburgh as well as of revealed religion. The council which picked this professor from a list of 'several able Divynes' on 2 May 1711 was headed by a Whig, John Ross of Clachan and Arnage, who in 1704 married the daughter of Arthur Forbes of Echt.[52] In 1697 and 1711, the town council was not prepared to support Jacobite Episcopalians even though such men had the support of local notables. The town fathers' choices made good political sense. To have chosen otherwise would have led to litigation in Church courts where Aberdeen Jacobites were unlikely to win.

From 1690 to 1715 the cultural distinctiveness of Aberdeen and its hinterland had been largely preserved. While the proponents of a local school of mystical divinity had been forced from the divinity halls, they had fought a rearguard action with the support of local aristocrats which had not wholly failed until 1714. Ousted from their kirks, these men had not been proscribed and forced underground as some were after both 1715 and 1745.[53] Their political message was equally clear and was accepted by many of the local gentry who rose in rebellion in 1715 and 1745. Most of those men had been educated in the Aberdeen colleges where regents still taught the doctrines favoured by the mystical divines. Efforts to remould the thinking of the men of the North East to resemble that of the South and South West had failed, despite both the visitation of 1690 and constant pressure from more orthodox Calvinists like William Carstares and his protégés. The result of this failure was the persistence in 1715 among many ministers of the established Presbyterian Church of Episcopalian sympathies and of a deviant piety, one form of which (Bourignonism) had been denounced as heretical in 1700 by the General Assembly. Moreover, a shadowy Episcopalian Church continued to exist, one which embraced members of the social *élite* such as the Countess of Erroll, but also many who were to shoulder guns in 1715 or provide shelter for the beaten Jacobites. The northern universities thus helped to keep alive ideas and organisations which were helpful to the Stuart cause. Without the backing and protection of men such as the Earls Marischal, the Earls of Erroll and Mar and many other local gentlemen, it is doubtful that the colleges would have been able to preserve their character and perpetuate for another generation ideas effectively stifled at Glasgow and Edinburgh in 1690, and revived with difficulty at St Andrews after 1690 where the purge left in place only one of sixteen professors. This was a considerable achievement. The true measure of its subversive tendencies came in 1715.

III 1715 and the Purging of the Colleges

In 1715 the Aberdeen area erupted in rebellion as harassed Episcopalians and disaffected Jacobites sought to overturn the Hanoverian succession. At King's College, Principal Middleton, Civilist John Gordon and two regents, Gordon's son Richard and James Urquhart, were implicated in the rising. Suspicions fell on the humanist, Alexander Gordon, and the mediciner, Patrick Urquhart. Only David Anderson, and George Gordon—the core of the Whig faction—were beyond reproach.[54] At Marischal College, there were fewer reported bonfires and riots but the masters, with the exception of Thomas Blackwell, were more deeply implicated. It was correctly alleged that they were guilty of the following crimes:

1 attending 'the illegal Election of the Jacobite Magistrates by the Earle of Marischall' (Principal Paterson, Regents Peacock, Moir and Smith).
2 admitting to a regency William Meston even though 'the said Meston, previous to his Admission, came riding in with the Earle of Marischall, To proclaim the Pretender with sword in hand' (all the Masters save Profesors Liddell and Blackwell).
3 'Mrs. Peacock, Moir, Smith & Meston delivered an address to the Pretender at Fetteresso under the title of King James, which address being from the College, It is highly probable, was signed by the Principal . . .'
4 'The Whole forsaid Masters attended daily the Episcopal Jacobite Clergy in their treasonable Sermons, and prayers and particularly on their publick Fast & Thanksgiving dayes.'[55]

Given this record it is not surprising that Marischal College should have been purged.

The 1716–17 Aberdeen visitation commissions (the life of the com-

4   Thomas Blackwell II, by Jonathan Richardson. The Pierpont Morgan Library, New York. BULL ALBUM, f.16.

mission was renewed in 1717) were picked by Squadrone politicians whose protégés played a large part in their proceedings. This was especially true of men dependent upon James Graham, 1st Duke of Montrose.[56] The duke had resigned as secretary of state for Scotland in August 1715, but his party was strong enough to secure control of the visitation commissions. These were used to entrench its supporters in the northern universities. The preliminary to that was the quasi-judicial proceeding which purged the colleges.

In August 1716, and then again in April, June and July 1717, most of the masters were summoned before the visitors first in Aberdeen and then in Edinburgh.[57] Witnesses were called, but not for the accused, who objected to this as violating 'Procedure in any legall Civill or Criminal prosecution whatsomever'.[58] They also objected because the commissioners refused to allow them to hear the charges made against them or to see evidence given concerning their conduct, or to have copies of this information. The commission did not even allow the errant masters fully to explain their actions. Objections were to no avail. On 19 April 1717, James Urquhart and Richard Gordon of King's were deposed and their colleagues were 'Inhibite from taking upon them to supply the Vacancies'.[59] On 19 June, Principal Middleton was also deposed, followed by John Gordon, the civilist, on 22 June. Thomas Bower had already resigned, and old Dr Urquhart was, or said he was, too feeble to be active. The chancellor had demitted office on 14 May 1716 before the commission came to Aberdeen. There was no rector. These depositions effectively destroyed the Jacobite faction at King's College.

At Marischal College the visitation was equally summary and the purge more thorough. Meston and Keith had fled so there was little need of a serious inquiry into their actions.[60] The principal had died. Regents Peacock, Moir and Smith and George Liddell, the professor of mathematics, had all clearly and publicly been guilty of rebellious, even treasonous acts.[61] They were all ousted by the summer of 1717, leaving Thomas Blackwell as the sole member of the corporation whose former chancellor had been forfeited in 1715. The ground was now cleared to build anew.

Chapter 3

The Squadrone and the Argathelians, 1717–1730

I The Squadrone Years at Marischal College, 1717–24

In the political upsets of 1715 one of the first casualties had been the Duke of Montrose. He had resigned as secretary of state for Scotland in August 1715 because of the growing power of his rival, John Campbell, 2nd Duke of Argyll.[1] Throughout 1715 and the first half of 1716, Argathelian and Squadrone politicians battled in London for precedence, patronage and the control of Scottish affairs. When Argyll went into opposition in June 1716, the Squadrone had won. It was that victory, or rather the succession of small victories which led to it, which allowed the Squadrone men to control the 1716 visitation commission and to pack the northern colleges with their protégés. The process is most clearly visible at Marischal College where the forfeiture of the Earl Marischal made the crown the principal patron with six regius chairs at its disposal.[2] The earl's forfeiture had also left the chancellorship of the university vacant.

No chancellor was named by the crown or by the visitation commissions and no means of picking one was specified. Moreover, it was the opinion of the lord advocate that the crown's college patronage ought to vest in the Trustees of the Forfeited Estates. That would have been too great a self-denying ordinance for any eighteenth-century politician; it did not happen. Initially patronage was dealt with by the visitors and the 1st Duke of Roxburghe, the new secretary of state for Scotland. Thereafter it was dispensed by politicians in Edinburgh and London who advised the secretary for Scotland. No chancellor served again until the 3rd Earl of Bute was elected in 1761. The visitors were not so backward in filling other vacancies.

By 30 September 1717 Thomas Blackwell had been installed as principal, along with three new regents and professors of mathematics and Greek. A professor of medicine was named the following month. In November Blackwell, who continued to hold the chair of divinity, gained access to the college's records and property, from which he had been locked out by the ousted masters. Indeed, it was not until 28 November that the college was formally surrendered to him by the town council, an occasion presided over by Arthur Forbes of Echt, a member of the visitation commission, who was to be rector of King's College from 1718 to 1727.[3] These changes made Marischal College a Squadrone institution useful in the control of the burgh and of the North East generally. They also created there a Whig political faction which was to cause problems once the Argathelians returned to power in Scotland in 1725.

When the Marischal College chairs were being filled in 1716–17 a good deal of activity amongst Squadrone politicians and their dependants was directed at the securing of those posts. Montrose's friend Charles Morthland, the clerk of the visitation commission, tried to 'obtain . . . an Arm Chair [i.e., a professorship] in one of the Colleges of Aberdeen'. Gershom Carmichael, Morthland's colleague at Glasgow University, had a similar idea. Later that year the Duke of Montrose urged Glasgow's Principal Stirling, a visitor, to keep 'Mr. Carmichael in your eye'.[4] David Warner or Verner, a relative of Glasgow's former professors of divinity, James and Alexander Wodrow, was recommended for a place at Marischal by Glasgow University faculty members, most of whom were either related to Glasgow's principal or rector or tied, as those men were, to Squadrone politicians. Like Verner, Colin Maclaurin was at the same time given a similar commendation. Later, in 1722, he was to become the travelling tutor to the son of the Earl of Marchmont, one of the Squadrone leaders.[5] Both Verner and Maclaurin were appointed, but Carmichael and Morthland were not.

A third man with Glasgow ties was Thomas Blackwell whose friends in the Kirk were gathered around Principals Carstares, Stirling and Hadow. His brother-in-law, Dr John Johnston, had obtained the regius chair of medicine at Glasgow in 1714 through the efforts of Principal Stirling and his friends. Blackwell's son, Thomas the younger, was later (falsely) to claim that the family had always been loyal to the Squadrone interest or at least to Roxburghe.[6] These were all things which might recommend Blackwell to Squadrone politicians.

In September 1716 the new town council, imposed by the Whig government advised by Roxburghe and his friends, recorded in its Register an 'Act for the Magistrates to use their Endeavours with the Government to get Mr. Blackwell to be Principal of Marischal College'. This was followed by other decisions to lobby the visitation commission about Blackwell's appointment 'and to see to get grave and Learned men admitted Regents'.[7] It was presumably these discussions which regained for the burgh its right to pick the professor of mathematics, Dr Blackwell, and two regents, who were the sons of town merchants, John Anderson and George Cruden.[8] Finally, it seems quite likely that James Hadow, another of the visitation commissioners, secured a place for the son of a St Andrews minister.[9] All

5 John Ker, 5th Earl and 1st Duke of Roxburghe, by an unknown artist. Scottish National Portrait Gallery.

this tends to confirm the claim made by Robert Pringle to Principal Stirling in 1716 that since the Aberdeen visitation commission's report 'will come into the hands of the Duke of Roxburgh under whose direction the concerns of North Britain, doe more immediately fall, I doubt not but his Grace will take due care of it'.[10] The crown's presentations to these men would have borne Roxburghe's signature or those of his assistants.

The Squadrone continued to make appointments in Marischal College between 1721 and 1724, by which time its power had begun to slip in Scotland and in London. To Squadrone influence the college owed the appointment of George Turnbull (1721), Thomas Hadow (1723), Thomas Blackwell II (1723) and Daniel Gordon (1724). The evidence for this claim is largely circumstantial but in the end convincing. Turnbull was a close friend of Charles Mackie whose patrons were the Squadrone-supporting Earls of Rothes and Leven.[11] Turnbull's brother-in-law was Robert Wallace, the Squadrone manager of Kirk patronage 1742–6. In London, after his resignation from Marischal College in 1727, Turnbull was to be found among opposition politicians whose Scottish friends were in the Squadrone, not amongst the Argathelians. Like Thomas Hadow's, Turnbull's father had been allied to Squadrone men in Church affairs.[12] Daniel Gordon's antecedents and the circumstances surrounding his appointment are not known, but it is known that Gordons recently had been active in burgh government where one served as dean of guild in 1724.[13] It would have been surprising had their wishes counted for nothing. Furthermore, Gordon became an ally of the Blackwells in scrapes occurring in 1725–7 and 1731–2. Thomas Blackwell II claimed to have come in with help from Roxburghe.[14] These four appointments were the last made by the Squadrone without opposition until they returned to dispense patronage for the ministry formed after Walpole's fall in 1742.

The Squadrone-appointed professors and masters at Marischal College completed their friends' political revolution by judicious choices of rectors: Sir William Forbes of Craigievar, 1720–1, probably a brother-in-law of the Rose of Kilravock who had served on the visitation commission, and Thomas Forbes of Echt and Pitrichie were elected for 1723–6. The Forbes family then had the largest electoral interest in Aberdeenshire. In 1727 this was thrown behind Sir Archibald Grant to defeat Ilay's brother-in-law, Alexander Fraser of Strichen.[15] It is most unlikely that these rectors or the majority of their assessors were Argathelians.

II King's College and University, 1717–25

At King's College the process of reconstruction followed a somewhat different course. There a majority of the pre-1715 staff remained in place.

The government could not simply fill the vacated professorships. It had to negotiate with professors who might legally appoint men obnoxious to the politicians. Indeed, they had to be prohibited from doing so. In late July or early August of 1717 Sir Alexander Ogilvie of Forglen went 'North in order to treat with the members of the University yet remaining anent filling the vacancies and to know if they would agree to such persons as the Commission would name'. His efforts aimed at securing the election of a proper principal and professors but they failed.[16] The unpurged masters were censured for mismanagement of funds and not allowed a voice in the selection of the new professors. It seems likely that even Whiggish Gordons, their Fraser relative and the other two masters, David Anderson and Alexander Burnet, would have sought to elect family members, friends or local men less politically reliable than themselves. The purge at King's had left a remnant neither fully committed to the new order nor satisfied with the means which brought it about. Even if the masters had been content to accept the nominees of the commission, there is no certainty that a proper principal could have been chosen. That was certainly recognised by William Dunlop, professor of ecclesiastical history at Edinburgh. Writing on 20 October 1717 to his brother Alexander, professor of Greek at Glasgow, William analysed the necessity for the crown's imposition of a principal in the following terms:

> You'll have heard that Mr. [George] Chalmer's Commission for Principall of old Aberdeen is come down; the Sollicitor [Sir James Steuart] is to prosecute it, and its designed that he should be immediately transported and settled by Martinmass, I do not know how that College will take it without the Government hazarding ane election of persons as disaffected as those turned out for besides that only 3 of the present Professors would give any tolerable assurances of the folks they should pitch on [;] according to their statues 4 Procurators chosen by the students (who probably would have been Tories) must have a vote in the election[s] which must render any security from these 3 or even more ineffectual.[17]

From this it would appear that the unreliability or unpredictability of the procurators of the four nations as well as the masters led the government to impose men upon the college. The visitors' charges of mismanagement may have been merely a screen to justify a political necessity.[18] That necessity resulted in five appointments which resembled the ones made in Marischal College.

The first of the new men to be admitted to office was Alexander Garden of Troup, the younger. He had been made sheriff-depute of Aberdeenshire on 14 August 1716. His sinecure position in the university would pad out what was, given the times, an inadequate salary. One suspects that he was also seen as an eligible candidate for the post because his father-in-law, Sir Francis Grant of Cullen, sat on the visitation commission.[19] Other additions to the college staff were made in November when the Rev. Mr George Chalmers, and two regents, Daniel Bradfute and John Ker, were installed in a similar manner.

George Chalmers, like Blackwell, had come north from south-west Scotland; again, like Blackwell, he was quite friendly with Glasgow's professors and Principal Stirling. Chalmers was later distrusted by Lord Ilay, Argyll's younger brother, and was not likely in 1717 to have been a friend to their party.[20] Ker seems to have been a distant relative of Roxburghe (John Kerr) whom he called his 'Chief' in a 1719 letter to Principal Chalmers.[21] In 1734 Ker was translated to the Edinburgh University chair of humanity with the support of a number of advocates and judges who belonged to the Squadrone connection.[22] Bradfute's antecedents are unknown, but he too seems to have come up from the south and may have been the man whose name appears on the Edinburgh matriculation roll for 1701. By the end of 1717 the college had four new men, three of whom had fairly clear ties to the Squadrone interest. But the corporation still lacked a chancellor and rector.

The former chancellors at King's had supported a party not only in the university but in the region as well. For example, David Anderson wrote to William Carstares on 4 April 1715, 'if the affair of the Chancellor be not expedite with all diligence, I can have no prospect of any possible information of this university and consequently of the north country'.[23] The government would want a man who could do as much. The masters also needed a protector who could find them funds, who would perhaps help to repair the college's buildings, add to equipment and ensure that they remained safe in a region whose Episcopalian and Jacobite loyalties had not really changed. In 1716 the professors began the search for a new chancellor.

As noted earlier, one of the first political casualties of the 'Fifteen' had been Montrose. Argyll's party in the summer of 1715 seemed as if it would become the paramount force in Scottish affairs, a prospect reinforced by Argyll's military role in the suppression of the rebellion. Those King's professors who had not been involved in the uprising clearly saw things that way when they decided to choose Argyll's brother, Archibald, 1st Earl of Ilay, as their new chancellor. The earl had been paid this 'Compliment' by 14 May 1716. Ilay was an intellectual interested in science and mathematics who had no great liking for stiff-necked clerics. He was also a moderate man who did not seek punitive measures after 1715, or even 1745.[24] Perhaps the Gordon-Fraser votes cast for his election were cast in the hope that some of those ultimately expelled by the visitation commission might be saved. In any case, this 'Compliment to the Argathelian party', as Professor Thomas Gordon later called it, was a very sensible political move. Ilay, however, may also have realised that it would do his party no good to accept an honour conferred by a corporation which in 1716 still contained recently active Jacobites. He refused the chancellorship, perhaps already knowing that the college had given meal to Jacobite troops.[25] As Thomas Gordon noted in the 1780s, 'the Argathelian party... had lost much of influence by that time'. Ilay declined a position likely to be a costly honour of little use.[26] Another source is more explicit about what happened next:

> Sometime after the rebellion was over the Masters of the College did formally elect the Earle of Iyla for their Chancellour and thereupon ordered a patent to be drawn in his favours which they Signed and caused append thereto a Silver box with the College arms, but before his patent was sent up there happened some changes at court as well as in the College, so that Such of the old Masters as wer keeped in wer by the influence of the new made [to] believe that his Grace the Duke of Roxburgh was more capable to support that new footing their College was now on than the former therefore resolv'd to made choice of his Grace for their Chancellour. But in order to save charges to the College they were so good manadgers as to make the same Patent serve [their] turn. Accordingly the Earle of Iyla's name titles and armes were eras'd, and instead thereof those of his Grace Insert, and this was not all for the Subscriptions of some of the Masters who had signed this very Patent in favours of the Earle of Iyla were quite taken out and others of the Masters whose Subscriptions were left intire and who had not been privy to these fine contriveance when they saw their names at a Patent in favours of the Duke of Roxburgh they had almost taken the same for a forgery: And of this new reformed Patent adorned with all those embellishments they were pleas'd to make a present to his Grace.[27]

This is such a fine story that one wishes it could be confirmed. Its kernel of truth may be that the old masters were, or became in 1716, Argathelians who would later reject Squadrone leading-strings. However that may be, it is clear that the choice of Roxburghe was made more than two years after the offer went to Ilay and that it was suggested by the new men who were also involved with its making and presentation.

On 18 September 1718 Professor John Anderson wrote to Principal Chalmers then in London on a fund-raising mission, that the masters had 'This day ... unanimously chosen the D. of Rox: for our Chancellor'. He went on to say, 'As for the diploma or patent we intend to have it handsomely don; and in order to that must have an exact account of his graces tittles and coat of arms'.[28] The diploma was signed piecemeal as the professors came to town, but there is no reason to think that the duke got a strange-looking parchment even though he got it late.[29] There is, however, reason to think that Roxburghe, after initially accepting the office, refused to act.

The duke's problem seems to have arisen from an opinion given by the lord advocate, Sir David Dalrymple, some time in the summer of 1718. Roxburghe had solicited the crown for funds for Marischal College. The lord advocate, however, was 'of Opinion that what is desired . . . wou'd be agreeable to law provided . . . his Maj^{tie} was to become Patron by the Attainder of the late Earl Marshall, but he takes the Right of Patronage of the said College to be vested by Act of Parliament in the Commiss^{ers} and Trustees of the forfeited Estates'.[30] Sir David's opinion made no political sense; the management of Marischal College patronage was retained by the politicians who did the king's business and was not given to the Commissioners of the Forfeited Estates. But, if the Earl Marischal's rights had come to the crown by the earl's forfeiture, had not the bishops' rights to be chancellors of King's College reverted to the crown along with their other patronage and property rights? It was presumably this scruple which had occurred to the duke by early 1719.

That the duke had qualms about his election as chancellor is certainly reported in the correspondence of Principal George Chalmers. From the surviving letters one can infer that Roxburghe thought that there was no clear right by which the masters could elect a chancellor. This right might be vested in the crown or require its permission for a valid election. If that were the case, Roxburghe's chancellorship lacked a legal foundation. These points and others were all addressed by professors and regents writing to their principal in London during the spring of 1719. Subprincipal Alexander Fraser wrote that although there was:

> No rule about it yet we have been in use to elect our Chancellor not only since the revolution but in K: Charles the i time. when episcopacie was abolished we elected the marquis of huntley who was then protestant and accepted of the office by advice of Sr Thomas hope who was then kings Advocat for it was his opinion that since by our institution we have the election of all the members so we have the election of the Chancelour and accordingly we have always elected without any inhibition save in the time of episcopacie which is all we know about it.[31]

Fraser's friend, the humanist Alexander Gordon, strengthened this case by grounding it in Hope's 'Opinion that in such cases wee should make the most probable conjecture what wold have been the mind of the Founder's in case they could have foreseen that Episcopacy was to be abolished in Scotland'. Bishop Elphinstone would have allowed this election, Fraser thought, just as Charles I and later parliaments allowed Huntly's election in 1645. Moreover, the legality of actions of the Jacobite 12th Earl of Erroll had been upheld by the court of session which had found him to be a real and not 'only [a] pretended Chancellour', as members of that court would still remember. Visitation commissions had also acted as if the Earls of Erroll were real chancellors, a point which had been made by those Jacobites who now questioned the rights of Roxburghe and Principal Chalmers.[32] In the end, the duke was probably not persuaded, since Thomas Gordon's short account of Roxburghe's election ends: 'But [Roxburghe] also politely excused himself on account of the E. of Ilay having a subsisting nomination and patent under the College seal.'[33] By 1719, then, the masters had failed to secure as chancellor the protector and patron whom they so much needed. They had, however, elected a rector.

On 27 March 1718 the masters chose Arthur Forbes of Echt as their rector, the first they had had since 1712. Echt had been 'out' against the Jacobites in 1715, and was described by William Orem, the Jacobite local historian of Old Aberdeen, as a 'bigot Presbyterian'.[34] Forbes had been a member of the 1716–17 visitation commissions. He was to remain rector until 1728, giving the Squadrone control over one university court until around 1724 when the Forbeses shifted their allegiance to Argyll. Serving as his assessors in these years were the Revs Alexander Mitchell, William Dyce and James Howie. Mitchell, the minister of Old Aberdeen, had been excluded from his kirk from 1714 until 1716 by Jacobite intruders backed by some King's professors.[35] Dyce was son-in-law to Professor David Anderson, while Howie held livings in the gift of Whig heritors.[36] Another assessor, Alexander Thomson of Port Lethen, an Aberdeen advocate, had first been named an assessor in 1705. His loyalty to the crown was ensured by his possession of minor but lucrative posts in government.[37] Such men, and they formed the majority of the rectorial court until 1725,[38] were far different from the assessors of the Jacobite years.

By 1719 King's College had failed to secure the protection and support of a powerful politician interested in the corporation's welfare. Lacking a real chancellor was to lack not only a head and judge but a lobbyist. Roxburghe did nothing for the college which by 1719 even hesitated to approach him for funds.[39] A poor college got poorer and found no substantial new grants from the crown to remedy this condition.[40] It could not even sustain its professorship of mathematics for which Principal Chalmers sought funds in 1719, and again in the 1730s.[41] Worse yet, the Squadrone was rather ineffectual in the North. Unreconciled Jacobites sought other educational establishments, apparently reluctant to send boys to the Presbyterian and Whig regents of Old Aberdeen. Others were too poor to do so. College enrolments and the status of the students dropped after 1717 until in 1723 William Orem lamented: 'this year there is no

6 Archibald Campbell, 3rd Duke of Argyll, by Allan Ramsay. Scottish National Portrait Gallery.

college table kept in the college of Old Aberdeen; the like has not been these many years bygone, for this year there are no gentlemen's sons of distinction at the college.'[42] Benefactions did come to the college, but not from the crown or from the men in power or from the local gentry.[43] Finally, the ousted Principal Middleton fought a long rearguard legal action which cost the new men many pounds that could have been better spent on the fabric, books and much else.[44]

III The Growth of an Argathelian Interest

The Squadrone politicians were not very efficient, not very well organised or led, and may indeed have lacked the landed power necessary to govern Scotland for their London friends. Neither Montrose nor Roxburghe was clever enough to retain the patronage power he had been given. By 1720 it was clear that Argyll and Ilay were not to be counted out. Argyll had already returned to court in March 1719. After his success in many Scottish burgh elections in 1721-2 he was able to get patronage for his friends; Ilay was organising to drive Squadrone MPs from their seats. At the general election in the spring of 1722 the Argathelians wrested seats from Squadrone incumbents. Among them were the Aberdeen Burghs' seat in which Col. John Middleton defeated William Kerr, brother to the Duke of Roxburghe. Aberdeenshire continued to be held by a Squadrone man, Archibald Grant of Monymusk, and neighbouring Kincardineshire remained with Lt-Col. James Scott, a government pensioner in 1720-1, who had fought against the Jacobites in 1715.[45] If this was a confused result, all London could see that Ilay and Sir Robert Walpole had become friends by 1722-3 and that Argyll's fortunes were improving.[46]

With that improvement came a greater involvement of Argathelians in Aberdeen politics. A letter from D[aniel?] Campbell in favour of Thomas Blackwell Jr, may even indicate a 1723 interest in the affairs of the Aberdeen colleges. A clearer sign is the election of Patrick Duff of Premnay to the rectorial court at Marischal College in 1723. Duff was soon to become, if he was not already, one of Ilay's principal Aberdeen advisers. The rectorial court was not a court Ilay could pretend to dominate in 1723, but it was one on which he now or soon after had at least one or two friends, the Rev. Colin Campbell (the father of George who in 1759 became principal with Ilay's help) and Patrick Duff.[47] In August 1725 Roxburghe was dismissed as secretary of state for Scotland. He had been unable or unwilling to act effectively to prevent the Scottish malt tax and had done nothing to forestall the riots which the imposition of this tax provoked in June of that year. To Ilay and his party fell the task of bringing order into Scottish affairs. For the earl and his chief aides this meant the domination of every

7   Patrick Duff, from a portrait by William Mossman. AUL, LAE1 SCN 10.

Scottish corporation by one means or another. There could be no neutrals in this game in which few holds were barred.

Ilay and his friends interfered in every Scottish university between 1725 and 1728. Glasgow was visited in 1726 and its Squadrone professors and principal were disciplined and some were even threatened with deposition. In 1727 Neil Campbell replaced Principal Stirling who died in that year. In Edinburgh the town council had earlier shifted its allegiance. The creation of a medical school in 1726 was probably part of the effort to control the burgh and its corporations. Colin Maclaurin's appointment to the Edinburgh mathematics chair in 1725 was acceptable to Ilay, who was already using Maclaurin as a political agent by 1724. At St Andrews Ilay sought to help Alexander Scrimgeour, the Episcopalian professor of divinity who had long been harassed by the Kirk and by his colleagues. In 1730, after several years of indecision, it was Ilay's man and namesake, Archibald Campbell, who became the new professor of ecclesiastical history at St Andrews. In Aberdeen the attempt to manipulate and control the two colleges certainly had begun.[48]

Marischal College, like King's, had suffered a drop in enrolments after 1715 from which it had not recovered. Here salaries were also lower which, with reduced fees, meant smaller incomes for the professors whose wages were derived from both these sources.[49] For bright young men not content with £50 a year, Aberdeen was a place to leave. The first to do so was Colin Maclaurin who in 1722 went abroad as a tutor to Lord Polwarth, the eldest son of the Earl of Marchmont. Maclaurin taught little in Aberdeen after that date—only in the winter and spring of 1724–5 and only then after his charge had died in France. His prolonged absences quite understandably displeased Principal Blackwell, and the town council which had appointed Maclaurin. Blackwell may have persuaded the council to reprimand Maclaurin in 1724 and to sack him in 1725—but only after he had accepted a post at Edinburgh. The principal's conduct was resented not only by Maclaurin but by George Turnbull who in 1725 also had to be summoned home to teach his classes.[50] These resentments led to a fight with the principal just as the political control of patronage in Scotland was changing.

Joining Maclaurin and Turnbull in their controversy with Principal Blackwell were Matthew MacKaile and David Verner.[51] Both were also looking for ways to improve their incomes and positions. Maclaurin found his in Edinburgh with Ilay's help. Maclaurin had known Ilay since the early 1720s when he discovered that the earl was something of a mathematician. Colin Maclaurin in later life was to say that he 'had it always in [his] View to make some Interest amongst those that are in Power to see if by their favour I could get myself made easier. This made me so much concerned in Sir Robert Menzies ... the Marquis of Lothian ... [Argyll and] ... Lord

Islay' whom he hoped might obtain for him in 1731 'some of those places about the Exchequer which when vacant they bestow sometimes without much attachment perhaps'.[52]

Verner and MacKaile were later supplicants for Ilay's favour, but Turnbull is not known to have sought help in that quarter. His attitude was similar to Maclaurin's in the 1720s, but later his most significant job in England was as chaplain to the Prince of Wales, a post likely to have gone to a Squadrone Scot.

Ilay was the logical man for all of these young men to turn to, and all four did so then or soon after. The way in which they did is interesting. They opposed the principal over the rectorial election in 1725. Principal Blackwell sustained his position by successful appeals to the court of session. Thomas Forbes of Echt was again elected rector in 1725, but in the following year the post went to Ilay's Aberdeen adviser, Patrick Duff. From the point of view of Principal Chalmers at King's College, Maclaurin seemed responsible not only for the unseemly commotions at Marischal College but also for the increasing political divisions in the town council over the appointments of ministers.[53] That was a party matter involving, among others, the Rev. James Chalmers whose nomination for the principalship of Marischal College Ilay was to scupper three years later.

A further view of the politicisation of Aberdeen University life is provided in a letter dated 20 December 1725 from Matthew MacKaile, MD, to Ilay's political manager in Edinburgh, Andrew Fletcher, Lord Milton. MacKaile sought the King's College post of mediciner to which he believed 'Dr Gregory, Principall Chalmers's Son in Law will Succeed unless Something be done by our Friends to prevent it very Speedily By a Methodes being fallen upon to pull the Electors by the Mouth'. MacKaile suggested a comparative trial. Arthur Forbes of Echt, the King's rector (and father of the then Marischal College rector) was to be 'rightly address'd'. He went on to say, 'I think it would be no Difficult matter to disappoint Ch[alme]rs Project for it might be brought into the Kings Hands & then I think our friends might over rule them'. MacKaile probably had in mind using the commissary of Aberdeen to block the professor's admission to the university; or, he may have contemplated an assertion of a royal right to the chancellorship. Both ideas were in the air soon after.

MacKaile and his friends were very much a party working in Ilay's interest, or at least one hoping to use the Argathelians for their own ends. That helps to make intelligible later squabbles amongst the Marischal College professors.

What is equally clear is the Argathelian intention of dominating both colleges and using the rectors to effect those ends if it were possible to do so. If it were not, then legal manoeuvres or 'a Lett[r] from the Secretary [of

8 Lord Milton. AUL, Macbean Portraits, box 2.

state] recommending a part^r person might as King's now Stand overawe Some of them & make them alter their Measures'. Professor MacKaile's reference to Baillie Forbes, another of 'old Echt's' sons, makes it clear that the town councillors also had fingers in these pies. By hook or by crook both colleges were to be made amenable to Ilay's direction. What is also not surprising is that there was a Gordon candidate for the mediciner's post but 'one who would reckon himself Injur'd if any should think him a friend to Church or state'. Gordon loyalties at King's could still run more to their family than to Whig Presbyterianism. MacKaile did seem to think that some 'of our friends' might support such a man. To make that less likely, Dr MacKaile 'desyr'd my Friend Mr. McLaurin [then in Edinburgh] to act along with you [Lord Milton] in this affair'. Both Maclaurin and Ilay's agent would have found useful 'ane abstract of the Foundation' which MacKaile sent down.[54] Dr James Gregory was elected to his post as mediciner three days after Dr MacKaile sent his letter, long before Lord Milton or Ilay could have acted. Gregory's admission to King's College strengthened the position of his father-in-law and very probably irritated both the Gordons and the Argathelian party, if they were not already one and the same.

In 1726 Patrick Duff was elected rector at Marischal College, a position which he held until 1729 when his father-in-law, William Duff of Braco, was chosen. After 1726 most of the Marischal College assessors ceased to be clerics who were likely to agree with the Rev. Dr Thomas Blackwell. Replacing them were advocates, town councillors and merchants more dependent on politicians and more agreeable to Ilay. That pattern was to last, and characterised the secularity of outlook brought to most of the institutions Ilay managed. It nicely reflected his anti-clerical tendencies and his distrust of the 'Levites'.[55]

At King's similar developments also came after 1725 and reflect the accommodation made by men who recognised that their bread was no longer likely to be buttered by Squadrone politicians. When Patrick Duff became an assessor in 1725, the rectorial court ceased to be mainly a body of clerics, becoming instead one dominated by lawyers and landed gentlemen. Some of these men, such as Thomas Hay, sheriff clerk of Aberdeenshire, and John Paton of Grandholme, who became rector in 1728 and served until 1733, were old Jacobites who had seen the light.[56] Ilay, some of the staff, and those students who also chose rectorial court electors were probably more tolerant and forgiving than Principal Chalmers. The evidence of politicking in the colleges is far better in 1727. Then the death of the king (22 June) and the survival of Walpole's ministry and Argathelian power allowed Ilay and his friends to assert themselves more vigorously in Aberdeen and elsewhere.

Prior to George I's demise, a patent for a Marischal College regency had been secured for William Duff, replacing George Turnbull who had resigned. Duff was the son of Hugh Duff, minister of Fearn, Ross-shire, and very likely a relative of both Patrick Duff of Premnay, who was chosen rector in 1726, and of his father-in-law, William Duff of Braco, rector at Marischal College in 1728. The latter controlled the Banffshire parliamentary seat. In 1727 the Duff interest supported the government and was untainted by Squadrone sympathies.[57] Professor Duff's later behaviour was erratic and violent but it also suggested a deep and long-standing dislike of the Squadrone Blackwells.

The other 1727 Marischal College appointment was equally significant in the politics of Aberdeen because it involved an attempt by Ilay and his friends to cow the town council. They failed in a battle whose origins went back to 1726 and to the removal of Colin Maclaurin from the chair of mathematics in January 1726.[58]

The chair of mathematics was by its foundation to be filled by a comparative trial with some regard paid to the founder's kin, but the place was really in the gift of the town council. Between 1714 and 1727, the provost had for ten years been either Robert Stewart of Bridgeford or George Fordyce of Broadford. The first had been restored to his office in 1716 by the Squadrone; the latter was a son-in-law of Principal Blackwell. Their politics were hardly in doubt. Indeed, throughout 1727–8 a town council faction composed of Fordyce, Baillie William Cruden and Provosts William Cruickshank and William Chalmers opposed Ilay's choices for jobs in the Aberdeen universities and the kirks. These men were not thought of by Patrick Duff as being 'of our Syde'.[59] If Ilay and the crown were to be able to make an appointment to the mathematics chair, they had to produce a plausible candidate who could stand a trial, and they had to convince the town council to appoint him. In the end they found a man, but they were unable to place him because the town fathers were as insistent upon their rights as Ilay was determined to deny them. The struggle for this job had begun by 26 March 1726 when Charles Erskine (Ilay had made him solicitor general in the previous year) wrote to someone, possibly Argyll, that Marischal College professors had 'applyed to me, Representing the Interest the Crown had in filling the Imployment, and offered the Memorial herewith inclos'd'. Erskine went on to give legal advice about the rights of the crown to act as patron or perhaps as chancellor to that university and college:

> I have seen a Copy of the Mortification, and it appears to me, the Crown has really an Interest in the Matter; and for that reason I am humbly of opinion it may not be improper such power as in the Memorial is mention'd be directed to Mr. Duff who I believe is a person fit enough to discharge that trust.[60]

What Erskine had in mind was for Duff to 'give his Majestys votes at the election of [the] professor of mathematics', a vote representing the crown's interest in the college and in each of its chairs.[61] This is confirmed by a 'Note [of] what seems to have been communed upon betwixt Mr. Erskine his Majestie's solicitor and Mr. Garden of Troup [the former King's civilist and sheriff-depute of Aberdeen who was now an Argathelian] anent settling the Professor of Mathematicks in the Colledge of new Aberdeen'. This memorandum says that the college should protest against the trial programme set out by the magistrates and appoint as judges of the competition 'the four [Scottish] Professors of Mathematics ... And that the Delegate from the King, should consent to that choise'. The trial would be held in the college in the presence of 'the Masters of the Colledge & the Delegate, should be present with the Magistrates and Councell, But the Judges only should act'. They were to give their judgement in separate papers to the council and to 'the Colledge and Delegate, And that the Councell give one presentation to the person chosen, And the Colledge & Delegate should give a separate Presentation to the same person that happens to be chosen'. The memorandum also says that 'the Magistrates should declare under their hand That if Mr. Campbell be found the dignior [worthy] person by the Judges, They should concurr in settling him'.[62] These arrangements would have brought an end not only to the independence of the council but also to that of the masters since it is hard to believe that friends of Walpole would have made the delegate only an *ad hoc* presence in the college.

The town fathers were clearly not prepared to accept this arrangement. The next deal with Troup was inscribed in their letter book in rather different terms. The judges were still to be the other Scottish mathematics professors, but the trial was to follow its usual procedure and neither they nor the college were to 'emitt any Program'. Neither the college nor town fathers were to comment publicly on the case or upon the delegate's presence and concurrence with the masters upon the election. If the judges found for Campbell, he was to be preferred. This was entered on 10 June 1726 but it clearly did not end the matter.[63] The question of who had a right to elect went to the court of session whose decreet found 'that the Magistrates & Town Council of Aberdeen have the only power of naming and appointing a Professor of Mathematicks in this Colledge'.[64] Once this had been received, John Stewart, the son of Provost Robert Stewart, petitioned to be tried.

The council which considered his petition on 21 August 1727 included Provost Fordyce, Baillies Cruden, Morrison and Cruickshanks, Dean of Guild William Gellie and John Stewart's father. Five of these men had already appeared in Lord Milton's correspondence as unfriendly or unreliable; Gellie had been a Marischal College assessor in 1720–1 and 1723–4, years in which Ilay's friends were not yet in power. The council deliberated and then exercised its rights. It appointed the St Andrews mathematics professor, Charles Gregory (he happened to be in Aberdeen), Alexander Burnet of King's College and Regent Daniel Gordon to meet on 22 August and to try any who might appear.[65] John Stewart was duly tried, found worthy and appointed but not without protest.[66] The Argathelians had been beaten and Principal Blackwell's faction had been afforced with an extra vote. That outcome made it more important for Ilay to win the next contests which had in fact already begun. These concerned the principalship, the professorship of divinity (both held by the ailing Principal Blackwell) and the church livings which would be shuffled as a consequence of Blackwell's expected demise. Before turning to these one must note the effect which the king's death in June 1727 had upon Aberdeen politics.

With the king's death all grants made only for the life of George I lapsed. These included some grants of money to the colleges, a royal chaplaincy held by David Anderson, the deputy collectorship of bishop's rents belonging to George Gordon, like Anderson a King's College man, and the offices of JP and commissioner of supply held by Patrick Duff and some of the assessors at both colleges. It was important to their holders to get these renewed as quickly as possible. At King's this was especially important because the 1718 fund-raising tour undertaken by Principal Chalmers had gained little from the government or from private sources as far away as Holland which Chalmers also seems to have visited.[67] The £1,400 given by Dr James Fraser of Chelsea did not yield all that much income, and substantial sums had had to be spent on repairs to the college fabric. In 1727 Professor George Gordon was pessimistic about the renewal of the royal bounty to King's. Indeed, he feared that Thomas Blackwell the younger and Ilay's friend Maclaurin, both then in London and looking after Marischal College interests, would hurt the chances of King's College and, perhaps, his own. He clearly hoped that friends of either David Anderson or Principal Chalmers would come to power as new 'favourites' but he also seemed willing, as was Thomas Blackwell Jr, to cultivate any politician who might serve King's College.

Something of the uncertainty, excitement and anxiety which a change in monarchs produced is captured in George Gordon's letter from Edinburgh to his 'R[everen]d & D[ear] C[olleague]', probably Principal Chalmers, written on 21 June 1727:

> Addresses are you may easily beleeve flying throng to our Gracious Soveraign. I should wish wee were not among the last, Our great friend the Doctor [James Fraser] I suppose would be angry, if wee are not on this occasion earely in the road of our duty. I doubt not our envious Neighbours

will endeavour to prevent us Now that they have young T. Blackwell at London, to him (notwithstanding of old family quarrels) will I'm informed be assisting Mr M^claurin Who went post for London yesterday afternoone—you see by inclosed Print [lost] that he is one of those who signs our Proclama'n & is a very throng man like to excell in Politicks as well as mathematicks.

Robin [Provost Robert?] Stuart & one or two more of his Colleagues told me that he [Blackwell] was to mannage the affaire of their Society above, to get their Gift of the Royall bounty renewed (for you know all Gifts & pensionse doe now fall) & farther insinuat that they thought the other Universities in Scotland could not doe better than apply to him for getting their Gift renewed & taking care of their Interests at Court. I doubt not but you'l easily beleeve that I heartily wish Wee could promise any safety to our selves from such Conduct. I freely owne to you I dread the contrary however, as I presume you'l communicat this to the Society so I shall be glade to have their sentiments.—Sure I am that if wee had money it were much the Societie's Interest to have one of their owne Number there on this extraordinary occasion, for takeing care of our Concerns, setting our great friend the Dr in a right roade, & timeously plying those who shall be discovered to be favourites which will ere long appeare & I hope you may have the honour to be well with some of them, & be a proper Plenipo.[68]

When the new favourites turned out to be the same old servants of the crown, the King's College men seem to have made peace with Ilay who was willing to buy them. Professor Anderson kept or got his royal chaplaincy which he saw 'not only as an accommodating to my family but also as a seasonable mortification to a certain Sett of men [Episcopalians] who have long endeavoured by all means to crush me with their party rage'. He also promised 'that Mr. Wallace only shall be the man upon any terms Your Lop shall think fitt'. Clearly a bargain had been struck. George Gordon kept his post as 'depute Collecter of Bishops rents' and was no doubt grateful to the same lords.[69] The college got its grants renewed, but it is clear that Principal Blackwell's son had tried to divert funds to Marischal College. He had tried so hard that he overplayed his hand.[70] Ilay had been fair and even generous to King's. In the general election of 1727, Principal Chalmers cast the college's vote not for the Forbes interest, as he had been instructed by the masters to do, but for Ilay's brother-in-law, Alexander Fraser.[71]

Principal Chalmers in 1728 became minister of Old Machar and Ilay's friends seem to have helped to get him admitted when he was opposed and barred by parishioners and the General Assembly.[72] In doing that Ilay ignored the advice of his ally Lord Grange. Ilay's favourable attitude towards the college persisted at least until 1733. In 1730 George Gordon was allowed to succeed his father as regius professor of oriental languages. Principal Chalmers had recommended this with the support of his staff and Col. John Middleton, the MP for the Aberdeen Burghs.[73] The king's death and the emergence of the Argathelians among the favourites allowed Ilay to buy goodwill at King's College by the simple expedient of renewing grants, fairly awarding funds and giving support to Anderson and the Gordon-Fraser connection which had not opposed him. Principal Chalmers had been helped and Ilay could expect to be repaid for the favours he had conferred.

At Marischal College the political situation in these years was somewhat different. There was no chancellor, but Ilay's agent in Aberdeen, Patrick Duff, was rector. Principal Blackwell was no friend to the Argathelians, but he could not afford to offend them since he too needed to have both university and personal grants renewed or augmented. The ambivalence of his position was clear to Patrick Duff who informed Lord Milton that Principal Blackwell 'has much to say with many of our Council and I believe not to be of our Syde if his friends [Provost Fordyce in particular] would come along with him'. In the end Blackwell aided the Argathelians in the parliamentary general election of 1727.[74] And, as we have seen, Thomas Blackwell the younger joined with Colin Maclaurin to try to promote the fortunes of the college. In the college meetings, however, there were signs of trouble because the majority had shifted from Ilay's friends to his opponents with the selection of John Stewart as professor of mathematics. This meant that the next appointments would be very important. Before any were made to professorships there occurred a bizarre bit of flattery of the royal family, probably related to the general parliamentary election which took place in Aberdeenshire on 7 September and in the Aberdeen Burghs on 9 September 1727.

The rector, Patrick Duff, Principal Blackwell, Professor MacKaile and Regents Verner, Gordon and Duff met on 29 August to elect as their chancellor 'The High & Mighty Prince William Duke of Cumberland'— then aged five. This certainly told the new king that the college was loyal. Such sycophancy was probably also an attempt to extract larger grants from the crown. Perhaps this was one of 'young Tom' Blackwell's schemes which that year had so shocked Principal Hadow and Professor Hamilton. The grotesque election, which joined the two college factions in an assertion of their collective interests, was one which would have ensured that the college would come more completely under political control and that there would indeed be a 'Royal Delegate' able to participate in all important matters. Until Cumberland could act himself, this would also have ensured a greater authority to political managers like Ilay. Intriguing as these documents are, their consequences are unknown. Probably they served an ephemeral purpose and were never received by the guardians of the prince.[75] From 1727 until 1742 Ilay himself served as the *de facto* chancellor and protector of the university and college, but there is no reason to believe that he was a legally elected official, as is sometimes claimed.

In 1728 Principal Blackwell died and the crown had two vacancies to fill, the principalship and the chair of divinity.[76] Ilay's problem, as he well knew, was to find trustworthy men for these places who could help him manage the college and the burgh. The fly in the ointment was that the principal's salary from the college was a derisory £20. His real stipend came from a city church which was in the gift of the town council. The case was even worse with the chair of divinity since the right of presentation belonged to the town. The council's recalcitrance had been displayed in the Stewart case and was again in evidence even though it had voted in 1727 as Ilay wished. Of the town councillors only Baillie William Cruickshank had been especially active for Ilay's candidate, Col. Middleton, who had again been returned for the Aberdeen Burghs. Provosts Stewart and Fordyce and their friends had been unreliable if not obstructive and their ability to cause trouble still remained, since they retained places on the burgh council. The Argathelian game was to lessen their influence by making appointments in the college which would please a majority of the town council and make it, the presbytery and the college more manageable.

On 20 February, the day Principal Blackwell died, ex-Provost George Fordyce and Baillies William Cruden, William Cruickshank and William Chalmers all signed a letter to Lord Milton asking that Blackwell be speedily replaced by James Chalmers, then the minister of the East Church. Milton warned Ilay against this appointment, saying that Chalmers was unfit and politically in the enemy camp.[77] By that time Milton would have received Patrick Duff's two letters of 21 February sending a copy of the foundation charter and a recommendation of John Osborn 'another of our Ministers who is a man of excellent Judgement & learning who has been alwise a firm friend & has many good wishers in the town, and who was a favourite with the Magistrates till he lost his [illegible] by opposing Mr. [George] Chalmers was the man I proposed to [the Rector's Court]'. Duff added that the rectorial court, on which Osborn had sat in most years since 1720, had a majority in his favour.[78] Osborn was the son of a former dean of guild but also the nephew of an Edinburgh merchant who was to become lord provost there with Ilay's help in 1733. He seems, as well, to have been related in some fashion to Forbes of Craigievar, and had married Margaret Mitchell who was probably the daughter of an Aberdeen minister.

Duff's suggestion was an astute one as was his action in putting the matter to his assessors. That made the candidate publicly known, gave him backers in the university and showed councillors that there was an alternative both for them and Ilay. A week later, on 28 February, Duff wrote again to suggest that if Osborn became principal, Chalmers might get the professorship of divinity. That was a compromise but not one much liked by the town council. On 1 March, Duff urged delay and thought that if Blackwell's salary were continued to his widow for a year that could help ease tensions.[79] Those were rising. On 1 April the magistrates informed Milton that they were not plotting or upset at the delay, but they asked for more favours. Could not Blackwell's third son, Charles, have a Glasgow bursary? On 26 May they sought the recently deceased Daniel Gordon's place for George Blackwell, the second son.[80] And, again, on 12 April, William Cruickshank asked that Chalmers be made principal.[81] Only a week before, Duff had reported that the baillies had denied seeking advice (presumably legal advice) about what to do should Chalmers not get the post. By then it was also clear that these two appointments were being related to that of Principal George Chalmers to the kirk living of Old Machar, a place from which he had been barred by Church courts.[82]

The ways in which Ilay sorted out all these problems tells a good deal about the nature of his success as a government manager. Everyone got something, while he increased his power. On or about 8 April John Osborn wrote to Ilay's secretary that he was to be made principal.[83] The Fordyce faction was annoyed but they had not come off so badly. Mrs Blackwell had her year's pension. Ilay had taken the trouble to inquire of Colin Maclaurin about George Blackwell. He turned out to be 'under Age & but of mean parts'.[84] Despite that, Milton seems to have recommended him for the librarian's post at Marischal and for an Aberdeen regency in 1728. The youngest son did go to Glasgow in 1735.[85] By July, Chalmers had got his consolation prize and Baillie Cruickshank, who had been willing to accept that deal, got the provost's job and positions for his sons. Those who followed his leadership came to dominate the town council and seem to have remained with Ilay until 1742, some until 1761. Ex-Provosts Fordyce and Stewart were no longer the dominant local politicians. The principalship had gone to the right sort of man whose casting vote would give the Argathelians control of Marischal College. Osborn would be useful in Aberdeen and in the General Assembly where he sat for at least six years.

Lord Ilay was not so fortunate with Professor James Chalmers; he turned out to be, and to remain, an enemy. Twice in 1729 he was to embarrass the Argathelians. When the time came to elect the rector, Chalmers engineered the election of William Duff of Braco.[86] He thus ousted Patrick Duff of Premnay from that post, but Braco may have kept it only one year.[87]

What lay behind this move was certainly the control of the corporation and perhaps plans to object to Osborn's presentation in either the rectorial or civil courts. It coincided with Braco's joining the opposition in parliament and it was part of a scheme in which MacKaile believed Principal George Chalmers to be somewhat implicated.[88] Perhaps that explains why in 1733 when Principal Chalmers applied for the late Professor Anderson's royal chaplaincy nothing came of the proposal.[89] Personal animosities and party feeling kept an Aberdeen opposition alive among men whose original political loyalties were to Squadrone patrons.

In late 1728 or early 1729 Professor Daniel Gordon died and one Argathelian opponent in Marischal College was gone. His place went to Dr MacKaile whose diligence as an informer was well rewarded. By 1729 he held the sinecure chair of medicine, the post of librarian and after November 1729, a regency. It is also noteworthy that he tried to have the warrant for this chair specify that he was to be 'professor of Natural & Experimental philosophy'. In that, however, he was unsuccessful.[90] More successful was his harrying of Thomas Blackwell the younger.

Blackwell, after his father's death and the discomfiture of the Fordyce faction in the town council, became the leader of Marischal's Squadrone men. By 1731 MacKaile and the Argathelians had tried to 'break' his class, suspended him from teaching and wished to drive him from the college. Blackwell saw this as a party-political move by a faction which had one more vote than his. He was ultimately forced to seek protection from Lord Milton.[91]

By 1730 Lord Ilay, the Argathelians and their friends were clearly in control of four of the five Scottish universities—only St Andrews eluded them. Until 1742 Ilay would work to maintain that dominance against increasing odds. Opposition challenges after 1733, the defection of his brother, the Duke of Argyll, from Walpole's ministry in 1738, and the decline in Walpole's power up to 1742, made the manager's life a difficult one.

Chapter 4

The Argathelians, 1730–1761

I Marischal College, 1730–42

Marischal College was now an institution in which recruitment was determined by the servants of the crown, but within the college there were those who kicked against the pricks. Party tensions and the insecure majority of the Argathelians in the college meeting probably explain the lack of rectorial elections in 1730 and 1731. The following year the post went to Sir Alexander Ramsay of Balmain, as a compliment for founding in 1732 the chair of oriental languages.[1] Professor James Donaldson, MD, chosen by Sir Alexander, almost certainly sided with Ilay's friends.

The death of Dr MacKaile in 1734 allowed the crown to make three appointments. All went to safe men. The chair of medicine was given to Dr James Gordon of Pitlurg, Professor Donaldson's brother-in-law, who was recommended to Lord Milton by Patrick Duff.[2] Francis Skene[3] got MacKaile's regency, while the librarian's post went to Thomas Reid who was later to make a name for himself as a professor at King's and Glasgow. The only other appointment before 1742 went to Alexander Innes. He had been a substitute for William Duff, chosen first by the regent himself and then by the masters when Duff's conduct had become impossible. With the backing of the town council the masters all asked that Duff's deposition be recognised by Ilay, and that Innes be appointed. To remove any shadow of illegality from their proceedings, the masters advertised a comparative trial. As they no doubt expected, no one came to it but Innes. He was also appointed by Ilay in 1739 but only with reluctance. The Aberdonians had shown too much initiative in this case.[4]

II King's College, 1730–41

At King's there was far more turmoil because the masters were divided politically and because they lacked a strong figure to whom their differences might be appealed. Ilay could intervene very little. There was no real chancellor and the rectors, when they sat, did little. As politics heated up in the late 1730s and early 1740s, King's too came to the boil.

At King's, Ilay arranged for the appointment in 1730 of George Gordon the younger, but he seems to have had nothing to do with the selection in 1732 of James Gregory the younger as mediciner, or of Alexander Rait as professor of mathematics. Gregory's stepmother was the principal's daughter; Rait seems to have been related to both Alexander Burnet and Daniel Bradfute. Rait's appointment gave a title to someone already teaching in the college. These elections were family affairs which Ilay and his friends could not much influence. Apparently not consulted, they would feel little need to find Rait a salary; when asked they did not do so.[5]

All that no doubt seemed more important to Ilay in the spring of 1733 when Walpole's Excise Bill occasioned an all-out attack upon the government by the Squadrone and Jacobites. Something of the atmosphere of the time is conveyed in a 1733 letter of James Erskine, Lord Grange, once an ally of Argyll and Ilay but then in opposition:

> Ilay used sillyly to boast, some years ago, with a haughty disdainful air, and to cry (I have heard him), where is now the Squadron and opposing party? have I not annihilated them? It had been strong enough and vain enough to have said he had buried them. But they have had a resurrection. The excise scheme on the back of so many other grievous things, the threatening speech they made for the King at the end of the parliament, the violent measures of resentment for differing from them in parliament, and turning out men of the best characters, Chesterfield, Cobham, and very near Scarborough, etc had awakened men from their lethargy. Among us seem to be firmly united against them Tweedale, Aberdeen, Stair, Roxburgh, Montrose, Marchmont, Duke Hamilton, Duke Queensberry, Dondonald etc.[6]

In Aberdeen this attack gave rise to a protracted contest between John Lumsden and James Gordon involving the professorship of divinity at King's.[7]

This has been seen as a fight between Evangelicals and Moderates but that is unlikely. Principal Chalmers was an Evangelical friend of Robert Wodrow, but in this case the principal was defending the rights of his corporation and of a candidate who turned out to be a Moderate. Ilay was not always a supporter of such men. In 1743 he was to back for the Glasgow chair of divinity John Maclaurin, a high-flying supporter of Whitfield who had been involved with the 'Cambuslang wark'. In that election the Squadrone backed the Moderate candidate, William Leechman. Making either appointment an ideological religious struggle within the Kirk obscures its essentially political nature and, in this case, its relation to an opposition's attack upon the ministry. That is brought out in correspondence concerning the former affair. James Gordon was as much a Squadrone candidate as he was one who belonged to a particular religious party. That was equally true of John Lumsden, the man whom Ilay backed and the one who ultimately got the chair.

Lord Milton was informed of the impending election by Patrick Duff as early as 14 February 1733.[8] Principal Chalmers, on 8 October 1733, reminded Milton that 'I was encouraged to engage in it partarly when I had the honour to wait on the E. of Ila and your Lops when last att Edin[r] so I particularly depend on your good offices in my favours which I shall always be ready to acknowledge with the greatest Gratitude and the best services for the common Interest I am capable of.' On 25 October 1734 Chalmers asked for support for Lumsden, for £60 addition to the money already sent and said that Gordon's expenses were being underwritten 'by liberal Contributions from that party who espouse his cause'.[9] The attack on the Argathelians in this case made Chalmers an ally, as he usually had been since 1728, but the principal's greatest concern was to protect his university's rights.

The electors to this chair of divinity were principally the delegates of the synod of Aberdeen joined by delegates from the college. The foundation required a comparative trial but that provision had been long ignored. The real process of selection had been under way since 1729. John Lumsden was Ilay's man, but the Rev. James Gordon, the minister of Alford, was elected by a stacked electoral body over which he presided on 26 August 1733. Principal Chalmers believed that the electors' right to present had lapsed because they had not exercised it within the prescribed time limit. Chalmers appealed to the General Assembly which said this was a civil case. The principal then pursued Gordon in the court of session. Gordon, who had been chosen as Moderator of the General Assembly in 1734, lost there but appealed to the House of Lords, presumably with the backing of some of the lords mentioned in Lord Grange's letter. Chalmers certainly believed that the appellant 'particularly depends upon the friendship & countenance of those called Patriots [the Squadrone] for promoting his Interest'. The same letter makes it clear that Col. Middleton and Ilay were expected to bear some of the principal's legal costs.[10] Gordon won his case but he did not appear at the rescheduled trial and election at which John Lumsden was chosen. Gordon's absence makes it highly likely that this affair was carried on in the interest of others such as William Gordon, 2nd Earl of Aberdeen. If Lumsden's election was a victory for Moderates, it was also one for Ilay over the synod.

In March 1734 the Squadrone leaders were trying to rally supporters in the parliamentary constituencies.[11] It was amidst such commotions that three other appointments were made at King's in 1734. These vacancies went to Daniel Bradfute, Alexander Rait and Thomas Gordon and were occasioned by John Ker's translation to the chair of humanity at Edinburgh University. That was made possible by Squadrone politicians then dominant in the Faculty of Advocates. Bradfute took Ker's Greek chair; Rait became a regular member of the college as a regent. Gordon was named assistant and successor to his relative, Alexander Fraser, who remained subprincipal. Just as the principal had taken care of his relatives so too had the Gordons and Frasers.

By 1734 there was a third family group forming around Alexander Burnet. This was to be significant in later years, more significant perhaps because the election of rectors ceased in 1733 when John Paton of Grandholme was not re-elected.[12] There were to be no more known rectors until 1760. That left the masters free to quarrel amongst themselves with no intramural mediators and only the civil courts to which appeals could be made.

King's College by the time of the annual rectorial election in the winter of 1733–4 was a college evenly balanced between two family factions, each of which had divided political loyalties. On the one hand there were the 'new men' of 1718 put in by the Squadrone to whom they probably still felt some obligation and personal ties. These included Principal Chalmers, Daniel Bradfute and John Ker. The mediciner, James Gregory I (d. 20 December 1733), was the son-in-law of the principal, and in 1734 was followed in office by his son James. The latter was married to Helen Burnet who may have been a relative of the subprincipal but who was certainly related by marriage to Daniel Bradfute. This group had few roots in Aberdeen and was probably disposed to look abroad for support as Chalmers had done in 1733 when he asked Ilay to help pay legal bills incurred in the suits over the professorship of divinity.

The other family faction centred on the Gordon-Fraser connection which was locally rooted and had continued in the college for many years. In 1734 the Gordons were represented by: Alexander, the humanist; George II, his nephew and professor of Hebrew; Thomas, another nephew and assistant and successor to Alexander Fraser I, regent and subprincipal, who was also related to the Gordons by marriage; and Fraser's son, Alexander II, the civilist. The professorship of divinity was vacant since David Anderson, the friend of Chalmers and George Gordon I, had died on 13 February 1733. Anderson had been indebted to Ilay for the renewal of his chaplaincy in 1727 although he owed his original appointments as professor and chaplain to Squadrone politicians. By 1733 the Gordons owed something to Ilay for the appointment of George Gordon II, although they may have felt more obliged to Col. Middleton or even to the Duke of Newcastle. The Gordon family's earlier political dealings, like George Gordon the elder's scepticism about Ilay in 1727, suggests that their Whig loyalties ran to the Squadrone not the Argathelians or that they may not have been much committed to either party.

The Argathelians weathered the attacks of 1733–4 and the universities in Aberdeen were peaceful until 1741. By that time Walpole's Scottish team was in disarray. Argyll had broken with his brother Ilay in 1739 and had gone into opposition to Walpole's government. Ilay was left trying to manage Scottish affairs without the prestige, patronage and economic power of the Duke of Argyll who had had military as well as civil jobs to dispense. This situation was made worse in Aberdeenshire because the MP, Sir Arthur Forbes, had followed Argyll into opposition. The Burghs' seat still remained safe with John Maule, Ilay's secretary, who had won it after Brigadier Middleton's death in 1739.[13] Problems were bound to arise in Aberdeen's universities as politicians tested one another. They did so first at King's College in 1741 when the civilist's chair fell vacant upon the death of Alexander Fraser II. The ensuing contest pitted Sir William Forbes of Monymusk against James Thomson of Portlethen. The fight which followed was, like so many in the academic world of the eighteenth century, political, principled and centred on family concerns. The principles are easiest to deal with.

III Family and Party Contests at King's and Marischal Colleges, 1741–5

Civilists were originally chosen by the rector, the principal, subprincipal, mediciner, the grammarian or humanist and by the procurators of the Four Nations, an *ad hoc* electoral body chosen by the masters.[14] The regents and other professors had no direct vote prior to 1711. In that year, as we have seen, the court of session in William Simpson's case had found that the professors of mathematics and Hebrew were entitled to vote in elections. The professor of divinity joined the list of the enfranchised in 1713.[15] By 1741 that left only the regents excluded from the election and from the selection of the procurators who were usually local notables with some connection to the college. In 1741 the Burnet faction (Burnet, Bradfute, Rait) was disenfranchised in both elections when at the college meeting Principal Chalmers ruled that they could vote neither for the procurators nor the civilist. That decision left six voters and a tied vote which the principal claimed to be able to break with his casting ballot.[16] Having his way would have restored to Chalmers a measure of control, and it would have helped his political friends outside the corporation. The principal could also plausibly argue that he was following the ancient constitution of the college. The foundation required a resident civilist which one candidate, Sir William Forbes, a practising Edinburgh lawyer, could not be. James Thomson of Portlethen, the other candidate, was certainly resident. This issue had caused problems earlier when it had been settled in favour of residents and, incidentally, of men native to Aberdeen who belonged to its Society of Advocates.[17] The family issues were almost equally clear.

The principal's supporters included John Lumsden whom Chalmers had brought into the college as professor of divinity and the mediciner, James Gregory, who was his step-grandson. Thomson, their candidate for civilist, was the mediciner's distant relative, as was Andrew Thompson, one of the procurators. Another procurator, William Thomson, was very probably related to both, while a third, John Burnet of Elrick, may have been kin to Gregory's wife, Helen Burnet. James Thomson, Gregory and Burnet all had Jacobite antecedents which would not have bothered Ilay greatly. Opposed to Principal Chalmers were Alexander Burnet, Alexander Rait and Daniel Bradfute, all regents and relatives. Voting with them for Sir William Forbes's procurators were George and Thomas Gordon both of whom married Forbes women in 1741 and 1742.[18] The procurators whom they chose included Thomas Forbes of Echt, the son of the 'bigot Presbyterian' rector of 1718–28. Others were the Rev. Theodore Gordon, who owed his kirk to his Gordon relatives at King's, and Alexander Strachan, minister of Keig (he had been appointed to his church living by heritors named Forbes and Gordon). These connections are more significant when one remembers that Thomas Forbes had been friendly with Ilay since about 1724, and that Sir Arthur Forbes was a member of the 'duke of Argyll's Gang' in 1741. The principal's men were Ilay's; the other side belonged to his brother and/or the Squadrone; the Gordons formed a third party, siding against the principal in this case.[19]

The political nature of this contest can also be confirmed by the counsel feed by each side. Sir William's principal advocate seems to have been John Murray, who was made principal clerk of session by Roxburghe in 1723. The other side was represented by William Grant, then solicitor general, a man usually but not always loyal to Ilay, and by Robert Dundas who in 1742 was to become solicitor general for the Squadrone. Chalmers's friends were perhaps hedging their bets; both sides were also employing some of the best talent at the bar of Scotland.[20]

The fight over the civilist's sinecure post (worth about £40 a year) was eventually settled by the court of session which forced the admission of Sir William Forbes. The regents were given votes in future elections and the power of the principal was curbed. The decision left a legacy of bitterness discernible in the King's College minutes where the principal noted on 7 August 1741 that the court's order violated the college charter and the masters' rights. The lords of session had ordered the installation of a professor who would not reside, teach or serve the corporation in its local legal business. The principal's chagrin was again evident in 1743 when another civilist had to be elected. Again family and political interests were at stake, and principles justified what faculty cliques chose to do. The big difference this time was that neither Ilay, nor his brother, was any longer in the ministry in London.

By 1743 Walpole had fallen and in Scotland the Squadrone interest (led by the Marquis of Tweeddale) had been returned to power. The Town of Aberdeen had voted in 1741 for a new MP, Alexander Udney, even though Provost Alexander Robertson, ex-Provost William Chalmers and Baillie Fordyce were listed in 1742 as 'all strongly attached to Mr. Maule' who again carried the Burghs' seat in 1741.[21] The council would have still been split in its loyalty a year later. At Marischal College the new political managers found support.

Marischal's professors might owe much to Lord Ilay, but his party, now lacking Argyll's support, was clearly waning by the late 1730s. In 1737 the masters had elected as rector George Skene of Skene, an Argathelian who remained loyal to the duke and deserted the government in 1739. Skene's assessors in 1737 were probably all friends of Ilay, as was William Cruickshank. By 1739 the rectorial court included one William Fordyce and three men who had never held this office: Alexander Robertson, provost (1740–1), James Morrison, provost (1744–5) and James Catanach. All by 1743 supported the Squadrone faction. From 1741 to 1745 the rectorial court included at least one member of the Forbes family. Its political complexion had clearly changed. So too had the allegiance of the rector. Loyal to Argyll after 1739 but not to the government, Skene had changed sides.[22] That the majority of the masters accepted the necessity of this change is evident from the fact that Skene remained rector until 1745. Voting for him would have been his protégé, Francis Skene,[23] and David Verner who seems also to have trimmed.[24] Joining them would have been Ilay's old enemies Professors James Chalmers, John Stewart and Thomas Blackwell. By June 1742 the latter was professing loyalty to the Squadrone and pleading for funds for the college.[25] In September of that year they were to be joined by another regent, David Fordyce. He was Blackwell's cousin, a son of the former provost whom Ilay had deprived of power in 1728, and the only Squadrone appointment made at Marischal between 1742 and 1746.[26]

At King's similar shifts had occurred. On the death in January 1742 of Regent Alexander Fraser the elder, the college had elected his assistant and their clerk, John Chalmers, as his replacement. Chalmers was an ideal man since he also appears to have been a nephew of the new subprincipal, Alexander Burnet, a cousin to the Gordon brothers and a relative of Alexander Rait either by blood or marriage. This would not strengthen Principal Chalmers's hand but it could be expected to help the friends of the Marischal College professor of divinity, James Chalmers, to whom John Chalmers was also related. John Chalmers's appointment made the Burnet connection the largest in King's College. It could reasonably try for another member and it did so in 1743 when the civilist's place was again vacant. These men, but not the Gordon brothers, then joined with Principal George Chalmers to support James Catanach.

On 8 June 1743 the King's College masters gathered to elect their new civilist, but were unable to agree on who he should be. They split into two factions led respectively by Principal Chalmers and Subprincipal Burnet. Principal Chalmers, who in 1724 and 1741 had so wanted a local resident lawyer, now supported the candidacy of Charles Hamilton Gordon, an Edinburgh lawyer who practised much in Church courts. Gordon was the son of Sir William Gordon of Dalfolly. In 1744 he applied to Lord Milton to become collector for the Widows' Fund and it is likely that in 1743 he looked to the same connection for support in his attempt to secure this sinecure.[27] Voting with the principal were his friend, the divinity professor John Lumsden, and the Gordon brothers, George and Thomas, who doubtless knew a kinsman when they saw one. The procurators for this side included Arthur Gordon of Whitehouse, the Rev. Theodore Gordon of Keithall, Patrick Duff of Premnay[28] and a John Maxwell. By picking the right man, the principal's side had found new friends.

As one might expect, the other side was also a family connection as the principal noted in his protest at their election of James Catanach. John Chalmers and Alexander Rait were Subprincipal Burnet's 'two Nephews and Mr. Catanachs near relation'. He could have added that Daniel Bradfute was also a relative, as James Gregory may have been. These men picked as procurators: James Thomson, who had failed to get the chair at the last election; George Turner, an Aberdeen advocate who seems to have become commissary-depute in Aberdeen in 1743 and six years later was to marry Catanach's sister Margaret;[29] and two Marischal College professors, Francis Skene and David Verner. The loyalty of these men was certainly not to Ilay, perhaps not even to Argyll who died in October 1743. Only a year before, Thomas Blackwell had written to Tweeddale that every 'Member of our society' had for him 'Gratitude, Esteem and true Attachment'.[30] Like the civilist's fight in 1741, this looks like a family struggle with political overtones. Both these unmentionable aspects of the case were certainly of more initial importance than the issues of principle which sent this case to the law courts and ultimately to the House of Lords. The issues which could be litigated centred on James Catanach's qualifications for office and on the rights and privileges of Marischal College and University which had bestowed upon him an LLD.

James Catanach seems not to have matriculated at either of Aberdeen's colleges; instead, he served an apprenticeship with George Keith, a noted

Aberdeen advocate. In 1743 he was examined by Verner 'by appointment of the [Marischal] Faculty, and being found truly well qualified, In Strict Examination, The Faculty unanimously agreed to create the said Mr. James Catanach Doctor of Laws'.[31] The granting of this degree qualified him for the office of civilist which required a licentiate or degree in law, a condition which had not in the past been regularly observed. The King's College men opposed to his election objected to his lack of university training and to his degree. Marischal College, they argued, was no university. Even if it were, it had no law faculty; no one taught law or was qualified to examine a candidate for a law degree. Moreover, no Aberdeen advocate could really be thought to hold a licence within the meaning of the foundation charter since these advocates could not practise in the kingdom's higher courts but only in local ones. Those charges were enough to set off a long legal battle.

Marischal College had to vindicate its status as a university; the Society of Advocates and Procurators of Aberdeen clearly wished to assert its right to supply men to the civilist's chair when its members were nominated, and Verner had to defend his learning and honour. He claimed to have studied law at Edinburgh with James Craig and said that in 1722 he 'began to profess and teach the Civil law; which he has ever since continued and has at present Students under him at that Science'.[32] That record and his own Marischal College LLD seemed to qualify Professor Verner. The university could show that there had been many legal confirmations of its status as a university. Because of these considerations, the commissary of Aberdeen, Robert Paterson (he was not even an Aberdeen advocate) had no right to refuse admission to Catanach. These arguments did not move Paterson or the court of session where a majority of the 'Whole Fifteen' had received appointments with Ilay's help and where corporate solidarity would have led them to denigrate the status of their humbler brethren of Aberdeen. The House of Lords, however, on 11 April 1745 reversed these decisions and found Catanach's qualifications good and his election valid. It thus vindicated the honour of Dr Verner and of Marischal College and University. The Society of Advocates ordered the decision 'to be engrossed in the publick records and a notarial copy thereof, with the printed debate, to be laid up along with the writings belonging to the Society'.[33]

Once again it is interesting to look at the political affiliations of the advocates who represented Catanach and Gordon. Catanach's Edinburgh lawyers were William Grant, James Graham and Charles Maitland of Pitrichie; those in London were Alexander Hume Campbell and Charles Erskine. Three of these five men had clear ties with the Squadrone. Hume Campbell was the younger brother of the Earl of Marchmont, a Squadrone magnate who had long opposed Walpole's ministry and Ilay's politics. Hume Campbell's 1741 election as MP was contested and the decision in his favour helped to bring down Walpole's government.[34] Graham was almost certainly a Squadrone man since he came from the Glasgow area where most Grahams followed the political lead of their 'chief', the Duke of Montrose.[35] Maitland of Pitrichie was a cousin of Lord Arbuthnot, a Jacobite non-juror who in 1748 backed Maitland's winning challenge to Ilay's candidate for the Aberdeen Burghs seat. In 1742 other Arbuthnots were helping Tweeddale to manage Edinburgh politics.[36] Grant's loyalties were usually to Ilay, as were those of Charles Erskine. However, in 1744 Erskine's relations with the Squadrone men had been good enough for Robert Dundas to have 'owned before [to Tweeddale that] I had no aversion to Charles being a judge' of the court of session. If they had

9 Thomas Reid, by James Tassie, Scottish National Portrait Gallery.

discussed such an appointment, Erskine's loyalties were at least suspect in 1744. That is made more probable by the fact that Patrick Duff, Ilay's Aberdeen agent, was backing Gordon.[37] On the other side Gordon's lawyers included Alexander Lockhart, Robert Craigie, William Murray and Robert Dundas. Lockhart came from a Jacobite family but married into a Squadrone family, that of the Pringles of Edgefield. Both Craigie and Dundas held offices given them by Tweeddale between 1742 and 1746 while the William Murray was probably the later Lord Mansfield, a friend to Newcastle but a Scot who had no great liking for Ilay.[38] When one makes allowances for the party in power and the uncertainty of the times, one is still left with the impression that none of the King's College men were very sympathetic to Ilay and his friends. Catanach's lawyers in these years all had Squadrone ties while on the other side, legal prowess and interest in what appeared to be the rising political connection seems to have dictated the men employed.

After 1746, when Catanach was finally admitted to his chair and John Chalmers became principal, King's College seems to have withdrawn into itself, having little or no contact with the politicians. The next few appointments—John Gregory, regent (1746); Roderick McLeod, regent (1749); Thomas Reid, regent (1751)—all went to men connected with or nominated by the Burnet family faction.[39] Old opponents were punished: John Lumsden, the principal's ally, had his salary reduced in 1746.[40] By 1747 things appear to have settled down and relations between the professors had again become amicable.[41] By then the Burnet-Gregory faction was dominant, having captured the principal's chair and a majority in the faculty meeting. It was under their regime and auspices that union with Marischal College, now again under Ilay's tutelage, was considered and rejected in 1747 and again in 1751–5; and it was largely owing to their efforts that the course of study was transformed in 1753.[42] The change which this brought to the college set off disagreements which again divided the faculty into new factions which by 1760 had made necessary the selection of both a rector and chancellor. The new factions had again defined themselves in a fight over the appointment of a civilist in 1760.

At Marischal College, where the professors had more reasons to accommodate the crown's ministers than they did at King's and elsewhere in Scotland, the early 1740s was a period of Squadrone ascendancy. We may disbelieve Thomas Blackwell's claim that all of the professors were attached to Tweeddale, but the salaries of regius chairs were paid by the crown. The Squadrone party could undoubtedly count on Professors Chalmers, Blackwell, Stewart, Skene and, after 1742, David Fordyce, whose appointment made a majority of Squadrone men in the college meeting. Moreover, the rector was no longer an Argathelian. Fordyce's placement, like many earlier ones, had clearly been made with an eye to the management of the town. After 1740 the assessors included at least one member of the Squadrone-sympathising town council and at least one member from old Squadrone families who no longer served when Ilay, then Duke of Argyll, returned to power in 1746. Indeed, rectors and assessors were no longer chosen during the duke's regime which ended in 1761.[43] During this period (1740–6) there was only one vacancy in teaching posts other than that filled by David Fordyce.[44] That came in the divinity chair when Professor James Chalmers died in 1744. The town picked as its new professor Frederick Carmichael, whose connections were as much with Argathelians as with their opponents.[45] By then the Squadrone was a failing party. It was known to be so in Aberdeen by the appointment of Patrick Duff as commissary of Aberdeen, a job secured by Argyll. The choice of Carmichael may have been made with an eye to shifting power, a phenomenon closely watched by the town council. In any event, Carmichael turned down the council's offer and refused to be translated. He was replaced by Robert Pollock who was helped into this chair by Argyll's friends.

Pollock had been noticed in a 1744 letter from Francis Hutcheson to Gilbert Elliot, Lord Minto, who was often friendly to Argyll.[46] In April 1745 Argyll's secretary, John Maule, intervened in the case, apparently urging Carmichael to accept. When it was clear that he would not go to Aberdeen, the town's Edinburgh lawyers, George Chalmers and James Burnett (later Lord Monboddo), were told to 'wait on Mr. Pollock in person and pleade with him that he would make no opposition in the Judicatory and show him that his Election was harmonious'. This they probably did since Pollock was presented on 5 May 1745 and installed on 28 August without any trouble.[47] In addition to Hutcheson's good opinion of him, Pollock could surely count on the recommendation of the sheriff of Argyllshire whose children he had tutored.[48] This family belonged to the Argathelian connection but the other one in which Pollock is said to have tutored, Callender of Craigforth, probably did not.[49] Like Carmichael, Pollock had friends in both camps, which may have made for harmony among Whigs in 1745. In later years Pollock had no trouble serving Argyll, whose support made him principal in 1757.

IV Argyll's Second Period of Power, 1746–61: Marischal College

The Jacobite rebellion of 1745 gave the *coup de grace* to Squadrone hopes of continuing in power; Ilay, now 3rd Duke of Argyll, resumed his management of Scottish patronage in 1746. At Marischal College that change presented real difficulties only to Thomas Blackwell. In 1748 Blackwell applied for the Marischal College principalship and sought

10 James Beattie and 11 James Hay Beattie, AUL, LAa P14 Stu 122.

Argyll's blessing, even journeying to Glasgow to get it. Nevertheless, he relied for his real support upon his friendship with the Pelhams and others in England.[50] Other professors trimmed and in so doing emulated their relatives on the town council. They accepted the new regime and got what they could from it. There was very probably something for all of Argyll's old party in the college. Verner asked for and probably got patronage for his son David, a surgeon who had served as a volunteer with Lord Loudoun's troops in 1745.[51] In 1749 Pollock became King's almoner, while in the following year Francis Skene got the librarian's post. Drs Donaldson and James Gordon became physicians and surgeons to the new Aberdeen Infirmary.[52] Only Fordyce, Stewart and Blackwell seem not to have been rewarded in some fashion—but then they were Squadrone men.

Throughout the remainder of Argyll's career as a patronage dispenser, he used the college to help manage the burgh and to reward protégés of friendly country gentlemen. Neither he nor his loyal aide, Lord Milton, was oblivious to merit but they sought to use Aberdeen patronage to control local affairs and thus to strengthen their parliamentary interest in the area. Because they often chose from a number of candidates equally well recommended and loyal, they could often follow their personal proclivities and appoint men who were as tolerant, polite and as interested in science as they were, in short, the more enlightened of their applicants. That they did so at Marischal College can be seen when one looks at the men who came into office with their help or acquiescence. These included Regents Francis Skene, Alexander Innes, Alexander Gerard, [53] William Duncan,[54] William Kennedy,[55] George Skene[56] and James Beattie,[57] Principals Robert Pollock[58] and George Campbell[59] and professors of medicine James Gordon[60] and Alexander Donaldson.[61] Of these men Innes, Gerard, Duncan, Kennedy, Skene and Pollock had town council backing for one or another of their appointments. Five or six others (Donaldson, Innes, Gordon, both Skenes and James Beattie) were essentially the nominees of local gentlemen with parliamentary interests. Five (Innes, Pollock, Gerard, Kennedy and Campbell) were also appointees with ties to the local clergy whose roles in the presbytery and synod of Aberdeen could not be ignored. Finally, the masters themselves played some role in the placements of Innes, Duncan and George Skene. All these groups had had their disappointments over the years but none was ignored.

The relative openness of the appointment process had produced a professoriate which was responsive to the needs of diverse groups and patrons. It had also given Marischal College an exceptional staff which included many innovators who had helped to modernise the scholastic attitudes of the college and to introduce into it new studies which in the long run worked to transform the Scottish mind. Principal Pollock, still the professor of divinity, encouraged his students to learn Hebrew and 'recommended to the students of divinity to draw their information with regard to the Scriptures from the original, not from translations'.[62] That view was later espoused and exemplified by George Campbell, whose teachings in numerous religious works prepared Aberdonians for the higher criticism and historical accounts of religion given in the nineteenth century. They did so, however, without eroding a belief in miracles, in mysteries and in the gift of faith which has always marked the theology of Calvinists. The theology of the northern Moderates in the Kirk owed more to Campbell than to anyone else before George Hill began to lecture on systematic theology at St Andrews in 1788.[63] In Francis and George Skene

12 George Campbell, Principal of Marischal College, 1759–96. AUL, MS U 591.

and Alexander Donaldson the college found men who, like MacKaile and James Gordon earlier, advanced the study and teaching of science. They purchased instruments, started a chemistry laboratory[64] and began a natural history museum.[65] Both MacKaile and Gordon may have taught medicine in some way and the latter is said to have taught clinically at the Aberdeen Infirmary which he helped to found in 1739.[66] Among Ilay's other men one finds polite scholars. Alexander Gerard won the Select Society of Edinburgh's gold medal for 'An Essay on Taste' in 1757. His numerous publications stemmed, as did those of some of his other colleagues, from papers read to the Aberdeen Wise Club.[67] William Duncan was well known for his work as a translator and for his contribution to *Dodsley's Preceptor*, a self-help course in polite learning for which David Fordyce also wrote the section on moral philosophy.[68] The achievements of James Beattie were greater and need no commentary even after two hundred years. Indeed, of these men only Innes and Kennedy seem to have been unremarkable.

V Argyll's Second Period of Power, 1746–61: King's College

King's College in the years 1745–61 was a far less flourishing institution. While neither of the Aberdeen universities had supported the rebellion, both, but particularly King's, had been hurt by it. Again it was King's College's enrolments that tended to drop because it recruited students in the Highlands. That situation was reflected in the selection of Roderick McLeod as a regent in 1749. He was recommended by John Gregory as 'a Sufficient & well qualified young man of good connexions & reputation in the country . . . [who] is very nearly connected with some of the most considerable families in the Highlands from which the College have always drawn a great many Students as often as any of their professors were of that country'.[69] McLeod came from a family which chose correctly in 1745; his election was to help remedy a slump in enrolments such as had followed 1715.

The college chose a new principal in 1746, John Chalmers, a member of the clique which had opposed Principal Chalmers in the Catanach affair. Unlike his predecessor, this Dr Chalmers was a local man who had few contacts outside the North East. His election did, however, advertise the college's loyalty to the government; Chalmers had been captured by Jacobite troops as he helped in the suppression of the rebellion. His tenure consolidated the hold over the college of the Burnet faction and made the election of other relatives almost inevitable. One of them was his replacement as a regent, Dr John Gregory.[70]

In 1751 another Aberdonian and Gregory relative appeared on the staff,

13 John Chalmers, Principal of King's College, 1746–1800, from a portrait attributed to Sir Henry Raeburn. In a private Scottish collection.

Thomas Reid. King's continued to be very inbred, a fact which the masters seemed to recognise with their 1754 appointment of John Leslie to the chair of Greek.

John Leslie was one of several men interviewed by Principal Chalmers and Thomas Reid on a trip to Edinburgh in the spring of 1754. Leslie had been a travelling tutor to Lord Aberdour and had seen how things were done at Westminster, Balliol, Leyden and Glasgow. In the end he too was made 'a member of the family'. He seems to have had no relatives on the faculty but his future wife was to be a distant cousin of the Gordons, being a daughter of Hugh Fraser of Powis, who was the son of Alexander Fraser I, the King's subprincipal who had died in 1742.[71]

By the time Professor Leslie was chosen the masters had begun to divide over questions of educational policy and over the future of their institutions. A plan for the union of the King's and Marischal Colleges had been proposed in 1747 but it foundered when the town council of New Aberdeen insisted that the united college be located in their burgh. There was more talk of schemes in the early 1750s, but these died in 1755 for the same reason. They had one permanent result. Consideration of educational matters led to curriculum reform in both Marischal and King's Colleges. The masters in each institution reorganised their courses so that the students would progress in philosophy, as the Marischal men said in their minutes (11 January 1753), from 'those Parts . . . which are conversant about Objects of Sense' to those 'which have the Mind and its Faculties for their Object'—from civil and natural history to natural and experimental philosophy to logic, metaphysics and morals. At both institutions those reforms entailed others. Marischal switched from a regenting to a professorial system with fixed and specialised professors in 1754, but King's rejected this reform. It did make many others relating to bursaries, housekeeping arrangements, and the length of the academic year, which was extended. These changes caused dissensions at King's which, as usual, followed family lines, although in this case the reactions of some professors were clearly more related to their perceived self-interest. By 1760 they were all quarrelling in earnest—a condition caused by the lack of outside direction which Argyll and his friends supplied at Marischal College.

Between 1717 and 1761 both Aberdeen universities had been marked by the struggles of Scottish parliamentary factions. At Marischal, where the dominant politicians controlled recruitment and could usually minimise professorial in-fighting, the political influence was benign. Marischal College taught more and better mathematics and natural philosophy than did King's. That was one response to the town fathers' interest in practical education. By 1761 it had also employed notable literary men—George Turnbull, Thomas Blackwell Jr, David Fordyce and James Beattie—three of whom are still of interest to historians of Scottish moral philosophy. In Turnbull and Verner it also had teachers who had lectured on law. Marischal College had not only switched from a regenting to a professorial system but had supported its educational reforms with useful collections of instruments, a laboratory and a museum. The play of outside influences had meant closer and more balanced relations between the burgh, local churchmen and the gentry than were to be found at King's. In Old Aberdeen things were rather different. Only two men of great distinction were appointed during these years—Thomas Reid and John Gregory. Both eventually left to make careers elsewhere. King's next most distinguished literary man, John Ker, left as well. The college was riven by family-based factionalism. Lacking the protection of great men who could also settle grievances, it was plagued by lawsuits. Situated in a small town, unfriendly to the religious and political outlook of some of its members and recruiting students in the counties north and west of Aberdeenshire, it is not surprising that it did less well financially than its sister institution. King's made the curricular changes which were accepted at Marischal, but the retention of regenting prevented them from having their full effect. Finally, politics impinged upon the university most clearly in the recruitment of professors of divinity and law. In these cases family feuding and the meddling of politicians worked to impoverish the college and to embitter its staff, but not to improve the institution.

Chapter 5

The Universities and Colleges, 1761–1800

I *King's College With and Without the Tutelage of Outsiders, 1745–85*

The great Duke of Argyll died on 15 April 1761 and with his death ended the political patronage regime which he and Lord Milton had operated with such efficiency. Milton remained for several years extremely useful to Lord Bute, who inherited his uncle's political machine, and to Bute's brother, James Stuart-Mackenzie. Missing after 1761 was system and the authority of a *sous-ministre* such as Milton had been. What also increasingly changed was the attitude toward the administration of patronage. The Squadrone and Argyll had, of course, used it for the parliamentary advantage of the ministries they served, but politicians in both factions had also over a long period of time deliberately appointed men whom it is easy to call enlightened. Montrose, Roxburghe, Tweeddale, Ilay and Milton all shared the tolerant, secular, pragmatic and scientific values of the Enlightenment which they did so much to institutionalise and to perpetuate in Scotland. After their regime ended these values continued to be found in the appointees of Lord Bute, but thereafter Enlightenment values were less important. What had been over many years the systematically followed personal preferences of the managers of parties, now were increasingly replaced by the political calculations of other less enlightened managers or of ministers in London. The appointments made by Bute's successors had far less to do with their cultural preferences than with votes. This was not true of Lord Bute. During his short period of power he focused even more clearly on the merits and abilities of applicants than his uncle Argyll had ever done.[1] And, when he went out of ministerial office in 1763, his attitude to some extent still guided his brother, James Stuart-Mackenzie, who continued to handle Scottish patronage for the government. By 1765, however, it seems to have largely disappeared. This happened partly because of ministerial instability in London. No ministry until North's, beginning in 1780, was really able to set up a well-run system for the administration of Scottish patronage such as Argyll and Milton had used. Baron William Mure and others who advised the somewhat unstable

14 South-east view of King's College, Old Aberdeen 1785. AUL LAa E Ken 15 vol 2.

governments between about 1763 and 1780 took advice from their friends and recommended men who would make Scotland more amenable to leadership from London. This meant in practice that gentlemen with interests in the universities and who were friendly with the politicians in power generally found support for their nominees. Those most concerned were the chancellors and rectors, the town councils of Edinburgh and Aberdeen and others whose rights to present to privately endowed foundations gave them claims to consideration. At Glasgow this gave increased influence to gentlemen with local political influence, men who had counted for less with Ilay. At St Andrews the chancellor, the Earl of Kinnoull, was a stronger figure than his predecessors had been. At Edinburgh it was easier to circumvent the town council as increasing reliance was placed on the advice of politicians outside the town. As we shall see, this also happened in Aberdeen.

The disappearance of a strong organisation from politics in Scotland also gave added weight to the one political party which the kingdom possessed—the Moderate Party of the Kirk led from 1755 to 1780 by the Rev. William Robertson, whom Bute had made principal of Edinburgh University in 1762. Moderate clerics in the Kirk had considerable power because they were necessary to any government which wanted the established Church to pursue policies which kept down dissent, enthusiasm and 'high-flying' Calvinism, which brought with it claims to ecclesiastical independence not sanctioned by law. During the period from 1760 to 1780 most of the more prominent politicians belonged to or worked with the Moderate Party. And, toward the end of the 1770s, Henry Dundas, the rising star of Scottish politics, found it easy to associate with and use a party led by Principal Robertson whose own start in life had benefited from Squadrone patronage requested by Henry's father, Robert Dundas, Lord Arniston.[2] The upshot of these developments was that in Aberdeen, university affairs after 1761 tended to come under the influence of the chancellors, Lord Deskford at King's (1760–70) and Lord Bute at Marischal College (1761–93). By the mid 1780s Henry Dundas and his friends were able to influence the recruitment and policies of these institutions.

The King's College men had lived in relative isolation from national political pressures during the years 1747 to 1760 but that came to an end in the latter year when another civilist had to be elected. The £50 a year sinecure again attracted the attention of men in Edinburgh and the election further embittered a faculty which had been scrapping since about 1757 over the consequences of a new course of study adopted in 1753.

The new curriculum had made necessary a longer academic year. That had cut enrolments and consequently the fees of teachers. This hurt the professor of Greek, the subprincipal and regents but not the professors of humanity, divinity, oriental languages, medicine and law, the last two of whom were sinecurists. The new factional alignment reflected these facts as well as the loyalty of men to their relatives. By early 1760 Professors Lumsden (divinity), George Gordon (Hebrew), Gregory (medicine)[3] and Thomas Gordon (humanity) with Thomas Reid (the regent who had sponsored the new curriculum), had formed a new faction opposed by Principal John Chalmers and his relatives, Subprincipal Burnet and James Catanach, the civilist, and Regents Leslie and McLeod. When Catanach became ill in 1759–60, 'The Principal and Sub-principal, sollicited publickly all the Members in ffavours of Mr. Thom Advocate in Aberdeen, brother in law to the first & in the same way Nephew to the other'. McLeod and Leslie promised William Thom their votes in the next election for a civilist.[4] Then, in the autumn of 1759, the masters differed on the use of bursary money with the principal's party favouring the awarding of more small bursaries to help enrolments while the other side wished for fewer but more sizeable ones. This dispute led on to one about the rights of regents, and of the boys awarded bursaries by individual regents and not by the college meeting. That issue was settled by the court of session which upheld the regents and the old foundation rules violated by the reforms of 1753. Having won this fight, the Chalmers faction then went on to shorten the academic year and to amend other features of the 1753 reforms.

This in turn led to attempts to exclude Professors Lumsden and George Gordon from 'surplus revenues' and most of the professors from real power in the college meetings which concerned bursaries and educational policy. Thomas Gordon, the humanist, also believed that he had been attacked and his fees lessened by the encouraging of students not to take his class.[5] All of these issues made the election of someone other than Thom of importance to the faction centred on the Gordon brothers. To them Reid, Gregory and John Lumsden adhered out of interest or family loyalty. Lumsden was also a relative of his party's candidate for the post of civilist, David Dalrymple.[6] When it became plain that neither side would give up its claims, the principal 'proposed as a remedy for their present disorders to make choise of some Gentlemen of Reputation and Character in the Neighbourhood for their Rector by whose Interposition the Society might be brought to rights in a constitutional way but this was intirely rejected'.[7] Thus things stood in February or early March 1760 when Catanach's illness and absence gave the Gordon faction a majority in the college meeting. The civilist's return to meetings in March restored the principal's control and his determination to act strictly according to the foundation charters. In April 1760 Alexander Fraser, Lord Strichen (Ilay's brother-in-law and the stepfather of the 3rd Earl of Bute) was asked to mediate the quarrels. He recommended that each side choose mediators and a chairman and that a rector be chosen.

The first attempt to carry out that plan involved William Thom and Arthur Forbes as arbitrators. They failed; so too did efforts to settle things by the mediation of advocates who later became court of session judges, Francis Garden and James Burnett, with James Ferguson of Pitfour as 'oversman'. On 13 May 1760 the masters at last met to select a rector and procurators for the coming year.[8] The two factions, being evenly balanced and still at odds, quite predictably chose two rectors and two sets of procurators. The Gordon faction also managed a minor coup when Professor Lumsden walked off with the college minute books. The stage was now set for the lengthy court battles which followed as Principal Chalmers tried to secure the election of his brother-in-law as civilist.

The masters on 13 May had first tried to elect a rector since his vote could also be counted in the election of procurators. The principal's faction, by his casting vote, named George Burnet of Kemnay, the later manager of the Earl Marischal's estates and political interests, and joined with him to choose four procurators. His opponents protested against the principal's casting vote and elected as their rector George Middleton of Seaton who joined with them to select another slate of procurators. On 13 May 1760 the sides were as shown opposite:[9]

As usual, these were family slates and, as in the past, they had a political tinge. Alexander Burnet's friends had not been sympathetic to Ilay in the 1740s; now they were joined by John Leslie whose loyalties would have run to the Squadrone, as his patrons and former employers were Squadrone men, Lords Morton and Dundonald. The Burnet family had never been active in Argathelian circles. They had, however, once employed Francis Skene as a tutor. Perhaps he now found loyalty to the Burnets stronger than loyalty to the political faction led by an aged duke which had not made him principal of Marischal College and which might pass over his son who was then seeking a post at Marischal. The lines on the other side were clearer. Patrick Duff was still in Argyll's camp. So too was David Dalrymple who in 1746 had been made procurator to the General Assembly and two years later was named sheriff of Aberdeen. George Middleton, the son of Argyll's old friend Col. John Middleton, MP, was also doubtless still loyal to the Argathelians. Lumsden owed his job partly to Argyll's support of the lawsuits required to obtain it. The Gordons, Reid and Dr Gregory were pursuing more principled lines, but they were related to at least one other member of their faction and to no one on the other side. They were not enemies of Argyll and had done his faction's work on other occasions.

The election of procurators by both sides prior to the existence of a vacancy was unusual since the procurators were an *ad hoc* body chosen to elect university officials. What this election of 13 May did was to ensure that the dying James Catanach could vote for the body which was to choose

The Principal's Faction Voting for William Thom

Principal John Chalmers
Subprincipal Alexander Burnet
James Catanach, civilist
Roderick McLeod, regent
John Leslie, regent and professor of Greek

Procurators
Andrew Burnet, merchant in Aberdeen
James Thomson of Port Lethen,
    Aberdeen advocate
Francis Skene, regent at Marischal College
John Robertson of Pitmillan, Provost of
    Aberdeen 1736–7

Who elected as rector George Burnet of Kemnay

The Gordon's Faction Voting for David Dalrymple

John Lumsden, professor of divinity
George Gordon, professor of Hebrew
    and oriental languages
John Gregory, mediciner
Thomas Reid, regent

Procurators
Patrick Duff of Premnay
David Dalrymple, advocate
Patrick Wilson, Esq.
Rev. Theodore Gordon

Who elected as rector George Middleton of Seaton

his successor. Without his vote the principal would have lost power and William Thom, Catanach's old apprentice, friend and relative, could not have been promoted. In the end this was not a prudent move since it violated the custom if not the letter of the university's constitution. The other side, while it also chose procurators in May, made another selection prior to the election for the civilist held on 27 November 1760. That came three days after Catanach had died and one day following the granting to Thom of the MA and LLD degrees by Marischal College. These qualified him for office. Dalrymple's friends had arranged for him to receive an LLD from Edinburgh in 1760. Thus equally qualified, he was chosen by the Gordon faction and their procurators who now included:

> Charles Forbes of Sheils
> Thomas Mossman, Aberdeen advocate
> Patrick Wilson, Esq.
> Rev. Theodore Gordon[10]

Dalrymple was admitted to the civilist's chair by the commissary of Aberdeen, Patrick Duff, who probably found it convenient that George Burnet of Kemnay seems not to have accepted his rectorial office while Catanach still lived. Equally important to the final resolution of the case was the fact that present at the Gordon faction's election was a majority of the masters; the principal had come to protest and had cast a negative vote.[11]

By early May it was clear that neither the election disputes nor the masters' other quarrels could be settled by arbitration or by the rectorial court. They went to the court of session and later to the House of Lords, both of which found the election of Dalrymple to be valid and ordered his admission in the spring of 1763.[12] By 1760, then, the factional fights had taken on a very serious aspect. They had disrupted college life and morale and they were also costly. If they were to end, the college would need more guidance and a court of appeal less expensive than the court of session or the House of Lords. King's would have to have a chancellor. It found one in James Ogilvie, Lord Deskford, whose father, the 2nd Earl of Seafield, had long been important to Aberdeen merchants.[13]

Lord Deskford (he did not succeed to his titles of Earl of Findlater and Seafield until 1764) was an astute choice. He had attended King's College (1730–4) and then studied law in Edinburgh.[14] In 1740–1 he was in Europe. When he returned to Scotland he became an enthusiast for agricultural and other improvements. The establisher of spinning schools and the builder of two new villages, his activities would have recommended him to the professors who had formed the Gordon's Mill Farming Club in 1758.[15] His interests, wealth and position in Banffshire led him into politics while his family's Squadrone connections had picked his allies. Deskford was made a member of the Board of Trustees (1749–70) through the influence of Newcastle. This post was followed by appointments as Commissioner of Customs (1754–61),[16] of the Annexed Estates Commission (1755–70) and Board of Police (1765–70). Deskford's ties to Newcastle and the old Squadrone interest probably made him look good to the principal and his friends, but he was also friendly with Thomas Reid. During the 1740s, 1750s and 1760s Deskford's was an important voice advocating change in Scotland, not just economic but cultural change as his membership in various societies showed.[17] Deskford's father had been an associate of the mystics of the Aberdeen region and active in the 1750s in promoting union between the colleges.[18] In 1761 his son was an ideal figure to breathe fresh air into King's College's mouldering precincts and to reconcile its contending factions. Finally, it should be noted that the masters chose their new chancellor only in May 1761, after Argyll's death, and a month after Lord Bute had become chancellor at Marischal. Deskford was almost certain to belong to whatever group came to domi-

15   James Deskford, 4th Earl of Seafield by Pompeo Batoni. In a private Scottish collection.

nate Scottish politics and patronage in the next few years—as indeed he did—but he had been no favourite of Argyll.

Lord Deskford's first tasks, after his appointment by a unanimous vote on 20 May 1761, were to sort out the tangled issues besetting the college both as a friendly mediator and as a chancellor sitting as a visitor and judge.[19] This was no easy task and for some time Deskford's advice was ignored more often than not. He told them to choose a rector. The masters conducted what was probably an illegal rectorial election in 1761. They did not listen to their arbitrators in November 1761 as his lordship urged them to do. In 1762 they quarrelled bitterly about the disputed rectorial election. Sitting as the civilist, William Thom and his friends again chose George Burnet of Kemnay, while the other masters re-elected George Middleton of Seaton.[20] In July Deskford ordered the principal to call to meetings and to count the votes of the professors of divinity and oriental languages. That only produced protests and another appeal to the court of session.[21] In November 1762 a series of rectorial court meetings went badly. Principal Chalmers, Subprincipal Burnet and Regents McLeod and Leslie got and retained custody of records and minute books which they refused to surrender to the visitors.[22] In exasperation, Rector Middleton left 'the Petitioners to apply to the proper Courts for redress, as his the Rector's authority has been despised and in the mean time continue[d] the present Visitation'.[23] By 21 March 1763, after the House of Lords had found for David Dalrymple, the principal and his friends acknowledged the rector's authority. This was spelled out in subsequent meetings which determined that 'the Rector & Assessors are a Court of Justice, the Rector being chief Judge & Assessors assistant Judges, who vote & give their advice' about most college and university affairs. All this was approved by the chancellor whose own position was strengthened by these decisions.[24]

Deskford's moves on the legal and administrative front had been paralleled by others clearly designed to give him a party of supporters within the college and to lessen the importance of the existing family connections. In 1761, not long after the chancellor's appointment, the masters gave 'all the security they can that Mr. [William] Ogilvy [a distant kinsman of his lordship], or any other person he names to assist Mr. Burnet shall succeed to any Vacancy, that may happen in a Regent's place'.[25] In 1764 Ogilvie replaced Thomas Reid, for whom Deskford had secured the chair of moral philosophy at Glasgow University.[26] By 1765 Deskford, now Earl of Seafield, was sponsoring another young man for the next vacancy. James Dunbar was appointed on 3 April 1765. Two years later the former tutor of Seafield's son and heir, John Ross, got the regius chair of oriental languages.[27] All three of these men seem to have been unrelated to one another or to sitting colleagues. That seems to have been true of only four of the twenty-one men appointed between 1717 and 1761. These additions to the staff, along with David Dalrymple and a new mediciner, Alexander Gordon,[28] chosen in 1764, gave a clear majority to the Gordon faction, and one which was not upset by the uneventful election of William Thom as civilist in 1765.[29]

After 1767 the chancellor was less in evidence at King's and on 3 November 1770 Deskford committed suicide. He was not replaced until 1793. Between 1767 and 1785 the university also lacked a rector and assessors, so for many years the professors again ran things as they wished. The college reverted to its old ways, although only one of the three appointments of new men made in those years went to a relative of sitting professors.[30] Few innovations are recorded in these years but William Ogilvie could and eventually did record instances of negligence, malfeasance and greed in the professors' administration of college property. He also noted their failure to promote educational ends by the establishment of a botanical garden and by book buying. After 1785 all these combined with tensions centred on the renewed proposal for union with Marischal to create even deeper divisions in the college.[31] By 1786–7 Ogilvie, Dunbar and Ross favoured union with Marischal, but were opposed by Principal John Chalmers and his relatives and friends. Family politics had surfaced once again. Indeed, it did its share to scupper the union proposals of the 1780s. Patrick Copland writing to the Duchess of Gordon in 1786–7 claimed that the union of the colleges was then opposed by Thomas Gordon because he wanted to secure a chair for his grandson; Alexander Gerard, whose son Gilbert succeeded to his chair, is said to have wanted the principalship.[32] All of the old problems seemed to revive as the college and university drifted without effective influence from outside. This was changed by three things: the agitation over the union with Marischal which forced the college to seek outside help in order to survive; Henry Dundas's interest in monopolising political power in Scotland; and the increasingly felt need to bring order and regularity into a world stirred and threatened by revolution. Before turning to those developments we must again look at Marischal College which also got a new rector and chancellor in 1761.

II *Marischal College and the 3rd Earl of Bute, 1761–85*

Ten days after the death of the great Duke of Argyll in 1761, Lord Bute was elected chancellor of Marischal College.[33] The masters presented this honour to him as if he were the heir not only of Argyll's political machine but also of his supposed honorific office. Unfortunately, there exists no documentary evidence that Argyll had ever been elected chancellor. He had refused the chancellorship offered to him by King's College in 1716,

16 John Stuart, 3rd Earl of Bute. AUL, f.Lib R 92 (ti) 08 Mib.

and in 1727 that at Marischal was still vacant. What the masters were undoubtedly doing was beguiling the new royal favourite, Lord Bute, who had been tutor to King George III as a young man, and was now to be his chief minister. They clearly hoped to enjoy patronage from a minister who could be expected to wield more power than Argyll ever had and whose tenure might be equally long. Thomas Gordon's hostile account of this business was probably quite accurate: 'Nothing can equal the effrontery of Members of Marischal College, who pretend that the E. of Ilay was Chancellor of their supposed University &, as is informed, to induce Lord Bute to accept the Office of Chancellor of the Marischal College, they sett furth, that his Uncle Archibald Earl of Ilay had accepted the nomination to the said office of Chancellor'.[34] In any case the masters chose well.

As a dispenser of university chairs Bute tended to pay attention to merit. The meritorious were recommended to him by intellectuals who shared his interests and to whom he felt closer than he did to manufacturers, importers of corn and wine or skippers who dealt in whatever could turn a profit. In the case of Marischal College, the local intellectuals tended to be the sitting professors, Moderate clerics and polite gentlemen. Of these, Bute relied almost exclusively upon the professors. His policy was explained by James Beattie the elder to Sir William Forbes in a letter written on 20 October 1788: 'the choice of our own members [has been with the Masters] . . . ever since Lord Bute became our Chancellor in the year 1761';[35] Bute's condition for the acceptance of a recommendation appears to have been unanimity among the masters, a requirement more easily fulfilled at Marischal College than at King's. Again, a Beattie letter is helpful: '[In 1777] every member of the College was applied to . . . by two or three Candidates of this place, to whom we could have no valid objection, who wished, in case of a vacancy, to be recommended by the College to the Professorship of Natural Philosophy'. No engagements were given 'but we settled it among ourselves that we should not oppose one another, and that if a recommendation should be given by the College in favour of any candidate it should be given unanimously'.[36] The earl seems usually to have ignored, at least until his last years, the wishes of the town council and of politicians. Indeed, during Bute's chancellorship there seems also to have been a drop in the number of merchants chosen as rector's assessors. The deans of faculty of these years also tended to be Marischal College professors and not watchful outsiders.

Bute gave his professors relative freedom from government intervention but he was known to expect the nominations of qualified and worthy men. These he got. Most of those whom he presumably recommended for crown warrants or admitted to office also had interests in science. Prominent among them were Patrick Copland, Robert Hamilton,

William Morgan and James Beattie the younger. All shared with Bute interests in astronomy or botany.

Patrick Copland, who in 1774–5 had been assistant to Dr George Skene, the professor of natural philosophy whom he replaced in 1775, had been in contact with members of London's astronomical community since at least 1773. While there is no clear indication of how Copland got his post, it most likely came from the recommendation of Skene. Copland was also 'a Cousin of Provost Jops, at least Mrs. Jops',[37] which would have helped in gaining the two chairs to which he was presented. Of his first appointment James Beattie wrote: 'Mr. [Andrew] Greenfield proposes to stand for [the Natural Philosophy Chair] in case Mr. Copland should be chosen Professor of Mathematics. I know the Crown has the disposal of the former, but without doubt the opinion of the College will in a great measure determine the matter'.[38]

In 1779 the natural philosophy chair went to Robert Hamilton who had made a good impression on the masters in 1766 when he had come to Aberdeen to compete for the mathematics chair. He had then come second. Between 1766 and 1779 he had run a paper mill and served as rector of Perth Academy. He had been helped to jobs by Henry Home, Lord Kames, George Dempster, MP, and Henry Dundas. He had relatives of some political importance in both Edinburgh and Glasgow, but he was also known as the author of *Introduction to Merchandise* (1777) and, perhaps, as a man with interests in actuarial mathematics. Later he was to publish in that field and help to set up insurance schemes in Aberdeen.[39] Little is known of Morgan except that he was connected with Bute and certainly brought with him from Jamaica a valuable natural history collection.[40] James Beattie the younger was a botanist of some celebrity and the discoverer of *Linnaea borealis* in 1775.[41]

Other men appointed during Bute's chancellorship had other virtues including John Stuart[42] and James Hay Beattie.[43] James Hay Beattie might have become a minor literary figure had he not died in 1790 at the age of twenty-two. Stuart was an antiquary who wrote a number of historical papers and pamphlets on controversial subjects.

During Bute's tenure as chancellor, the town council appointed one professor of divinity and three professors of mathematics. The Rev. George Campbell, already principal, was recommended to Lord Kames by Dr David Skene and to the town council by the masters in 1770.[44] He was appointed to the divinity chair but there may have been another local hopeful. In 1766 a competitive examination for six candidates gave the mathematics chair to William Trail.[45] Its value had clearly risen since 1726, partly because of the growth of extra-mural opportunities for its holder. Ten years later Trail picked Dr John Garioch as his successor and recommended him to the council 'as a person whom by long acquaintance and particular Examination he had found to be very fit and well qualified for discharging the said Office'. Three days later, after an examination but not a comparative trial (perhaps no one else competed), Garioch was 'chosen Assistant & Successor to Dr Trail'.[46] Garioch did not live to inherit the post. That went to Patrick Copland upon Trail's resignation in April 1779. Copland's application was backed by Principal Campbell and James Beattie senior, 'the only Members of the College in Town'.[47] The town did not insist upon trial of its former examiner of Garioch. Sometime later it allowed Copland and Hamilton to exchange teaching duties although they did not formally swap chairs until 1817 when the imminent retirement of both required this for the settling of their successors.

As a university chancellor Lord Bute was a somewhat distant figure whose physical remoteness must have worked against his frequent involvement in college affairs.[48] This was hardly compensated for by the choice of rectors who could be useful. In 1761 the college elected Sir Arthur Forbes, one of the leaders of a political coalition opposed to the electoral interests of the Gordon family[49] which was, however, represented among the assessors chosen in that year and, indeed, until 1770. Sir Arthur remained rector until 1764. He was then replaced by John Gray, a Londoner who had founded two mathematics bursaries and who is better known as a friend of the poet James Thomson who had sought his help in writing on Newtonian science.[50] In 1770–1 Gray was succeeded by Alexander Fordyce of Colpna, the London banker whose spectacular failure in 1772 brought down many Scottish banking houses and contributed to the British economic crisis of that year. From 1772 until 1782 there were no rectorial elections, the post now 'being regarded as a thing of no consequence'.[51] That was probably its status throughout Bute's tenure.

During that interim the professors' political connections with the local gentry strengthened. James Beattie was on easy terms with both the Earl of Kinnoull and the earl's brother, the Archbishop of York, as well as with their relatives at Slains Castle, the Earl and Countess of Erroll. Patrick Copland was an intimate of the Duke and Duchess of Gordon. These and other professors also found friends in less exalted but quite genteel circles. The long-term consequence of these friendships was a reorientation of the politics of the college away from the town council and towards the political machine being constructed by Henry Dundas with whom Kinnoull, Gordon and most of the rectors of the last years of the eighteenth century were to be connected. The revival of rectorial elections in 1782 is related to these developments.

Cosmo Gordon, a friend of Henry Dundas who made him a baron of the Scottish exchequer, thanked James Beattie the elder for his election as rector in 1782. It was owing to the same professor's good offices that Gordon was re-elected in 1783, 1786 and 1787.[52] He was to aid the college men in their attempts to unite with King's College.[53] Francis Garden, Lord Gardenstone, followed Gordon in 1788. He was then described by William Adam as 'Connected at present with Mr. Dundas and his friends'.[54] In 1790 and 1791 the college honoured Sir William Fordyce, the great London physician and a brother of the late Professor David Fordyce and the late Rector Alexander Fordyce. Sir William was to make substantial gifts to the college. In 1792 and 1793, however, the rector was again a man from the Dundas connection, Sir William Forbes of Pitsligo. Sir William was an Edinburgh banker who handled government monies and whose banking house had been saved from bankruptcy in 1787–8 by the Royal Bank of Scotland, which was controlled by Dundas's friends and used for their political advantage.[55] Throughout the 1790s this pattern persisted. James Ferguson of Pitfour (1794–5) was kept in parliament by Dundas.[56] So too were Alexander Allardyce of Dunnottar (1796–7) and Sir Alexander Ramsay Irvine of Balmain (1797–9).[57] As these minor political figures succeeded one another, the town fathers were also returning to the rectorial court.

Throughout the 1760s there had seldom been more than one merchant or town councillor among the four assessors and the dean of faculty. In 1782 two merchants were elected and a third sat as dean. In most years thereafter at least two of the five positions were held by merchants and at least one other man was in some way beholden to the Dundas interest. The importance of these political connections was made clear to the college by the union attempts of 1785–8 and by appointments made in the 1790s. Bute had backed the union scheme, but it had been defeated by Dundas who was unwilling to see property rights upset or the feudal superiorities and votes held by his henchmen brought into question.[58] The appointees of the post-Bute period show once again a political cast. Professorial interests were disregarded by politicians eager to look after their own.

Bute had been a benefactor to the college, an enlightened patron and a benign influence upon a corporation whose scientific bent he had increased. Those who followed him as chancellors had no substantial interests in the college or even, perhaps, in Scotland. David Murray, 2nd Earl of Mansfield, elected chancellor in 1793, was to all intents an Englishman who served Pitt and was advised by Dundas on Scottish affairs. During the three years of his chancellorship, he and Dundas foisted upon the college two men the masters did not want, Dr William Livingstone[59] and the Rev. William Lawrence Brown.[60] The first owed his place to the town council, the other to the influence of William Eden, Lord Auckland. In 1796 Auckland was elected chancellor at Brown's request. A third appointee during Murray's time, George Glennie, did come in with the support of the rector and some masters, including James Beattie I whose niece's husband he was.[61] Auckland had no ties to Scotland save those of an anglified Scottish wife and a friendship with Dundas, with whom he had long been associated in Pitt's administration. His only real intervention in college appointments up to 1800 was the securing for W L Brown of the principalship from which George Campbell retired in 1796. This is significant as much for those excluded as for the man chosen. James Beattie I had sought the post with some support both in Aberdeen and London. The Duke and Duchess of Gordon probably backed Patrick Copland, while William Nairne told Henry Dundas that Cosmo Gordon and Ferguson of Pitfour supported Dr George Skene.[62] There is no indication that Brown had any local support. The decision to appoint him was made to gratify Auckland whose protégé he was. Seemingly, the choice of a principal had been made without regard for local interests and had strengthened the position of Dundas in a corporation which had long enjoyed independence in its recruitment of professors. Principal Brown and Professor James Kidd were also to make the college less of a centre of Moderatism in the North East as they shifted theological teaching in an Evangelical direction.

III   The Union Crisis and the Consolidation of Henry Dundas's Regime, 1785–1800

At King's College the regime of Lord Deskford had involved the revival of rectorial elections which returned George Middleton of Seaton to this post until 1767. Then the elections ceased; at the same time Deskford gradually withdrew from the affairs of the college. It was not until 1786 that King's elected another rector. Seven years later the professors chose a chancellor to fill a post vacant since 1770. These moves came in response to crises, one created by the humanist William Ogilvie and the union proposals, the other by the French Revolution. Both helped Henry Dundas to tighten his grip on Aberdeen's institutions and to increase his power in the North East.

The proposal to unify Aberdeen's universities and colleges originated (so it was said) with the Earl of Bute. The scheme involved a royal visitation which was expected to find a union feasible and to recommend it. Parliament would then charter a single reconstituted university and college, much as it had done in 1747 for the St Andrews arts colleges. Because of the ages of the King's professors, most of them would have been quickly retired but probably all would have lost something by the union. Old Aberdeen would have lost its principal claim to fame and sentimentalists would have regretted the demise of an ancient corporation. For others the benefits of a better equipped college and divinity hall and

17   Henry Dundas, 1st Viscount Melville. AUL, f.Lib R 92 (41) 08 Mit.

the existence of new medical and law schools were more apparent. In support of the union were most of the Aberdeen corporations and notables, most of the nobility in the North East and a number of presbyteries. Opposed were the synod of Aberdeen, which fought to retain patronage of the chair of divinity, King's College, and some proprietors of lands and superiorities alienated by King's in transactions almost certain to attract the attention of visitors seeking grounds for union in the mismanagement of property. Concerns for the rights of property, the rights of superiors (holders of the franchise) and the knowledge that suits and bitterness would result from a union moved Henry Dundas, Lord Sydney and the Scottish law officers to bar the proposals.

The union fight really began in 1785 and lasted into the winter of 1787–8. Concurrent with it, and a part of it, was a feud between William Ogilvie and his anti-unionist and conservative colleagues. This culminated in Ogilvie's appeals to a rectorial court in April 1786.[63] On 1 May a rector was elected, Sir William Forbes, 5th Baronet of Craigievar. Forbes turned out to be a poor choice for the majority of the masters. He was sympathetic to some of Ogilvie's concerns about the mismanagement and corruption of his colleagues, concerns which were also shared by James Dunbar who had joined in some of Ogilvie's protests and who continued to support him. Forbes also turned out to be a unionist. He was not re-elected as a rector in May 1786. On 14 May 1786 Ogilvie and Dunbar joined again in a condemnation of their colleagues' denial to Sir William of the rector's usual second year-long term. This they called an act of deposition.[64] The embarrassment of Principal Chalmers and his friends did not end there. Their public and printed statements implying that the rector had opposed the union scheme were curtly denied in the *Aberdeen Journal* of 9 October 1786 where Sir William wrote: 'I highly approve of the proposed plan of Union and . . . I have not yet heard of any objections to the "Outlines" which may not, in my opinion, be easily removed'.[65] If the college had sought a protector and spokesman for the interests of the majority of its members, it had blundered greatly in its choice of Sir William. Yet it needed a rector and more political support if the plans of Lord Bute and his Marischal College associates were to be frustrated. On 7 May 1787 the masters elected a new rector, Alexander Burnet of Kemnay, who answered and contained Ogilvie's protests. Burnet would have made the college look better to politicians had it been visited.[66]

Alexander Burnet was listed in 1788 as 'Connected with the Duke of Gordon' and in receipt of a 'Salary of £200 a year from Government'.[67] Here was a rector whose local connections were impeccable and who was likely to follow the lead of important politicians to whom he had access. The most important of these residing locally was the Duke of Gordon. Initially both the duke and his duchess had been sponsors of the university consolidation scheme; by the autumn of 1786 the duke was seeking to arbitrate the differences among the professors.[68] In 1787 neither he nor his duchess seem to have supported the union; at least they no longer show up as supporters in the records which survive. Probably they had been won over not only by the arguments of the King's professors but by the knowledge that Henry Dundas was quite prepared to see the scheme fail. Kemnay's election in 1787 may well signify that shift in the duke's opinion. What it also did was to put in place a man very sensitive to the views of the political managers in Edinburgh and London, of whom Dundas was the most important.

From the late 1770s onwards, Scottish politics had been increasingly dominated by Dundas, who served successive governments as the manager of Scottish affairs and as their principal adviser on patronage. By the late 1780s the Duke of Gordon had become a Dundas supporter.[69] Given Dundas's attitudes, the apparent uninterest of the duke in the union, and a rector sensitive to the loss of government patronage, King's had become relatively secure by May 1787. It did not need to elect a chancellor and there were good reasons not to do so. Any chancellor might still have to oppose Lord Bute publicly with more force than was seemly. That would have been insulting, and the appointment of a chancellor might have been construed in a similar way. When Bute's health had failed beyond recovery by 30 February 1793, the Duke of Gordon was elected chancellor of King's College. This merely recognised officially the power which Dundas had held over the college since at least 1786.

By 1793 political conditions in Scotland made it desirable to proclaim one's loyalty and orthodoxy. From 1787 on there are numerous signs of the King's professors' eagerness to express their loyalty to the government. Burnet of Kemnay was returned as rector until 1795. Then, after a three-year term accorded to Sir John MacPherson, a former governor general of India, Kemnay served again until 1801. On 3 March 1792 a majority of the professors resolved 'that no petition to Parliament respecting the Abolition of the Slave Trade should be made at present'.[70] Dundas favoured a gradual abolition and no reforms during that turbulent period. Professorial support must have been welcomed. Throughout the spring of 1792 the home secretary (as Dundas now was) was burned in effigy 'in almost every village in the North of Scotland', and in the larger towns including Aberdeen, Dundee, Perth, Edinburgh and Peebles.[71] On 2 July 1792, three months after the London Corresponding Society had called for reforms, and after the government had begun its repression of radicals sympathetic to the French, 'the Rector, Principal, Professors and Masters of the University and King's College of Aberdeen' addressed the king to affirm their loyalty. Their letter went through Dundas's office as did the king's acknowledgement.[72] In 1793 the Dundas party was paid a sort of double compliment. Three of the professors nominated and voted for Henry Dundas's nephew and political aide, Lord Advocate Robert Dundas, to become their new chancellor. The others chose the Duke of Gordon who 'from his rank and fortune was well as local situation . . . of all others [was] the most natural choice'.[73]

Gordon as chancellor related King's College to those who could help it financially but who expected it to defer to their wishes. In 1796 the duke approached Dundas and David Scot, MP, for aid to the college which, in time, was granted.[74] Job applications, however, began to flow to Dundas, bypassing the chancellor, rector and professors in whose gift the offices officially lay.[75] The perpetuation of family interest within the college became contingent upon the will of outsiders to whom the professors now felt increasingly indebted. This is not to say that nepotism was not allowed. Robert Eden Scott succeeded his grandfather, Thomas Gordon, in 1788; Gilbert Gerard followed his father in the divinity chair in 1796[76] and James Bannerman in 1797 got the mediciner's post to be held conjointly with his father. Bannerman and Gerard almost certainly had Dundas's backing and were most likely 'nominated' to him by the Duke of Gordon. Three regius professors were named to the chair of Hebrew in the 1790s: Alexander Bell,[77] Hugh MacPherson, James Bentley. Hugh MacPherson was the choice of the Duke of Gordon in 1793, but approved by Dundas,[78] as almost certainly were the nominations of Alexander Bell (1790) and James Bentley (1798). Only two other new faculty members were recruited during the 1790s, Alexander Dauney and William Jack. The first had several relatives in the college in 1793 and was to become the Colonel Commanding the Aberdeen Light Infantry in 1799. He had earlier been an officer in the Royal Aberdeen Volunteers which the Duke of Gordon had helped to raise. Of the appointment of Dr William Jack (1794) nothing is known. It was probably managed much as was the choice of the subprincipal in 1800. The preliminary proceedings in that case had bothered the Duke of Gordon who described his reactions and what was likely to have been his usual way of operating to Professor Patrick Copland of Marischal College:

> I wrote to the Principal to desire him to tell the Candidates for the Sub Principal's Chair to state their claims, and to get an attested Copy of the Foundation Charter made out, that I may lay the whole before the King's Council here, for their opinion and give my decision accordingly—this plan from what I learnt from you, may not be agreeable to some of the Society but that will not give me uneasiness for one single moment.[79]

King's College in 1800 had lost its autonomy through the ability of the chancellor to manipulate it and the eagerness of the politicians both to

18 John Kay's caricature of the 'Seven Wise Men' who dominated King's College and in 1786 opposed the proposed union with Marischal College. It was first published as a handbill and did not appear in a collected edition until 1877.

Key:
1. ***The Beauty of Holiness, Lecturing.***
   Dr Skene Ogilvie, minister of Old Aberdeen, whose nickname mocked his ugliness. He was not one of the seven.
2. ***Had you not sold your Patronages, First Minister might have been annexed to my Divine Chair of Verity and Taste.***
   Alexander Gerard, professor of divinity, and author of the *Essay on Taste*, had transferred from Marischal to King's in 1771.
3. ***Annually for 45 years and upwards have I beat up, even to the Ultima Thule have I recruited our University.***
   Roderick Macleod, subprincipal, who was active in securing Highland students for King's, and also in touring the presbyteries of the north to gain support for the anti-union cause.
4. ***I have rendered Vernacular the Greek Language from Aberdour to Aberdeen.***
   John Leslie, profesor of Greek, who had been tutor to Lord Aberdour, and is said to have made the boast here attributed to him.
5. ***Agriculture is the Noblest of Sciences, mind your Glebes, the Emperor of China is a Farmer.***
   John Chalmers, principal, who had a farm at Sclattie, near Aberdeen.
6. ***Has not the Effulgence of my Countenance been a light unto your feet, and a lamp unto your Paths.***
   Thomas Gordon, regent, commonly called 'Humorist Gordon'.
7. ***College property, Patronages are unalienable, so says the Law, the Noble Patron has rewarded most justly your rapacity.***
   Dr William Thom, advocate and professor of civil law. He disapproved of the college's sale of patronages and declared that the Earl of Fife, who had bought them cheap, had justly rewarded his colleagues' greed.
8. ***Degrees Male and Female in Medicine and Midwifery, sold here for ready money.***
   Dr William Chalmers, mediciner.

control it and to sweeten the pill to men who had once controlled their own affairs.

The Aberdeen universities had quite different experiences with politicians during the last forty years of the eighteenth century. At Marischal College, where recruitment had long been managed for the political benefit of the ministry and its Scottish supporters, the professors, thanks to Lord Bute, discovered in 1761 that they were almost free to co-opt colleagues. Bute's requirement that they be unanimous in their choices forced them to avoid both nepotism and weak candidates. With the end of the earl's active role in college patronage in the late 1780s, the professors lost their influence. Henry Dundas as he brought order to Scottish politics returned to a more politically motivated management of university appointments. His methods resembled Ilay's, but Dundas lacked Ilay's concern for merit. Too often he was ready to settle for a commitment to Tory political principles.

At King's College the respite from the pressures of political machines had less meaning since the corporation was virtually closed to outside influence or could be if it chose to be so. The condition for its effective operation as a closed corporation was agreement among the professors and regents. That was impossible to realise. Factional in-fighting over appointments, administrative matters, teaching routines, money and even over the principles which guided the curriculum reforms of 1753 became increasingly bitter after 1756.[80] By 1760 these could only be ended by the intervention of outsiders—judges, arbitrators, rectors and chancellors. The price of that service exacted both by Lord Deskford and by the Duke of Gordon was some control over appointments. Deskford started to build an interest within the university, but died having made only three appointments. Two of his men—James Dunbar and William Ogilvie—were among the most scholarly and innovative of the eighteenth-century professors; they were also often at odds with their other colleagues after 1785. Their criticisms, the strains caused by the proposals for union with Marischal College in the mid 1780s and then the Revolution in France made it easy for outsiders to intervene in the affairs of the college. This brought no great benefits but it did open the college to men more unrelated to their colleagues than had been true earlier. King's continued in these years to look away from the concerns of the New Town[81] and preserved its ties to the gentry of the region. While it ended regenting in 1799, there were not many other notable achievements after the 1750s. The college could not point to a collection of distinguished men such as Marischal possessed in the 1790s. There was not, and had not been a distinguished divine at the university since the 1690s. King's had no mathematician of note. There was no natural philosopher of stature after Thomas Reid departed in 1764. William Ogilvie was a good naturalist but his colleagues were unwilling to support his teaching of botany.[82] None of the mediciners had been willing to co-operate with those at Marischal who sought to begin medical education in the region. When medical education began in Aberdeen, it was with the blessing of Marischal College which also sheltered the Medico-Chirurgical Society, whose assets were held in trust by the Marischal College professors. James Dunbar was a moralist of interest, but hardly to be compared as a philosopher with Marischal's Principal Campbell or even James Beattie. King's, because of its closure to outside influences, had as undistinguished a career in the late eighteenth century as it had had during much of the period 1690–1760.

Conclusion

The story of academic recruitment in the Scottish universities is one with many interesting aspects. At one level it clearly shows the increasing involvement of the state with education. In 1690 the crown appointed no professor in Aberdeen. By 1800 it presented to one chair at King's and six at Marischal College. Indirectly its power was even greater. Moreover, between 1690 and 1800 it had purged the colleges (1716–17), tried to fix upon them a standard curriculum (1690–1702), mandated new rules of appointment (1695) and increased its regular and occasional funding to the point where the Scottish colleges were dependent upon its largesse for their continued operation at levels of efficiency and brilliance. In the first third of the nineteenth century the provision of state funds would account for most of the innovations and developments seen in the universities. And political patronage would continue to create chairs for those whose loyalty could be best rewarded in this fashion.[1]

The administration of patronage in the Scottish universities also reflected the increasing political integration occurring in Britain. After 1715 most Marischal College appointments were made by men in Edinburgh or London and were usually made with some concern for the control of the politics of the burgh and its parliamentary constituency. This political dimension of university patronage can be clearly seen even in rectorial elections which responded quickly to real or perceived changes in London which affected the power of Scottish politicians. At King's College politics seems to have exacerbated factional fights. Sustained if not promoted by outsiders, several of these were finally adjudicated not in Aberdeen but in the court of session in Edinburgh or the House of Lords in London. In the smooth operation of both Aberdeen colleges was reflected the efficiency of the 'machines' which controlled, or tried to control, Scottish patronage. That was even true of Bute's long period of dominance at Marischal. Initially his cause was that of his friends in the Moderate party; later his position was tacitly and explicitly upheld by Dundas. All of that tends to bear out the claims of Namierites about the nature of eighteenth-century British politics, but it does not do so completely. Ideology and the personal preferences of patrons and managers remained of importance in Aberdeen's universities as they did elsewhere.

It is also important to note that the extension of political control over the recruitment of professors did not rob the teachers of their freedom to teach what seemed to them true and useful. The universities, which had always been seen as public institutions, were less state-dominated than many in Europe where governments' presence in the institutions had also grown at the expense of clerical authority and influence. Scottish professors with life-long rights in their corporations were in 1800 still able to control most of their own affairs, although they usually found it prudent to keep at least one eye on what their patrons might want. During the 1780s in Aberdeen, professorial and patronage interests, and the status of the chairs as a species of property, had been upheld by the government when it refused to unite the universities. That view would long impede reforms, but it also worked to limit the extension of state control over these colleges.

The power of the crown, exercised either formally or informally, needed direction and organisation if it were to be deployed to the maximum advantage of politicians. How this could be ensured and brought to bear upon professorial appointments had been shown by the Squadrone managers, by Lords Ilay and Bute and after 1780 by Henry Dundas. The strong assertion of government influence tended to make the colleges peaceful. Marischal had been so after 1715 except in those years in which there had been uncertainty over who was to exercise ministerial power and patronage. King's, which had been more insulated from outside influences, was far more disturbed. The absence of concerted political influence upon the colleges which marked the years 1763–80 was also not to be repeated in Scotland until nineteenth-century reformers strengthened senates and somewhat insulated universities from local and regional politics. By that time these institutions had also lost some of their local identity as they became more British in their staffing. That they remained Scottish in their outlook on education, in their curricula, in their student recruitment patterns and in the work expectations of their teaching staff points to the continued resistance of Scots to incorporation into a homogeneous British society—homogenised to English tastes.[2]

There is a very real sense in which the Scottish Enlightenment was the product of the patronage of the anglified and progressive Scots who controlled and managed patronage throughout most of the eighteenth century. Without their interests, and their willingness to promote those who shared those interests, many who made the Scottish Enlightenment would have lacked the leisure to write, the influence to institutionalise their views and the prestige which was necessary for the acceptance of them. Where enlightened outsiders were most able to influence appointments, the universities flourished as did Marischal, Edinburgh and Glasgow. Where this happened more rarely, they did not, which was the story of King's and the St Andrews arts colleges. There is a very real sense in which the Scottish Enlightenment was the creation of enlightened patrons and politicians: William Carstares, the 1st Duke of Roxburghe, the 2nd and 3rd Dukes of Argyll, the 3rd Earl of Bute, James Stuart Mackenzie, William Robertson and the 8th Earl of Kinnoull. Ably seconded by advisers who shared their views, these men, particularly Archibald Campbell, 1st Earl of Ilay and 3rd Duke of Argyll, changed the nature of Scottish education and culture. They did it partly because their own English colleagues wanted changes, but they also promoted changes and made appointments which reflected their own views and values. They, as much as the intellectuals, were the creators of the Scottish Enlightenment.

Political integration with England modified Scottish intolerance, just as it placed a premium on polite interests and skills already valued by the English and useful to any Scot hoping to make his way outside his own kingdom. The Revolution Settlement of 1689–90 had sanctioned Whiggism of some sort. Just what this meant was continually and painfully defined in Scotland until after 1746. Early on, however, it was clear that the majority of Scots in the political nation were committed to beliefs which sanctioned change. They limited government, produced some convergence of Scottish and English social institutions and ideas, and fostered an ideology of improvement, one rooted more firmly in English than in Scottish scientistic beliefs. After 1690 Scots who did not share these views were unlikely to manage the crown's affairs for long. Men like Roxburghe and Ilay adopted them with enthusiasm and helped to institutionalise them in Scottish universities. It was also during their tenure as patronage managers that polite Shaftesburians such as Thomas Blackwell the younger, George Turnbull and Francis Hutcheson came into the arts colleges. There they began to develop both the Scottish philosophy of common sense and the social analyses which characterised so much Scottish thought in the eighteenth century.[3] These same politicians and their agents, particularly Ilay, gave even greater encouragement to scientists and doctors. Colin Maclaurin, Matthew MacKaile and George Skene are three Aberdeen professors who exemplify their patronage. The Squadrone lords, the 2nd and 3rd Dukes of Argyll and their aides generally encouraged moderates in religion and not 'high-flying' Calvinists. As they promoted men who shared their own views, they brought Scotland and England closer, while at the same time creating in the North the conditions under which the Scottish Enlightenment could root and flourish. Not all of that was consciously done; not all of it related to university appointments.

CONCLUSION

One should not neglect either the continental or the native sources for eighteenth-century Scottish thought. But the cultural alignment of England and Scotland was politically and economically good for Scots and very probably necessary for the tolerant attitudes they came to accept. University patronage and politics played a part in those achievements and in the Scottish Enlightenment.

How much the interests and particular concerns of patrons mattered is not always clear. It is worth remembering, however, that men like Seafield and Carstares intended to have a moderate Church and a workable union with England. They intended to improve Scotland and its universities and their models were Dutch and English. Mar, Roxburghe and Ilay all gave patronage to mathematicians, doctors and scientists. Ilay not only had a library full of science books but he even finds a place in a volume dedicated to the *Mathematical Practitioners of Hanoverian England*.[4] Bute was a competent amateur astronomer and an even better naturalist. Deskford belonged to the Edinburgh Philosophical Society and supported improvers. Even the 4th Duke of Gordon was intensely interested in science and machinery. It is not surprising, given the personal interests of these politicians, that Scottish universities should have found places for distinguished mathematicians, doctors, natural philosophers or improvers. Where the influences of Ilay and Bute were greatest—at Edinburgh, Glasgow and Marischal—there science flourished best. The same patrons, however, sponsored notable moralists and Moderate divines.[5] Indeed, William Robertson, Adam Ferguson, John Jardine, like William Mure of Caldwell, Lord Kames and Adam Smith, had all been promoted by Ilay. Choosing one candidate for a chair over another equally well recommended by a man of equal power often became a matter of considering the intellectual merits of the candidates. The decisions made by and for Scots about their universities constituted a minor branch of politics not always closely tied to parliamentary elections. Where politicians with patronage to bestow most insisted upon worthy candidates or where the positions attracted numerous applicants, faculties were best. At King's and St Andrews the arts colleges attracted few applicants to the poorest livings. There the legal patrons—usually the masters—set low standards and favoured relatives whose placements allowed a man to retire without a substantial loss of income to his family. Where the institutional framework precluded such deals and where the livings were richer, men of greater scholarly attainments were promoted (see Appendix VI, Table 6). Unfortunately we do not know who the best teachers really were. They may, indeed, have been the non-publishing professors of King's College. Reading the surviving lecture notes, comments on the professors and much else does not support that conclusion. It suggests instead that where family influences were least apparent education was also best.

Any account of the Scottish professors of the eighteenth century must also, to some extent, be an account of families. Persistence in one's father's occupation was almost a norm for the professional men of the time. This was in part due to tradition and opportunity, but in some cases it was due to the possession of items of cultural capital such as books (one thinks of the Gregory collection in Aberdeen University Library), a cabinet or museum (such as the Skenes possessed), or equipment (such as Patrick Copland's machines), whose sale by a professor might also dictate a successor who was often a relative. In other cases posts were passed to younger family members as a means of providing retirement incomes. This was more important in poor colleges and happened more frequently at King's and at St Andrews than elsewhere. At Edinburgh and Glasgow, retirements tended to take the form of salary payments and perquisites to the older man while the new conjoint professor taught for fees. At King's, where chairs were worth too little to support such arrangements, nepotism was often the product of such circumstances. Everywhere it was attempted by professors. King's and St Andrews were exceptional only in their lack of checks to family ambitions. At Marischal, both before and after 1715, professorial families could not manipulate recruitment in their own interests without the aid of outsiders. In Appendix IV the patterns which emerged from the influences of families are set out along with other information which allows the Aberdeen professors to be situated in a wider Scottish context. The processes followed in the recruitment of professors were roughly the same in all five universities. These did, however, break into two patterns defined by the institutional constraints on outside interference with recruitment. King's and Marischal are representative of each type. Their varied careers in the eighteenth century, like those of the other Scottish colleges and universities, are largely to be explained by the politics of culture and by the contexts in which it was played.

Abbreviations

ATCA	Aberdeen Town Council Archives
AUL	Aberdeen University Library
AUR	*Aberdeen University Review*
BL	British Library
DNB	*Dictionary of National Biography*
EUL	Edinburgh University Library
GUL	Glasgow University Library
HMC	Historic Manuscripts Commission
KCM	King's College Minutes
MCM	Marischal College Minutes
NLS	National Library of Scotland
OSA	Sir John Sinclair, *The Statistical Account of Scotland, 1791–1799*, eds D J Withrington and I R Grant, 20 vols (Wakefield, 1973–83)
PRO	Public Record Office
RCPE	Library of the Royal College of Physicians of Edinburgh
SAUL	St Andrews University Library
SHR	*Scottish Historical Review*
SNQ	*Scottish Notes and Queries*
SRO	Scottish Record Office

Notes

Chapter 1, pp. 1 to 17

1. The Act Recissory of March 1661 annulled all legislation enacted after 1633 and consequently repealed the 1641 union of the colleges. *Acts of the Parliament of Scotland*, 7, 86–7; *OSA*, 1, 308–9.
2. T C Smout, 'Where had the Scottish economy got to by the third quarter of the eighteenth century?' in *Wealth and Virtue: The Shaping of Political Economy in the Scottish Enlightenment*, ed. I Hont and M Ignatieff (Cambridge, 1983), 45–72, 47–48; Bruce Lenman, *Integration, Enlightenment, and Industrialisation* (Toronto, 1981).
3. See, e.g., J C D Clark, *English Society 1688–1832: Ideology, Social Structure and Political Practice during the Ancien Regime* (Cambridge, 1985).
4. R H Story, *William Carstares* (London, 1874), especially 173–242; William Ferguson, *Scotland 1689 to the Present* (Edinburgh and London, 1968), 102–8.
5. Michael Hunter, forthcoming in *Atheism from the Reformation to the Enlightenment*, ed. Michael Hunter and David Wootton (Oxford, 1991).
6. J Bulloch and A L Drummond, *The Scottish Church 1688–1843* (Edinburgh and London, 1973), 1–63.
7. D P McCallum, 'George Hill, D.D. Moderate or Evangelical Erastian?' (Unpublished MA thesis, University of Western Ontario, 1989).
8. Christine Shepherd, 'The Arts curriculum at Aberdeen at the beginning of the eighteenth century'; M A Stewart, 'George Turnbull and educational reform', both in *Aberdeen and the Enlightenment*, ed. J J Carter and J H Pittock (Aberdeen, 1987), 146–54, 95–110; P B Wood, 'Science and the Aberdeen Enlightenment' in *Philosophy and Science in the Scottish Enlightenment*, ed. Peter Jones (Edinburgh, 1989), 39–66.
9. Recent studies of Scottish patronage and politics include Alexander Murdoch, *The People Above: Politics and Administration in Mid Eighteenth-Century Scotland* (Edinburgh, 1980); several books by P W J Riley of which the latest is *King William and the Scottish Politicians* (Edinburgh, 1979); R M Sunter, *Patronage and Politics in Scotland 1707–1832* (Edinburgh, 1986); J S Shaw, *The Management of Scottish Society 1707–1764* (Edinburgh, 1983).
10. David Anderson to William Carstares, 4 April 1715, EUL, MS DK.1-1^2;

William Carstares to Thomas Blackwell, 29 January 1711/12, EUL, Laing MSS, MS LaII 407.10.
11 NLS, Yester MSS 7044 ff 45–6, Lord Grange to Tweeddale, 1742.
12 Lenman, *Integration* 42–3; 76–80.
13 Richard Sher, *Church and University in the Scottish Enlightenment: the Moderate Literati of Edinburgh* (Princeton, 1985), especially Chapters 2 and 7.
14 Two recent works are good introductions to Jacobitism and its literature: Bruce Lenman, *The Jacobite Risings in Britain 1689–1746* (London, 1980), and Eveline Cruickshanks, ed., *Ideology and Conspiracy: Aspects of Jacobitism, 1689–1759* (Edinburgh, 1982).
15 William Carstares to the Earl of Mar, 30 November 1708, SRO, Mar and Kellie MSS, GD 124/15/796/3.
16 The Convention and the hysteria it produced are described in Christina Bewley, *Muir of Huntershill* (Oxford, 1981).
17 I have discussed this elsewhere: R L Emerson, 'Natural philosophy and the problem of the Scottish Enlightenment', *Studies on Voltaire*, 242 (1986), 243–91; 'Sir Robert Sibbald, Kt, the Royal Society of Scotland and the origins of the Scottish Enlightenment', *Annals of Science*, 45, (1988), 41–72.
18 John Hill Burton, *The History of Scotland* (Edinburgh and London, 1897), 7, 441.
19 'Marischal College Papers Concerning Visitations by Parliament', AUL, MS M 91.1/3; P J Anderson, *Records of the Aberdeen Universities Commission 1716–17* (Aberdeen, 1900, privately printed).
20 B Lenman, 'The Scottish episcopal clergy and the ideology of Jacobitism' in *Ideology and Conspiracy*, ed. Cruickshanks; Lenman, *Jacobite Risings*, 51–78.
21 These and others are discussed in G D Henderson, *Mystics of the North-East* (Aberdeen, 3rd Spalding Club, 1934).
22 Romney Sedgwick, ed., *The History of Parliament: The House of Commons 1715–1754* (New York, 1970), 1, 381, 395–6; Shaw, *Management of Scottish Society*, 106–13.
23 OSA, 1, 321.
24 R A Smart, 'Some observations on the provinces of the Scottish universities, 1560–1850' in *The Scottish Tradition*, ed. G W S Barrow (Edinburgh, 1974), 91–106, 97, 102–3.
25 King's was without a chancellor for fifty-five years between 1690 and 1800, Marischal for only forty-five years. The figures for the rectorships cannot be given because information about some years is lacking.

Chapter 2, pp. 18 to 34

1 G D Henderson and H H Porter, eds, *James Gordon's Diary 1692–1710* (Aberdeen, 3rd Spalding Club, 1949), 109.
2 William Orem, 'A description of the Chanonry in Old Aberdeen . . . 1728' *Bibliotheca Topographica Britannia*, ed. J Nichols, 4 (1782) 3, 57–8.
3 J A Henderson, *History of the Society of Advocates in Aberdeen* (Aberdeen, New Spalding Club, 1912), 318–19.
4 G D Henderson, *Mystics of the North-East* (Aberdeen, 3rd Spalding Club, 1934), *passim*, 35–6; Bruce Lenman, *The Jacobite Risings in Britain 1689–1746* (London, 1980), 25, 130–1. See also W G Sinclair Snow, *The Times, Life and*

Thought of Patrick Forbes Bishop of Aberdeen 1618–1635 (London, 1952), 161–70.
5 P W J Riley, *King William and the Scottish Politicians* (Edinburgh, 1979), 177.
6 Henderson, *Society of Advocates*, 291; H Scott, *Fasti Ecclesiae Scoticanae*, 7 vols (Edinburgh, 1915–28), 7, 356.
7 P J Anderson, *Officers and Graduates of King's College Aberdeen* (Aberdeen, New Spalding Club, 1893), 36.
8 Ibid., 47. Unless otherwise noted this book is the source for information concerning appointments at King's; Scott, *Fasti*, has been used for divines.
9 Riley, *King William*, 142, 170, 178. In the Union votes recorded by Riley, Erroll, Marischal and Moir of Stoneywood voted 'no' while Burnet joined the Squadrone voting 'yes'. Perhaps his change of political allegiance cost him the rectorship in 1705. P W J Riley, *The Union of England and Scotland* (Manchester, 1978), 334.
10 Riley, *King William*, 112, 167.
11 M A Stewart, 'The origins of the Scottish Greek chairs' in *'Owls to Athens': Essays on Classical Subjects Presented to Sir Kenneth Dover*, ed. E M Craik (Oxford, 1990), 391–400, 392–3.
12 Scott, *Fasti*, 7, 371, 541; 4, 301, 310; 5, 9; 2, 574; Henderson, *Mystics*, 61–5; G D Henderson, 'Professor James Garden', *AUR*, 28 (1940–1), 202–9; Alistair and Henrietta Taylor, eds, *The Jacobite Cess Roll for the County of Aberdeen in 1715* (Aberdeen, 3rd Spalding Club, 1932), 19.
13 The details of Bower's life can be gleaned or inferred from the following: Anita Guerrini, 'The Tory Newtonians: Gregory, Pitcairne, and their circle', *Journal of British Studies*, 25 (1986), 288–311; *A Letter from Dr James Walkinshaw to Sir Robert Sibbald* (London, 1709); *Philosophical Transactions of the Royal Society of London*, 354 (1717), 713–17; KCM, 3 May 1703–1713 *passim*; 'Information for George Middleton . . . against Dr Thomas Bower, and Mr George Gordon', NLS, Forbes MSS, Acc. 4796, Box 213; 'Proposals for buying mathematical instruments for the use of the King's College of Aberdeen' [1709], SRO, Mar and Kellie MSS, MS GD124/15/966/1–2; H W Turnbull et al., eds, *Correspondence of Sir Isaac Newton*, 8 vols (Cambridge, 1961–77), 6, 444, n.5; W G Hiscock, *David Gregory, Isaac Newton and Their Circle: Extracts from David Gregory's Memoranda 1677–1708* (Oxford, 1937), 17; Bower to Pitcairne, n.d. [6 February 1710], EUL, Sibbald Papers, Laing MSS, La III.353 (original at RCPE); John Chamberlayne, *Magnae Britanniae Notitia or the Present State of Great Britain . . . List of all offices . . .* Part II (London, 1736), 19; Charles Morthland to John Stirling, 10 July 1717, GUL, MS 27130; P J Anderson, *Records of the Aberdeen University Commissions 1716–17* (Aberdeen, 1900, privately printed), 6; AUL, MS K 282/3,1.5.
14 This is denied in M Bulloch, *A History of the University of Aberdeen, 1495–1895* (London, 1895), 131–3.
15 These struggles are discussed by G D Henderson, 'Professor James Garden', *AUR*, 28 (1940–1), 202–9.
16 R L Emerson, 'Sir Robert Sibbald, Kt, the Royal Society of Scotland and the origins of the Scottish Enlightenment', *Annals of Science*, 45 (1988), 72.
17 Pitachy had Jacobite nephews imbued with the mysticism taught by James Garden; Pitachy's mother was also a daughter of the Jacobite Earl of Kellie. Taylor, *Cess Roll*, 110, 114, 115; Henderson, *Mystics*, 46–51.
18 *The Manuscripts of the Duke of Roxburghe, et al.* (London, HMC, 14th Report, Appendix, Part II, 1894), 148–9; Scott, *Fasti*, 7, 368. His son, Thomas

NOTES to pp. 23 to 30

Gordon, later wrote that there was no legitimate legal reason to exclude George Gordon from the college meeting; AUL, MS 3107/4/5/1/109–18.
19 Professor David Anderson to Principal William Carstares, 4 April 1715, EUL, DK.1.1.².
20 AUL, MS K101; 'Information for Dr *George Middleton*, principal, Mr *William Black*, subprincipal, and the other masters and collegiate members of the King's College of *Aberdeen*', NLS, Fettercairn MSS, ACC. 4796, box 213/3, p. 10.
21 Anderson, *Officers and Graduates*, 59–61.
22 'Information' NLS, Fettercairn MSS (n.20, above), 9.
23 Ibid.
24 Anderson had been chosen without the required trial by an *ad hoc* body among whose members George Gordon sat as a King's College representative. The new professor was a Presbyterian but also related to the families of Gregory and Moir of Ferryhill. G D Henderson, 'Professor David Anderson (1711–1733)', *AUR*, 35 (1953–4), 27–32.
25 Ibid.; Henderson, 'Garden', *AUR*, 28.
26 Henderson, *Mystics*, 242.
27 KCM, 5, 19 and 21 February, 12 and 17 March 1711; Anderson, *Officers and Graduates*, 61; 'Memorial for George Middleton', NLS, Fettercairn MSS, Ms 4796 Box 213/1.
28 'Copy college minutes about Mr Burnet & Mr Simpson', AUL, MS K225 CT.
29 NLS, Fettercairn MSS (n.20), MS 4796/213/5. By 1711–12 John Gordon, the civilist, now voted with the Gordon family faction if he had not done so in 1709.
30 See Appendix III, Table 1.
31 A M Munro, ed., *Records of Old Aberdeen*, 1, 229; Scott, *Fasti*, 6, 20, 131; P J Anderson, ed., *Records of the Aberdeen University Commission 1716–17* (Aberdeen, 1900), 8–9. Alexander Mitchell was settled at Old Machar's Cathedral in 1717; the following year he was appointed assessor to the rector of King's University along with two sons-in-law of the professor of divinity, David Anderson.
32 Anderson, *Commission*, 7–11; KCM, 15 April 1716.
33 Riley, *The Union*, 21, 145; *King William*, 168.
34 Taylor, *Cess Roll*, 241–2.
35 Henderson and Porter, *Gordon's Diary*, 48.
36 A Moir, *Moir Genealogy* (Lowell, 1913), 144; E Wylie, *Families of Moir and Byres*, 80; A and H Taylor, *Jacobites of Aberdeenshire & Banffshire in the Forty-Five* (Aberdeen, 1928), 356–65; Taylor, *Cess Roll*, 248.
37 Scott, *Fasti*, 7, 362; ATCA, Letter Book 7, 8 September 1697. I thank Dr Gordon DesBrisay for this information about Sibbald.
38 ATCA, Letter Book 7, James Drummond, 4th Earl of Perth to the town council, 17 November 1686; Duncan Liddell to town council, 4 January 1687; Letter Book 8, 139; Bulloch, *University of Aberdeen*, 137–8.
39 Taylor, *Cess Roll*, 145, 158, 243; J A Henderson, *History of the Society of Advocates of Aberdeen* (Aberdeen, New Spalding Club, 1912), 235, 353; Scott, *Fasti*, 7, 356.
40 A list of the visitors of 1690 can be found in AUL, K 256/23/22; those for 1696 in M 91/18.
41 P J Anderson, ed., *Roll of Alumni in Arts of the University and King's College*

NOTES to pp. 30 to 32

of Aberdeen 1596–1860, 3 vols (Aberdeen, New Spalding Club, 1889–98), 48; KCM, 5 and 21 February 1711; Thomas Gordon thought this election was a ruse to gain time and that Smith was not expected to accept the offer. Gordon's account of the affair is somewhat garbled but he was probably correct on this point. 'Collections regarding King's College', AUL, MS K 34; 51, 80–2; Henderson, *Mystics*, 242; R H Campbell and A S Skinner, *Adam Smith* (New York, 1982), 10–11; Taylor, *Cess Roll*, 194, 242, 249.

42 The 9th Earl was a *virtuoso* and friend of Sir Robert Sibbald who listed him among those whom he thought fit to be founding members of a Royal Society of Scotland which he proposed in *c.*1700. See Emerson 'Sibbald' *Annals of Science*, 45 (1988); Taylor, *Cess Roll*, 171; E A Underwood, *Boerhaave's Men at Leyden and After* (Edinburgh, 1977), 86, 124.

43 BL, Sloane MSS, MS 3198/8. The commission is dated 17 February 1710. I thank Dr Andrew Cunningham for this reference.

44 Taylor, *Cess Roll*, 144–6, 242.

45 Ibid., 242; R Chambers, *A Biographical Dictionary of Eminent Scotsmen*, 4 vols (Glasgow, 1856), 4, 29–30. Meston continued his teaching career in a series of private schools patronised by Jacobites. In his later years he was a pensioner of the dowager Countess of Erroll, wife of the 12th earl. Meston never taught at Marischal College but on 24 June 1723 he successfully petitioned the town council for pay from 1715 to 1716. The council recorded that 'they were very well satisfied therewith' and paid him for one and a half years. ATCA, Letter Book 8, 24 June 1723.

46 Pitcairne was concerned that the chair might go to 'Dr [? Charles] Gregorie'. *The Manuscripts of the Earl of Mar and Kellie Preserved at Alloa House* (now at SRO), 2 vols (London, HMC, 1904), 2, 261; Pitcairne to Mar, 16 and 28 May 1706; Thomas Bower to Mar, 21 May 1707, SRO, MSS GD124/15/401/1, GD124/15/573; W T Johnston, ed., *The Best of Our Owne: Letters of Archibald Pitcairne 1652–1713* (Edinburgh, 1979), 43–5; Bulloch, *University of Aberdeen*, 137–8.

47 Scott, *Fasti*, 7, 362–3; C Innes, ed., *Munimenta Almae Universitatis Glasguensis*, 4 vols (Glasgow, Maitland Club, 1854), 2, 555; 3, 109, 261; GUL, William Carstares to John Stirling, 6 January 1709, Stirling Letters, MS Gen. 204/2/101.

48 Burnet had been recommended in 1687 to the town council by the Earl of Perth who may have wished to make him bishop of Aberdeen. In 1711 Burnet was the Jacobite candidate for the divinity chair. Scott, *Fasti*, 7, 356; ATCA, Letter Book 7, Perth to the town council, 29 June 1687; R Wodrow, *Analecta or Materials for a History of Remarkable Providences Mostly Relating to Scotch Ministers and Christians*, ed. M Leishman, 4 vols (Edinburgh, Maitland Club, 1842–3), 1, 329, 345.

49 T M'Crie, ed., *The Correspondence of the Rev. Robert Wodrow*, 3 vols (Edinburgh, Wodrow Society, 1842–3), 1, 215, 218–19.

50 Carstares to Stirling (n.47, above).

51 For this last heresy and its relations to the Jacobite Episcopalians, see Henderson, *Mystics*, 17–20, 35–8.

52 Taylor, *Cess Roll*, 159–60, 205; ATCA, Council Register 58, 2 May 1711; Scott, *Fasti*, 7, 358; M'Crie, *Wodrow*, 1, 345.

53 Munro, *Records of Old Aberdeen*, 6–12, 13–16, 41–6.

54 M'Crie, *Wodrow*, 2, 210–21; Anderson, *Records of Aberdeen University Commission, passim.* This includes 'A Memorial for the commission appointed by

his majesty for visiting the colleges and schools of Aberdeen', AUL, MS K 150; William Orem, 'A description of the Chanonry in Old Aberdeen, in *Bibliotheca Topographica Britannia*, ed. J Nichols, 4 (1782), 165–6.
55 'Memorial relative to the behaviour of the principal & masters of the Marischal College . . .', ascribed to Thomas Blackwell I, transcript from PRO, SP 54/12/1239 in AUL, MS U 581.
56 Principal Stirling's correspondence in GUL contains many letters dealing with the Aberdeen visitation; so too do various letters by Charles Morthland, the Glasgow University professor of oriental languages. Both were close to Montrose whose possession of the Barony of Glasgow gave him a great deal of local power and patronage in Glasgow and its hinterland, especially Dunbartonshire. See R M Sunter, *Patronage and Politics in Scotland 1707–1831* (Edinburgh, 1986), 199–210. The list of commissioners is given in Anderson, *Records*. Among the northern members were Sir Francis Grant of Cullen, Sir Alexander Ogilvie of Forglen, Arthur Forbes of Echt, George Monro of Culcain, [? Hugh] Rose of Kilravock, [? Duncan] Forbes of Culloden, and Robert Baillie, minister of Inverness. Among the clerical members beholden to Montrose or Roxburghe were Principals John Stirling of Glasgow and James Hadow of St Mary's College, St Andrews University. Charles Morthland and James Hadow served as clerks to the commission.
57 Professors George Gordon and David Anderson from King's were excused from attendance at Edinburgh while Principal Middleton and old Patrick Urquhart, the mediciner, pleaded illness and did not go down. Professor Bower resigned and did not come up from London. Principal Robert Paterson of Marischal died before the sitting at Aberdeen.
58 Munro, *Records*, 39–43, 49–51; 5; M'Crie, *Wodrow*, 2, 210–12; Orem (n.54, above), 165–6. Munro, *Records*, 1, 49–51.
59 'Memorial' (n.55, above), 16.
60 Keith had been excommunicated for adultery on 10 November 1714 which sentence, if sustained upon appeal, might well have disqualified him as regent. By the summer of 1716 he was in Copenhagen or Paris. Anderson, *Officers and Graduates*, 39–40.
61 Principal John Stirling may have interceded for William Smith with the Duke of Montrose who 'allways heard a good character of the man'. Montrose to Stirling, 26 January 1717, GUL, MS Gen. 204/1/14.

Chapter 3, pp. 35 to 58

1 John Stuart Shaw, *The Management of Scottish Society* (Edinburgh, 1983), 53.
2 AUL, MS M/361/10/6.
3 P J Anderson, ed., *Records of the Aberdeen Universities Commission 1716–17* (Aberdeen, 1900), 60–1; *Officers and Graduates of the University and King's College Aberdeen* (Aberdeen, New Spalding Club, 1903), 29, 50, 54; 'Marischal College papers concerning visitations' (transcripts by P J Anderson), AUL, MS M 91/1/20; Blackwell's protest over his exclusion from the college can be found in AUL, MS M 387/11/2–2; David Brown to Robert Wodrow, 2 November 1716, 31 July 1717, NLS, Wodrow Letters, 4°, vol. 11, ff. 256, 148.
4 Morthland to Principal John Stirling, 13 April 1716; Carmichael to Stirling,

13 April 1716; Montrose to Stirling, 29 August 1716, GUL, Murray MS 650/2.
5 Morthland to Stirling, ibid.; Maclaurin, aged nineteen, was technically too young for appointment; the Glasgow recommendation may have helped to overcome that barrier when the town council decided to appoint him. 'Marischal College register of presentations 1678–1857', AUL, MS M 93; Principal, dean and professors of Glasgow University to the town council of Aberdeen, 24 July 1717, ATCA, Letter Book 8, p. 239; Council Register 58, 1 May, 16 and 28 August, 11 September 1717; H W Turnbull, *Bi-Centenary of the Death of Colin Maclaurin (1698–1746)* (Aberdeen, 1951), 5.
6 Thomas Blackwell, the younger, to the Marquis of Tweeddale, 29 January 1745, NLS, Yester Papers, MS 7065/42.
7 ATCA, Council Register 58, 6 and 24 September, 3 October 1716; 30 January, 10 April, 1 May, 15, 16 and 28 August, 11 September 1717.
8 Anderson was the second, or first surviving son of Alexander Anderson of Bourtie. He married a daughter of George Skene of Rubislaw. Cruden was almost certainly the son of William Cruden, baillie in 1717.
9 Hew Scott, *Fasti Ecclesiae Scoticanae*, 7 vols (Edinburgh, 1915–28), 5, 234. Hadow's son Thomas was made a regent in 1723 on the recommendation of Robert Ramsay, provost of St Leonard's College, who in 1716 had been made a royal chaplain by Roxburghe. SAUL, St Andrews University Minutes, 25 June 1723, V, 109.
10 Pringle was the Squadrone's under-secretary of state for Scotland. Pringle to Stirling, 27 December 1716, GUL, MS Gen., 204/13.
11 Colin Drummond to Charles Mackie, 12 September 1716, Mackie Papers, EUL, MS La.II.91. Mackie was made the first professor of universal history at Edinburgh in 1719. He was a nephew by marriage to Principal Carstares and thus belonged to a family connection with Squadrone ties to men other than Rothes.
12 Note 9 above. The most recent accounts of Turnbull and his family are MA Stewart, 'Berkeley and the Rankenian Club', in *Hermathena*, 139 (1985), 25–45 and 'George Turnbull and educational reform' in *Aberdeen and the Enlightenment*, ed. J J Carter and J H Pittock (Aberdeen, 1987), 95–103.
13 A John Gordon was provost in 1706–7 and 1716–17; Duncan Gordon was city treasurer and John Gordon was dean of guild in 1724.
14 Thomas Blackwell the younger seems to have had the support of the Argathelian MP for Glasgow, D[aniel] Campbell of Shawfield, who recommended him to an unknown correspondent, 26 June 1723, PRO, SP 54/14, item 5; Patrick Duff to Lord Milton, NLS, Saltoun Correspondence (hereafter SC), 16535/61, 64.
15 Romney Sedgwick, ed., *The History of Parliament: The House of Commons 1715–1754* (New York, 1970), 2 vols, 1, 395–6. In 1725 the rectorial election ensured that Forbes would oppose Principal Blackwell. David Verner to Robert Wodrow, NLS, Wodrow Letters, 4°, vol. 16, f. 316.
16 Anderson, *Records*, 51–2; 'Memorial relative to the behaviour of the principal & masters of the Marischal College' (hereafter 'Memorial') ascribed to Thomas Blackwell the elder, transcript from the PRO, SP 54/12/239 in AUL, MS U 581; David Brown to Robert Wodrow, 31 July 1717, NLS, Wodrow Letters, 4°, vol. 11, f. 148.
17 GUL, MS Gen 357/24. The three most likely to have agreed to Ogilvie's proposals were the Gordon brothers and David Anderson. However, all the

old professors protested against the presentation of the men named by the crown as a violation of the King's charter, 'Memorial', 20–1. Other candidates for principal included Professor George Gordon; William Mitchell, minister at Old Machar; and John Brand, minister at Barrowstoneness. David Brown to Robert Wodrow, 1 January 1717 and 31 July 1717, NLS, Wodrow Letters, 4°, vol. 11, ff. 2 and 148.

18 Anderson, *Records*, 57–9.
19 Sir Francis J Grant, ed., *The Faculty of Advocates in Scotland 1532–1943* (Edinburgh, Scottish Record Society, 1944), 78. Troup was admitted to office on 3 November 1717 by an *ad hoc* body commissioned by the crown to swear him in, composed of the ministers and magistrates of Old and New Aberdeen. William Orem, 'A description of the Chanonry in Old Aberdeen . . . 1728' in *Bibliotheca Topographica Britannia*, ed. J Nichols, 4 (1782), 3, 166.
20 Scott, *Fasti*, 7, 367.
21 John Ker to Chalmers, 4 March 1719, AUL, MS K 282/8.
22 This chair was first offered to Francis Pringle who taught Greek at St Andrews. Upon his refusal, Scotstarvit, Newhall 'and other men of power' arranged for Ker to take it. T Bower, *The History of the University of Edinburgh*, 2 vols (Edinburgh, 1817), 1, 302; 'Francis Pringle's Common Place Book', SAUL, MS LF 1111. P81.
23 EUL, MS DK.1.1.2.
24 No biography of this great man exists but his interests are noted by Ian G Lindsay and Mary Cosh, *Inveraray and the Dukes of Argyll* (Edinburgh, 1973), especially 35–185; and Edmund and Dorothy Berkeley, *Dr. John Mitchell* (Chapel Hill, 1974).
25 'Memorial', 25; John Chamberlayne's *Magnae Britanniae Notitia or The Present State of Great Britain*, Book III, Part II, began to list Ilay as chancellor of King's in 1737 and continued to do so until at least 1748. That is the partial truth contained in the claim in *The Statistical Account of Scotland* that 'the Earl of Ilay, who notwithstanding his declining the office, yet always had among his other honourable titles that of chancellor of the University of Aberdeen', *OSA*, 1, 292. In 1736–7 there were political reasons to embarrass Roxburghe, reasons which had mostly disappeared by the 1750s.
26 Thomas Gordon, 'Collections regarding King's College', AUL, MS K 34, 5.
27 Anderson, *Records*, 59.
28 Anderson to Chalmers, 18 September, 1718, AUL, MS K 282/2.
29 George Gordon to Chalmers, 8 and 31 October 1718, AUL, MS K 282/3, 5.
30 Thomas Scott to Principal Thomas Blackwell, 5 August 1718, AUL, MS M 361/10/3. The issue had also been raised earlier by the visitors in 1716. Gordon, 'Collections regarding King's College', AUL, MS K 34/7.
31 Subprincipal Alexander Fraser to Chalmers, n.d., AUL, MS K 282/18.
32 Alexander Gordon to Chalmers, 6 March 1719, AUL, MS K 282/11.
33 Gordon, 'Collections', 5.
34 Orem, *Old Aberdeen*, 3.
35 Scott, *Fasti*, 6, 20. Ilay's friends show up on the lists of assessors at Marischal College in 1723 (Patrick Duff) and a year later at King's (John Moir).
36 Ibid., 6, 47, 63.
37 J A Henderson, *History of the Society of Advocates in Aberdeen* (Aberdeen, New Spalding Club, 1912), 351; Anderson, *Officers and Graduates*, 12.

38 Scott, *Fasti*, 6, 22, 24, 27, 38.
39 George Gordon to Principal Chalmers, 28 March 1719. AUL, MS K 282/13.
40 A poetic but not overdrawn statement of their poverty is contained in John Ker's *Donaides* (1725) (Los Angeles, Augustan Reprint Society, 188, 1978). This contains a translation by Barrows Dunham.
41 Colin Campbell to Chalmers, 29 April 1719, AUL, MS K 282/15; Patrick Duff to Andrew Fletcher, Lord Milton, 14 February 1733; Chalmers to Ilay, 14 February 1733, NLS, MS, SC 16552; 16553. Chalmers's plan in 1733 was not wholly disinterested since it involved making him a royal chaplain with his stipend used to defray the costs of attendance at the annual meeting of the General Assembly and the expenses of the revived chair. Nothing came of this proposal which was meant to 'procur[e] to the College and to me that mark of the Royal favour [for which] we shall endeavour to make the best return in our power to our Benefactor'.
42 Orem, *Old Aberdeen*, 174.
43 The £1,400 gift of Dr James Fraser of Chelsea is said to have gained the civilist post in 1724 for Alexander Fraser II, the son of the subprincipal. The civilist in 1729 was, by royal appointment, made baillie in Old Aberdeen. He was then no Squadrone supporter. With this election the faculty balance would have shifted to the Argathelians among whom were probably to be counted his father, Alexander, Alexander Burnet and the Gordon Brothers. Orem, *Old Aberdeen*, 173–5.
44 Ibid., 166–74.
45 Sedgwick, *History of Parliament*, 1, 395–6, 387–8, 381.
46 Shaw, *Management of Scottish Society*, 48–55.
47 Marischal College had elected no chancellor in these years perhaps because the masters were unsure of their right to do so.
48 George Gordon to Principal George Chalmers, 21 June 1727, AUL, KC Misc. Papers, CT Box 43.
49 AUL, MS M 387/11/3/4; Anderson, *Records*, 1, 18; Bruce Lenman, *The Jacobite Risings in Britain 1689–1746* (London, 1980), 175–6; P J Anderson, *Fasti Academiae Mariscallanae Aberdonensis: Selections from the Records* (Aberdeen, New Spalding Club, 1889).
50 Maclaurin to Archibald Campbell, 9 April 1725, Stella Mills, ed., *The Collected Letters of Colin MacLaurin* (Nantwich, 1982), 170–1; David Warner to Robert Wodrow, 28 February 1725, NLS, Wodrow Letters, 4°, vol. 16, f. 316.
51 Verner may also have been an absentee since he is said to have studied law in Edinburgh sometime before 1722 but not necessarily before 1717. In 1728 Verner was trying to exchange his Marischal College regency for the St Andrews chair of ecclesiastical history—a regius post for which Turnbull had applied in 1727. The Rev. James Innes, who became a Marischal assessor, recommended Verner to Lord Milton as one who showed 'Zeal for the Duke of Argyle's interest'. Innes to Andrew Fletcher, Lord Milton, 26 February 1728, 12 March 1728, NLS, SC, 16539/68, 72. Turnbull to Charles Mackie, 23 January 1727, EUL, La. II. 91.
52 Maclaurin to Martin Folkes, 25 March 1731, Mills, *Letters of Colin Maclaurin*, 31–3.
53 Chalmers to Principal John Stirling, 19 March 1725, GUL, MS Gen. 204/1/123. The views of Maclaurin's friends are given in David Verner to Robert Wodrow, 28 February 1725, NLS, Wodrow Letters, 4°, vol. 16, f. 316.

54 Dr MacKaile to Lord Milton, 20 December 1725, NLS, SC, 16532/56.
55 Ilay to Lord Milton, NLS, SC, 16535/131.
56 Alistair and Henrietta Taylor, eds, *The Jacobite Cess Roll for the County of Aberdeen in 1715* (Aberdeen, 3rd Spalding Club, 1932), 241.
57 Sedgwick, *History of Parliament*, 1, 382, 405, 525. By 1729 Braco was opposing Ilay's friends and supporting the college's Squadrone faction with whom William Duff now voted.
58 H W Turnbull, *Bi-Centenary of the Death of Colin Maclaurin* (Aberdeen, 1951), 5.
59 Duff to Lord Milton, 31 July 1727, NLS, SC, 16535/61.
60 Erskine's professorial correspondents were almost certainly MacKaile, Verner and Turnbull. PRO, SP 54/17/20a-c.
61 E M Walford to P J Anderson, 18 July 1885, with AUL, MS copies of PRD SP54, Bundle 46.
62 AUL, MS M 339/3. Mr Campbell was probably George Campbell, an extra-mural teacher of mathematics in Edinburgh.
63 ATCA, Letter Book 9, 127–8; this is also to be found in AUL, M 399/2.
64 'Register of presentations', AUL, MS M 93.
65 Daniel Gordon belonged to the Squadrone interest at Marischal; that was also dominant at St Andrews where he had studied. Burnet's views are unknown but he did not later belong to the Gordon-Fraser connection at King's which was friendly to the Argathelians.
66 'Register'; ATCA, Council Register 58, 23 August 1726. The protest came from Alexander Charles, an Aberdeen advocate married to a descendant of the chair's founder. He wanted the place for his son, George, who offered to compete. After this time the Liddell family interest in the chair is no longer apparent. William Knight MSS, AUL, MS 109/359.
67 *Reports ... into the State of the Universities of Scotland ... [1826, 1832]* (London, HMSO, 1837), XXXVIII, 192–267; Chalmers's trip can be partly followed in the collection of letters to him, AUL, MSS K 282/1-18.
68 AUL, 'Miscellaneous King's College papers', MS CT Box 43.
69 Anderson in 1726 seems to have had a pension from the deanery of the Chapel Royal. David Anderson to Lord Milton, 13 November 1727, NLS, MS SC 16535/34–5; Patrick Duff to Lord Milton, 30 September 1730, ibid.
70 AUL, MS K 255 Box 43 CT*; see also PRO, SP54/18/81 which gives the 1727 petition from King's College for the renewal of the grant from the bishop's rents shared with Marischal College. King's got £200, Marischal £100. Blackwell was trying to reverse the distribution.
71 Robert Wodrow, *Analecta, or Materials for a History of Remarkable Providences*, ed. M Leishman, 4 vols (Edinburgh, Maitland Club, 1842–3), 3, 484; Sedgwick, *History of Parliament*, 1, 381.
72 Scott, *Fasti*, 7, 367; Subprincipal Alexander Fraser to Lord Milton, 30 May 1729, NLS, SC, 16540/2; Lord Milton to Ilay, 24 February 1729, NLS, SC, 16540/25; Col. John Middleton to Lord Milton, 2 May 1729, NLS, SC, 16541/107c. Thomas M'Crie, ed., *The Correspondence of the Rev. Robert Wodrow*, 3 vols (Edinburgh, Wodrow Society, 1843), 3, 395; John Boyd to Robert Wodrow, 13 October 1728; David Verner to Robert Wodrow, 5 November 1728; David Brown to Robert Wodrow, 4 and 23 April 1729, 17 May 1729, NLS Wodrow Letters 4°, vol. 18, ff. 180, 190, 339, 340, 374.
73 George Chalmers to Lord Milton, 2 September 1730; and see NLS, SC, 16542/175; SC, 16543/33; SC, 16544/54; SC, 16545/184; PRO, SP 54/20/38.

74 James Gregory had also helped the Argathelians in this election. Patrick Duff to Lord Milton, 31 July, 1727; 3 November 1727, NLS, SC, 16535/61, 64.
75 Anderson, *Officers and Graduates*, 6–8; AUL, MS 387/9/7/1–2. These sources differ in the date; the first gives the 28th, the second the 29th. Cumberland never became chancellor at Marischal. Had he held this position, there would be some record of his interference in college affairs as there is at St Andrews where he was chancellor between 1746 and 1765. The Argathelians probably got some short-term advantage from the nomination and then scuppered it in London as inappropriate.
76 What follows draws heavily upon the fine account given by Shaw, *Management of Scottish Society*, 106–13; M'Crie, *Wodrow*, 485.
77 Shaw, *Management of Scottish Society*, 111; Milton's letters to Ilay were dated 24 and 27 February.
78 Duff to Milton, two letters, 21 February 1728, NLS, SC, 16538/178, 180; David Verner to Robert Wodrow, 5 November 1728, NLS, Wodrow Letters, 4°, vol. 18, f. 190.
79 NLS, SC, 16538/182; 184. The magistrates had asked this favour for Mrs Blackwell on 1 March as had Thomas II the day after his father's death. It was customary to pay the salary or 'ann' to a widow for six months but a year was not uncommon. NLS, SC, 16538.
80 NLS, SC, 16538/12.
81 Ibid., SC, 16538/160.
82 Baillie Cruickshank had originally opposed Principal George Chalmers's settlement but Ilay seems to have backed Chalmers to humble the town fathers and to ensure control of an unruly parish. James Innes to Lord Milton, NLS, SC, 16541/39.
83 Patrick Duff to Lord Milton, 8 April 1728, NLS, SC, 16538/19.
84 Milton to Ilay (scroll), n.d., NLS, SC, 16548/105; this letter is misplaced in the NLS catalogue.
85 Dr John Johnstone to ?, 22 August 1728, NLS, SC, 16539/87; Neil Campbell to Milton, 18 February 1729, NLS, SC, 16540/99; W Innes Addison, ed., *The Matriculation Albums of the University of Glasgow from 1728 to 1858* (Glasgow, 1913), 11, 15.
86 Dr MacKaile to Lord [Milton], 7 March, NLS, SC, 16541/74–5.
87 There are no surviving records of elections in 1730 and 1731 which may point to a longer period of tension.
88 Matthew MacKaile to Milton, 7 March 1729, NLS, SC, 16541/75; Sedgwick, *History of Parliament*, 1, 625.
89 Chalmers to Lord Milton, 14 February 1733, NLS, SC, 16552/203; The salary was to go to Alexander Rait whom the college had appointed as professor of mathematics. Rait seems to have been related to Regents Burnet and Bradfute and more distantly to the Gregory family and to Thomas Reid.
90 Neil Campbell to Milton, 18 February 1729, NLS, SC, 16540/99, f. 75; MacKaile seems to have been behind the 1726 'Proposals for setting on foot a compleat course of *Experimental Philosophy* in the Marischal College of Aberdeen'. Patrick Duff won from the Commissioners of Supply of Aberdeenshire a promise of aid (£9) if they had a surplus. Colin Maclaurin had been involved in earlier schemes to expand the instrument collections which perhaps included some 'Machines in husbandry and common-life' such as MacKaile sought to buy in 1726. AUL, MS 3017/10/18/2; M/361/1/4; William Knight MSS, AUL, M 111, pp. 1175–95.

91 Blackwell was accused of sexual improprieties with a lower-class local girl. Thomas Blackwell to Lord Milton, ? November 1731, NLS, SC, 16545/28; Blackwell to Sir John Clerk, 12 and 17 November 1731, SRO, GD18/5036/12–17.

Chapter 4, pp. 59 to 77

1 Ramsay was in Ilay's camp by 1735. Sir Alexander Ramsay to Lord Milton, 12 May 1735, NLS, Saltoun Correspondence (hereafter SC), 16563/27–28.
2 Duff to Milton, 14 June 1733, NLS, SC, 16553/53–4.
3 George Skene express to Lord Milton, 25 May 1733, NLS, SC, 16554/124.
4 Innes's sponsors included Rector George Skene, 'the Town, the College and the chief Gent^m of the Country'. Marischal College masters to Ilay, 23 January 1738; town council to Col. Middleton, MP, 23 January 1738, ATCA, Out Letter Book 1.
5 Patrick Duff to Lord Milton, 14 February 1733, NLS, SC, 16553/45–6; Principal George Chalmers to Lord Milton, 14 February 1733, NLS, SC, 16653/45–6.
6 'Letters of Lord Grange', *Miscellany of the Spalding Society* (Aberdeen, Spalding Society, 1846), 3, 45.
7 What follows is drawn largely from G D Henderson, 'Professor John Lumsden 1694–1770', *AUR*, 27 (1939–40), 106–15.
8 NLS, SC, 16553/45–6.
9 NLS, SC, 16556/1–2.
10 Ibid.
11 PRO, SP 54/22/23.
12 It is tempting to think that the failure to choose a rector was the failure of the Argathelians to keep a client in this place.
13 R Sedgwick, ed., *History of Parliament: The House of Commons 1715–1754* (New York, 1970), 2 vols, 1, 381, 396.
14 NLS, Fettercairn MSS, Acc. 4796/213/8, 'Memorial for Sir Wm Forbes', p. 2.
15 Ibid., p. 12; 4796/213/10.
16 KCM, 24 February 1741–7 August 1741.
17 'Memorial from Mr Alexander Rait', AUL, MS K 214/2/7; 'Remarks on the election of members in King's College', NLS, Fettercairn MSS, Acc. 4796/213/12.
18 Elizabeth Forbes of Disblair and her younger sister, Lily.
19 Sedgwick, *History of Parliament*, 2, 42–4; A and H Taylor, eds, *The Jacobite Cess Roll for the County of Aberdeen in 1715* (Aberdeen, 3rd Spalding Club, 1932), 115.
20 NLS, Fettercairn MSS, Acc. 4796/213/20; J S Shaw, *The Management of Scottish Society, 1707–1764* (Edinburgh, 1983), 73–4; Sir Francis Grant, ed., *The Faculty of Advocates in Scotland, 1532–1943* (Edinburgh, Scottish Record Society, 1944), 62.
21 Thomas Hay to Tweeddale, 5 August 1742, NLS, Yester Papers, MS 7049/8. Tweeddale made Alexander Udney a Commissioner of Excise in 1742; Udney to Tweeddale, 30 May 1742, ibid., 7049/110.
22 Milton to Ilay, 8 February 1757, NLS, SC, 16698/142.
23 Francis Skene's defection from the Argathelian party was not held against

him by Lord Milton, who in 1759 recommended him to Argyll as a man fit to become principal. Skene did not get that job but his son was made a regent. Contending for the principalship were Skene, John Home (Lord Bute backed him), Robert Pollock and William Wilkie. Skene to Milton, 14 June 1759; Milton to Argyll (copy), 8 February 1757; Pollock to Milton, 21 April 1757; George Skene of Skene to Sir James Carnegie, 19 February 1757; Carnegie to Milton, 15 May 1760, NLS, SC, 16712/34; SC, 16698/142; SC, 16701/208; SC, 16702/80; SC, 16714/128; SC, 16712/213; William Wilkie to Milton, n.d. [1759], SC, 16713/215; AUL, MS 38, George Skene to Dr David Skene, 5 June 1759.

24 Verner had been nominated for the Marischal principalship in 1729 by the Rev. James Innes who thought Verner's regent's salary might be partially used to supplement the other regents' salaries. In 1728 he also recommended Verner for the St Andrews University chair of ecclesiastical history. For both places Verner's chief asset seems to have been 'Zeal for the Duke of Argyll's interest' which may not have been quite the same thing as loyalty to Ilay who became Duke of Argyll only after the sides were chosen in this case. Verner, who was an outsider in Aberdeen, would not have seemed to Ilay an attractive candidate for principal. Innes to Milton, 26 February 1728, ? March 1728, NLS, SC, 16539/68, 72.

25 Blackwell to Tweeddale, 11 June 1742, NLS, Yester Papers, MS 7047/147–8.

26 For David Fordyce's appointment see: NLS, Yester Papers, MSS 7049/104; 7049/8, 10, 13, 45, 129, 106; 7075/23, 28; ATCA, Out Letter Book 2.

27 Gordon's legal battle to secure the chair was still going on in 1744, which makes this even more likely. Charles Hamilton Gordon to Lord Milton, 15 March 1744, NLS, SC, 16599/19. The new Widows' Fund was opposed by the Burnet faction at King's but supported by the principal's friends and generally throughout Scotland by Ilay's supporters. KCM, 9 February 1744. By 1744 Gordon was clearly allied with Argyll; NLS, SC, 16671/72.

28 Duff in 1742–5 may have been playing both sides of the street since he seems to have solicited both Argyll and Tweeddale for the post of commissary of Aberdeen which he was given in 1745. One of the losing candidates for that post was Thomas Blackwell; NLS, Yester Papers, Blackwell to Tweeddale, 29 January 1744/5, MS 7065/42; Thomas Hay to Tweeddale, 30 April 1745, MS 7065/42; [?Patrick Duff] to Lord Milton, 2 January 1743, 23 January 1745; NLS, SC, 16599/19, SC, 16607/705. Milton to Ilay (scroll) (n.d., 1741), SC, 16586/256.

29 J A Henderson, *History of the Society of Advocates in Aberdeen* (Aberdeen, New Spalding Club, 1912), 355, 385.

30 Blackwell (for Principal James Osborn) to Tweeddale, 15 November 1742, NLS, Yester Papers, MS 7051/44.

31 'Extract of Act of Admission . . .', AUL, MS K 214/3; the best accounts of this case are: P J Anderson, 'The Catanach Case', *SNQ*, 2/1888, no. 1, 114–30; AUL, MS K 144, K 214.

32 *SNQ*, 134. Verner himself had been given a Marischal College LLD in *c.* 1739 but that may have related to fund-raising activities rather than to his teaching of law. His private course in civil law is occasionally noticed in John Chamberlayne, *Magnae Britanniae Notitia or the Present State of Great Britain*, Book III, Part II, 15 [1727]; 15 [1728]; 18 [1743].

33 Henderson, *Advocates*, 114–15.

34 Sedgwick, *History of Parliament*, 2, 159–60.
35 Grant, *Advocates*, 86; Shaw, *Scottish Society*, 54.
36 Shaw, *Scottish Society*, 65; Sedgwick, *History of Parliament*, 1, 396; 2, 239–40.
37 Robert Dundas to Tweeddale, 20 November 1744, NLS, Yester MSS, MS 7064/92. This letter deplores the fact that Erskine's gown is said to have been secured by Argyll because that 'way of his coming in is terrible fatal to your interest and renders your friends here contemptible'.
38 Sedgwick, *History of Parliament*, 2, 285–6; Grant, *Advocates*, 125, 44, 62.
39 KCM, 27 May 1746, 13 June 1748, 8 September 1749, 25 October 1751. John Gregory and Thomas Reid were relatives of James Gregory; McLeod was nominated by him.
40 KCM, 27 May 1746.
41 There had also been fights over membership in the Widows' Fund in 1744, KCM 9 February 1744.
42 See 'Abstract of some statutes and orders of King's College in Old Aberdeen' (Aberdeen, 1753); AUL, KCM, 23 March 1753–16 August 1753. Curricular change is the subject of another monograph in this series by P B Wood.
43 The new rector elected in 1761 was Sir Arthur Forbes, 4th Baronet of Craigievar.
44 Perhaps the removal of William Duff in 1738, and his tardy replacement by Alexander Innes in 1739, should be noted in this context. William Duff had caned Thomas Blackwell the younger, had quarrelled fiercely with his other colleagues, had ignored three warnings from the principal and was living in London as a hack writer. Political disorder in London may have hindered the resolution of his case, about which Ilay had had to consult with Newcastle. The dismissal and replacement of Duff by his deputy, Alexander Innes, can be followed in the Marischal College Minutes but see also: AUL, MSS M 387/1/11/1; M 387/9/2/8/2; M 387/9/2/2/2; ATCA, Letter Book 9, 263; town council to Ilay and to Col. John Middleton, MP, 23 January 1738; 9 March 1739; town council to John Maule, MP, 11 February 1750, ATCA, Out Letter Book 1.
45 The evidence surrounding this attempted appointment suggests that Carmichael did not then belong to the Squadrone connection. His distant cousin and the head of the family was the Earl of Hyndford, an Argathelian. No correspondence regarding Carmichael's case seems to survive among the Tweeddale papers at the NLS—or for that matter in the papers of Lord Milton. The town council tried hard to persuade Carmichael to go to Aberdeen from Inveresk, claiming to want him because of the 'good Information given them of your great Character Ability & Qualification for supplying the Office'. Somewhat later they tried to enlist the support of northern presbyteries insisting that 'It concerns the whole Northern Part of this Nation That the Church Judicatorys Support this Call'. Town council to Frederick Carmichael, 26 November 1744; town council to presbyteries of Elgin, Inverness, Montrose, Brechin, Aberbrothick, 30 March 1745; ATCA, Out Letter Book 2.
46 Hutcheson to Minto, 4 July 1744, NLS, Minto Papers MS 11003/57.
47 Town council to John Maule, 15 April 1745; ? to James Burnet and George Chalmers, 7 June 1745, ATCA, Out Letter Book 2.
48 Thomas Blackwell II to Thomas Birch, 12 September 1748, BL, MS 4301/141 (supplied to me through the courtesy of Dr Dorothy Johnston). In 1757 Pollock was made principal of Marischal College by Argyll; Pollock to Lord Milton, 21 April 1757, NLS, SC, 16701/208.

49 R M Sunter, *Patronage and Politics in Scotland 1707–1832* (Edinburgh, 1986), 79, 81.
50 Blackwell to Thomas Birch, 12 September 1748, Correspondence of Thomas Birch, BL, MS 4301/141; Blackwell to Newcastle, 19 August 1748; 10 February 1753, Newcastle Papers, BL, MS 32716/152; 32731/158.
51 Verner got the Aberdeen town council to ask John Maule, MP, for favours to his son; ATCA, Out Letter Book 2, 3, September 1746. Had Verner failed in his request, it would not have been realistic for him to have applied for the principalship as he did in 1748; Verner to Lord Milton, 20 August 1748. NLS, SC, 16671; Loudoun's name was John Campbell.
52 E H B Rodger, *Aberdeen Doctors at Home and Abroad: The Narrative of a Medical School* (Edinburgh and London, 1893), 41, 89; E A Underwood, *Boerhaave's Men at Leyden and After* (Edinburgh, 1977), 86–7.
53 Gerard's father had sought the King's College chair of divinity in 1733 with the backing of Osborne and Patrick Duff. Alexander had deputised for David Fordyce in 1750 after failing in 1748 to get the Greek chair because Thomas Blackwell retained it with his principalship. In 1752 Gerard had the recommendation of David Scott, MP (Aberdeen Burghs), of the town council and the college. Provost and baillies of Aberdeen to Lord Milton, NLS, SC, 16671/213; Aberdeen town council to David Scott, 13 February 1752, ATCA, Out Letter Book 3. Argyll had told the magistrates that they should also thank Newcastle for this posting. Lord Morton had recommended a Matthew Wallace; Newcastle had probably decided between the nominations. Argyll's political position was precarious in 1752.
54 Duncan's appointment was requested by the college and town council. Town council to Argyll, 21 January 1752; town council to David Scott, n.d.; town council to the Duke of Newcastle, 8 February 1752; town council to David Scott, 13 February 1752. ATCA, Out Letter Book 3.
55 Provost and baillies of Aberdeen to Lord Milton, 6 September 1757, NLS, SC, 16698/3; Kennedy's nomination was opposed by the Marquis of Tweeddale whom Argyll quickly warned off his territory. Town council to David Scott, MP, 28 April 1757, ATCA, Out Letter Book 3.
56 Francis Skene to Milton, 14 June 1759, NLS, SC, 16712/34. This letter thanks Milton for having recommended Francis to be principal following the death of Thomas Blackwell II (1758). It goes on to say that the 'Magistrates have recommended a son of mine [George Skene] for a Regents place with a design to make way for the promotion of the Provosts brother (William Duncan)'. George Skene got his regency but both Francis and William Duncan were disappointed over the principalship which went to the Rev. George Campbell. He had local clerical support and is said to have appealed directly to Argyll for the post. J McCosh, *The Scottish Philosophy* (New York, 1875), 107, 239; H Scott, *Fasti Ecclesiae Scoticanae* (Edinburgh, 1915–28), 7, 359; *DNB*, 'William Duncan'. George Skene to Sir James Carnegie, 19 February 1757, NLS, SC, 16702/80; Sir James Carnegie to Milton, 15 May 1760, NLS, SC, 16714/128; SC, 16712/213; Robert Chambers and Thomas Thomson, *A Biographical Dictionary of Eminent Scotsmen*, revised edition (Glasgow, 1856), 1, 491; George Skene to Dr David Skene, 5 June 1759, AUL, MS 38; William Wilkie to Milton, n.d. (1759), NLS, SC, 16713/215; Town council to Ilay, 21 January 1752; same to David Scott, n.d.; same to Newcastle, 8 February 1752; same to Scott, 13 February, Out Letter Book 3.

57   Earl of Erroll to Lord Milton, 19 May 1760, NLS, SC, 16714/170; Argyll to Milton, 29 May 1760, NLS, SC, 16713/166; James Beattie to Lady Mayne, 2 January 1774, AUL, MS 30/1/201–25; Beattie says here that 'the persons who were instrumental in getting me that office [in Marischal College] were the Earl of Erroll, Lord Adam Gordon and Mr. [Robert] Arbuthnot' but Lord Adam Gordon wrote to Beattie on 9 September 1760 'you owe this entirely to the Duke of Argyll and Lord Erroll'; AUL, MS 30/2/1–776.
58   See Notes 45–8 above.
59   David Skene to Lord Kames, 26 September 1770, AUL, MS 38. ACTA, Aberdeen Council Register 63, 29 November 1770.
60   James Gordon of Pitlurg was a relative by marriage of James Donaldson whose appointment as professor of oriental languages preceded Gordon's by two years. Both were from Jacobite families but nothing has been discovered about Gordon's appointment in 1734. Donaldson was a presentee of the founder of his chair, Ramsay of Balmain.
61   Donaldson got his job in a three-way competition between himself, David Skene and John Gregory. Members of the town council recommended Skene to Argyll and David Scott, MP, on 4 November 1755 and n.d. [?1755], and again to Scott n.d. [1756?], ATCA, Out Letter Book 4. Baillies John Duncan and Robert Fordyce wrote on 4 November 1755 to the Duke of Newcastle saying that 'the Professors of this University earnestly wish that [Skene] may be Nominate Professor of Medicine'; BL, MS 32860/361. Thomas Blackwell, however, described Skene as 'a mere Youth' (he was twenty-four) and Donaldson as 'a notorious Jacobite'. Blackwell and three of the masters supported Dr John Gregory, formerly regent at King's College. Three others recommended Skene to Argyll. Someone else, probably Regent Francis Skene, solicited the support of an old Squadrone man, Andrew Mitchell, MP. Duncan and Fordyce to Newcastle, 4 November 1755, BL, MS 32860/361; Blackwell to Andrew Stone, 28 and 30 September 1755, 2 October 1755, BL, MSS 32859/259; 289; 343. Skene failed to get the post but in June 1757 he did get an appointment as physician to the Sick and Wounded Office's hospital in Aberdeen, ATCA, Out Letter Book 4. This is an interesting case because it shows not only the persistence of factionalism in the college but the perceived shakiness of Argyll's position in the Pelham ministry. Donaldson's earlier appointment to the chair of oriental languages (1754) at Marischal College had come from Ramsay of Balmain. Ramsay was on good terms with Argyll.
62   John Ramsay of Ochtertyre, *Scotland and Scotsmen in the Eighteenth Century*, 2 vols, ed. Alexander Allardyce (Edinburgh and London, 1888), 1, 469–70.
63   How much all this was resented by the 'High-flyers' then and later can be sensed in reading John MacLeod, *Scottish Theology in Relation to Church History since the Reformation* (Edinburgh, 1943, 2nd edn 1946), especially 208, 210–11. A more just appraisal of Campbell's Moderatism is given by Ramsay, *Scotland and Scotsmen*, 1, 482–504.
64   Donaldson in 1757 was to have built for him a laboratory whose cost was not to exceed £18. AUL, MS Marischal College Minutes, 8 May 1757.
65   P B Wood, 'Science and the Aberdeen Enlightenment', in *Philosophy and Science in the Scottish Enlightenment*, ed. Peter Jones (Edinburgh, 1989), 51.
66   Underwood, *Boerhaave*, 30, 86–7. Dr Gordon was recommended to Ilay by Patrick Duff and seems to have been chosen over another man nominated by Col. Middleton. Duff to Milton, 14 June 1733, NLS, SC, 16553/45–6.

67 The best studies of the group to which Gerard belonged are in: P B Wood, 'Thomas Reid, Natural Philosopher: A Study of Science and Philosophy in the Scottish Enlightenment' (Unpublished PhD thesis, University of Leeds, 1984); Stephen A Conrad, 'Citizenship and Common Sense: The Problem of Authority in the Social Background and Social Philosophy of the Wise Club of Aberdeen' (Unpublished PhD dissertation, Harvard University, 1980); H Lewis Ulman, ed., *The Minutes of the Aberdeen Philosophical Society 1758–1773* (Aberdeen, 1990).

68 The place of Duncan in British thought is assessed by W S Howell, *Eighteenth-Century British Logic and Rhetoric* (Princeton, 1971), 345–63, 408; the book also has sections on Campbell and Beattie.

69 KCM, 13 June 1748, 8 September 1749.

70 Gregory was related by marriage to Thomas and George Gordon.

71 KCM, 31 May 1754; J G Burnett, 'An Aberdeen professor of the eighteenth century', *SHR*, 16, (1915), 30–46. Leslie married Christian Fraser, the heiress of Fraser of Powis, see John George Burnett, ed., *Powis Papers 1507–1894* (Aberdeen, 3rd Spalding Club, 1951); the book also contains information on the Alexander Frasers and their cousin George.

Chapter 5, pp. 78 to 101

1 Roger L Emerson, 'Lord Bute and the Scottish universities 1760–1792' in *Lord Bute: Essays in Re-interpretation*, ed. Karl W Schweizer (Leicester, 1988), 147–79.

2 Thomas Hay to Tweeddale, 12 May 1753, NLS, Yester Papers, MS 7055/43. Robertson was later the receiver of much patronage from Lord Milton and Argyll as Richard Sher shows in *Church and University in the Scottish Enlightenment: The Moderate Literati of Edinburgh* (Princeton, 1985), especially 93–150.

3 The mediciner elected in 1755, John Gregory, was half-brother to his predecessor, and husband to the Hon. Elizabeth Forbes, a distant relative of the wives of the Professors Gordon.

4 Thomas Gordon to ?[Rector or Chancellor], 1 January 1760, 'Papers relating to William Thom', AUL, MS K 216/4, 5.

5 KCM, 26 January 1760. After 1754 all philosophy or arts students had been required to attend Thomas Gordon's Tuesday and Thursday lectures given for their benefit. Much of the foregoing paragraph is based on Gordon's letter (n.4 above); this account is largely confirmed in 'Memorial for William Thom . . . 10th December 1760', AUL, MS K 216/8/4.

6 Ibid., 7. 'The Professor of Divinity who was related to Mr. Dalrymple, tho' he had always disapproved of the late plan of education applied to the Humanist in favours of Mr. Dalrymple . . . for that reason now became a zealous stickler for the Humanists Interest, And for supporting that plan of Education.'

7 Ibid.

8 KCM, 13 May 1760.

9 P J Anderson, ed., *Officers and Graduates of the University and King's College Aberdeen* (Aberdeen, New Spalding Club, 1893), 14.

10 Ibid., 34.

11 'Memorial for William Thom'; 'Answers to certain queries', AUL, MS K 216.
12 Anderson, *Officers and Graduates*, 34.
13 From 1738 until his death in 1764 Deskford's father, the 2nd Earl of Seafield, had been Lord Vice-Admiral of Scotland. The Aberdeen town council acted as his not particularly scrupulous deputy.
14 He may possibly be the 'Jacobus Derkfort, Scotus' who matriculated at Leyden on 14 August 1734. Edward Peacock, *Index to English Speaking Students Who Have Graduated at Leyden University* (London, The Index Society, 1883), 28.
15 These included George Middleton of Seaton, rector 1760–6, Principal John Chalmers, Dr John Gregory, Thomas Reid, George Gordon, Roderick McLeod, Patrick Duff and David Dalrymple. Among the club's other members and correspondents were gentlemen who served both King's and Marischal College as rectors and assessors. 'Minute book of the farming club at Gordon's Mill 1758–1764', AUL, MS K 49; see also J H Smith, *The Gordon's Mill Farming Club 1758–1764* (Aberdeen, Aberdeen University Studies 145, 1962).
16 Argyll had him sacked from this lucrative office; J S Shaw, *The Management of Scottish Society 1707–1764* (Edinburgh, 1983), 48, 68, 69, 78–9.
17 He belonged to the Honourable the Improvers in the Knowledge of Agriculture in Scotland, the Edinburgh Musical Society, the Select Society of Edinburgh and to the Philosophical Society of Edinburgh.
18 G D Henderson, *Mystics of the North-East* (Aberdeen, Spalding Society, 1934), 39–44; ATCA, Out Letter Book 2, 13 April 1747; Aberdeen Council Register 60, 14 November 1754 to 26 May 1755; Letter Book 11, various entries 1755–7. Seafield was no honest broker in this attempt at union but had already determined to locate a united college in New Aberdeen when he was asked to arbitrate the outstanding issues between the colleges. The town council, but not the King's College professors, knew this. Argyll's reaction to this scheme was to support King's in its resistance to a union which would have relocated professors and tampered with the corporation's property. It was both just and politic, a conclusion to which Henry Dundas was to come over thirty years later.
19 These issues are traceable in KCM for these years; see also [Thomas Gordon's] letter to ?, 1 January 1760, AUL, MS K 216, Miscellaneous Papers; 'Copy minutes in the submission by the masters of the Old Town College', 1 April 1761, AUL, MS K 214; MS K 228; MS K 44; KCM, 27 November 1761, 5 and 12 July 1762; 21 March 1763, 10 and 14 May 1763; MS K 228, 4–24.
20 Anderson, *Officers and Graduates*, 14, 15, 39; no assessors appear to have been appointed.
21 KCM, 12 July 1762.
22 Ibid.
23 'Copy/rectorial visitation of King's College/1762 & 1763', AUL, MS K 228; Anderson, *Officers and Graduates*, 14–15. One interesting aspect of the rectorial elections of 1762 and 1763 is that they brought into the rectorial court as assessors men connected with Marischal College: Sir Alexander Ramsay of Balmain, Professors George Campbell and Alexander Gerard. The 1771 removal of Gerard to King's College likewise gave that corporation an intimate knowledge of the affairs of the town's college.
24 Ibid., 1–25.

25 KCM, 2, 6, 21 and 25 November, 1761. Burnet, despite this agreement, hired a Mr Temple as his assistant.
26 P B Wood, 'Thomas Reid, Natural Philosopher: A Study of Science and Philosophy in the Scottish Enlightenment' (Unpublished PhD thesis, University of Leeds, 1984); W R Humphries, *William Ogilvie and the Projected Union of the Colleges 1786–1787* (Aberdeen, Aberdeen University Studies, 117, 1940), 1.
27 For Dunbar see C J Berry, 'James Dunbar and the Enlightenment debate on language' in *Aberdeen and the Enlightenment*, ed. J J Carter and J H Pittock (Aberdeen, 1987), 241–50; Ross had been tutor to Dundonald's son in 1752 when both were at St Andrews. Seven years later Deskford sought the humanity chair there for Ross but was foiled by Argyll and Lord Milton. William Wilkie to Lord Milton, ? July 1759, NLS, SC, 16712/216; Ross was nominated for the King's College chair by Deskford: Thomas Gordon, AUL, MS K 34/70.
28 Alexander Gordon became a conjoint professor with John Gregory in 1764, succeeding to the chair upon Gregory's removal to Edinburgh in 1766. Gordon was a son of George Gordon I and a brother of the humanist, Thomas Gordon.
29 William Thom was a brother-in-law to Principal Chalmers and to William Dauney who succeeded him as civilist in 1793.
30 Alexander Gerard became professor of divinity on 9 June 1776. His translation from Marischal College greatly increased his income. Dr William Chalmers, appointed mediciner in 1781, seems not to have been related to Principal John Chalmers; but Robert Eden Scott, chosen in 1788 to assist and succeed his grandfather, Thomas Gordon, was but the most recent of a long line of Gordons to teach in the college. At least seven of the twelve appointments made between 1770 and 1800 went to relatives of sitting professors.
31 Humphries, *William Ogilvie*; Emerson, 'Lord Bute', 163–9.
32 AUL, MS U 557/3.
33 P J Anderson, ed., *Fasti Academiae Mariscallanae Aberdonensis*, 3 vols (Aberdeen, New Spalding Club, 1889–98), 1; *Officers and Graduates*, 8; Bute accepted on 10 August 1761.
34 AUL, William Knight MSS, MS M 113/1915; see Emerson, 'Lord Bute', 161.
35 NLS, Fettercairn MSS, Acc. 4796 Box 94.
36 So careful of unanimity were the professors that Beattie was even unwilling, independently, to aid his friend Andrew Greenfield to secure the chair of mathematics. Beattie to Robert Arbuthnot, 21 April 1778, AUL, MS 30 1/126; Andrew Greenfield to Beattie, 3 March 1778, AUL, MS 30 2/303.
37 'James Jopp of Cotton. Provost, and ruler of the town of Aberdeen. Very rich, attentive, economical man': Sir Charles Elphinstone Adam, ed., *Political State of Scotland . . . in 1788* (Edinburgh, 1887), 12.
38 Beattie to Robert Arbuthnot, 18 April 1778, AUL, MS 30/2/304; Alexander Innes to William Rose, Factor to Lord Fife, 4 March 1777.
39 *History of Aberdeen . . . with Biographical Sketches of Eminent Men of Aberdeen* (Aberdeen, 1811); 'Robert Hamilton', *DNB*; Thomas Gordon to John Gregory, 29 August 1766, AUL, Robert Hamilton Papers, MS 456.
40 Morgan's candidature in 1787 was backed by Dr George Skene, but since a Daniel Morgan had been recommended to Marischal College for a DD by

Bute in 1762 one suspects that Bute had a hand in the 1787 appointment too. The Rev. William Glennie, a local man, had also sought this place. Morgan's natural history collection was amalgamated with the one which Francis and Dr George Skene had assembled. Dr Skene sold their museum when he was forced by colleagues to vacate his professorship because he was not teaching. The £500 price he obtained may have included the value of his chair as well as his collection. Beattie to James Hay Beattie, 19 October 1787, AUL, MS 30/1; Beattie to Sir William Forbes, 20 October 1788, NLS, Fettercairn MSS, MS 4796/94.

41 James Beattie the elder arranged for this appointment of his nephew. A large loan from Beattie's friend, Sir William Forbes, was used to purchase Morgan's museum. Beattie II's application had been sent to Bute by 24 September but somewhat earlier to Lord Sydney. The town council tried very hard to get Dr William Glennie appointed, but failed because of Bute's interest in the case. Cosmo Gordon to James Beattie I, 24 September 1788, AUL, MS 30/2/575; James Beattie I to Sir William Forbes, 20 October 1788, NLS, Fettercairn MSS, Acc. 4796/94; H R Fletcher and W H Brown, *The Royal Botanic Garden Edinburgh 1670–1970* (Edinburgh, 1970), 96.

42 John Stuart's appointment came as a result of Professor William Kennedy's desire to retire in an age which lacked retirement schemes. Kennedy tried to sell Stuart his chair. This transaction did not please the masters. Kennedy resigned and Stuart, when he got his regius chair, gave him a bond for the payment of a lump sum and for what was, in effect, an annuity.

43 James Hay Beattie's appointment was arranged by his father with the rector, senatus, Bute and Henry Dundas, who had been lobbied by various English and Scottish supplicants. Beattie's efforts to secure a place for his own son went back at least to April 1786. Over a year later Bute still had not been informed. By then the Aberdeen magistrates seem to have had a candidate but were told by Dundas and Lord Sydney that 'the respect due to the Earl of Bute both as Chancellor of the University, and as a munificent Patron of learning was such, that the Person recommended by him would undoubtedly have the preference'. Beattie to Sir William Forbes, 20 October 1788, NLS, Fettercairn MSS, Acc. 4796/94; Beattie to Mrs Elizabeth Montague, 28 April, 29 November 1786, 9 and 16 April 1787; to the Duchess of Gordon, 9 and 14 April, 19 June 1787; Duchess of Gordon to Beattie, 4 April 1787; Cosmo Gordon to Beattie, 10 March, 17 April 1787, AUL, MS 30/1, 30/2/535, 542, 544.

44 ATCA, Council Register 62, 29 November 1770; Skene to Kames, 26 September 1770, AUL, Skene MSS, MS 38.

45 KCM, 7 July 1766; *History of Aberdeen . . . with Biographical Sketches of Eminent Men of Aberdeen* (Aberdeen, 1811), 382; AUL, Robert Hamilton MSS, MS 456.

46 MCM, 3 September 1776; ATCA, Aberdeen Council Register 64, 3 and 6 September 1776.

47 ATCA, Council Register 64; 8, 15 and 16 April 1779; AUL, MS M93; John S Reid, 'Patrick Copland 1748–1822: Aspects of his life and times at Marischal College', *AUR*, 172 (1984), 359–79, 362.

48 Bute did not learn until 1784 or 1785 why the union schemes of 1771 had failed. Patronage was a different matter. It could often be planned well in advance of the time at which an appointment had to be made.

49 Sir Lewis Namier and John Brooke, *The History of Parliament: The House of Commons, 1754–1790*, 3 vols (London, 1964), 1, 470.

50 Mary Jane W Scott, *James Thomson, Anglo-Scot* (Athens, Georgia and London, 1988), 106.
51 Anderson, *Officers and Graduates*, 17.
52 Gordon to Beattie, 5 March 1782, AUL, MS 30/2/3772. No rector was chosen in 1784 when Baron Gordon thanked Beattie for not choosing someone else and professed his 'readyness on all occasions to serve the University to the utmost of my power'. Gordon to Beattie, 11 March 1784, AUL, MS 30/2/447. Namier and Brooke, *The House of Commons*, 1, 512–13.
53 Emerson, 'Lord Bute', 166.
54 Adam, *Political State of Scotland*, 6.
55 S G Checkland, *Scottish Banking: A History, 1695–1973* (Glasgow and London, 1975), 217.
56 Namier and Brooke, *The House of Commons*, 2, 419.
57 Allardyce sat as MP for the Aberdeen Burghs. The papers of both Henry and Robert Dundas have numerous letters from him concerning political patronage matters. Sir Alexander Ramsay Irving of Balmain was a benefactor of the college and rewarded for that. In 1794 he had resisted pressure to appoint to the chair of oriental languages unqualified men including Professors John Stuart and George French who would have made the post a sinecure. He then ignored a recommendation from Sir Adam Gordon for a son of a Dr Robertson. John Stuart to Sir Alexander Ramsay, 29 January 1793; Alexander Donaldson to John Stuart, n.d. [1793]; Mrs Thomas Blackwell to [Marischal College masters], n.d. [1793]; AUL, John Stuart MSS, MS 3017/10/11–16. Ramsay appointed James Kidd who turned out to be a useful, pious and learned man—one of the few Aberdeen professors honoured by a biography.
58 Emerson, 'Lord Bute', 167–9.
59 Livingstone was the town council's nominee while Dr George Skene was the man picked by his former colleagues. ATCA, Letter Book 14, Alexander Allardyce to the magistrates, 25 May 1793; Livingstone 'was forced upon them by what is called Parliamentary Influence and besides absenting himself whenever he chuses to go Wrong in the Head, has never done any one Part of the little Duty formerly annexed to the Office'. Dr George Skene to Lord Buchan, 3 September 1797, NLS, MS 3873/253–4. That he was 'Wrong in the head' is borne out by another source, Adam, *Political State of Scotland*, 16.
60 Brown had been in correspondence with Dundas about jobs since 1788. He ultimately thanked him for this post to which he had been recommended by Lord Auckland who had known him earlier in Holland. There he had been a professor at Utrecht before being driven out by the revolutionaries in 1795. James B Salmond, *Veterum Laudes* (Edinburgh and London, 1950), 217; SRO, Melville Castle Muniments, MS GD51/6/817/1–2, 1073, 1140; George Hill to Henry Dundas, 9 January 1791, Melville Papers, SAUL, MS 41760.
61 Principal George Campbell to James Beattie I, 4 July 1794, AUL, 30/2/719; Mansfield to Beattie, 3 August 1795, AUL, 30/2; Beattie to Sir William Forbes (Glennie's old student), 25 January 1796, NLS, Fettercairn MSS, 4796/Box 94; Beattie's retirement deal with Glennie can be found in AUL, MS 30/31/2.
62 Beattie to Mrs Elizabeth Montague and to Robert Arbuthnot, 24 January 1791, AUL, MSS 30/1/318, 319; William Nairne to Dundas, 16 March 1796, SRO, Melville Castle Muniments, MS GD51/6/1151.

63 The story is told in Humphries, *William Ogilvie*, but see also KCM, 1784–1788; 'State of the differences which at present take place among the members of King's College, and which are now referred to the Rectoral Court', n.d. and incomplete, AUL, MS CT Box 43.
64 King's College Rectorial Minute Book, AUL, MS K 101, 14 May 1786.
65 Quoted in Humphries, *William Ogilvie*, 36.
66 Kemnay was a relative by marriage of James Dunbar whose allegiance to the proposed union and to his friend Ogilvie seem to have been unaffected by the appointment. C J Berry, 'James Dunbar and the American War of Independence', *AUR*, 45 (1974), 265.
67 Adam, *Political State of Scotland*, 14; it is not without interest that Sir William Forbes of Craigievar is listed as 'One of the Independent Friends' who would vote with Skene of Skene rather than the Duke of Gordon.
68 Thomas Gordon to the Duke of Gordon, 7 October 1786, AUL, MS 387/16/4/12/2; Patrick Copland to the Duchess of Gordon, 9 August 1786, AUL, MS U557/3.
69 Bruce Lenman, *Integration, Enlightenment, and Industrialisation: Scotland 1746–1832* (Toronto, 1981), 78–9.
70 KCM, 3 March 1792. Dissenting from this resolution were James Dunbar and Gilbert Gerard.
71 H W Meikle, *Scotland and the French Revolution* (Glasgow, 1912), 77–82; See also C Bewley, *Muir of Huntershill* (Oxford, 1981).
72 KCM, 2 July 1792.
73 Anderson, *Officers and Graduates*, 5.
74 Gordon to Principal John Chalmers, 12 March 1796;. David Scot to Roderick McLeod, 16 July 1796; John Menzies to Roderick McLeod, 9 December 1797, AUL, MSS CT Box 11; K217; Gordon to Henry Dundas, 17 December 1797, NLS, Dundas MSS, MS 5/17.
75 William Nairne to Henry Dundas, 16 March 1796, Melville Castle Muniments SRO, MD GD51/6/1151. Nairne's letter recommended Dr (George) Skene for the mediciner's place held by Kemnay's relative, Sir Alexander Burnet Bannerman. The Duke of Gordon and Ferguson of Pitfour were said to be for him, but no professor's opinion was given; probably none had been solicited. The post went to Bannerman's son, James, who was made a conjoint professor with his father. Neither man was interested in medical education and neither fostered medical education in Aberdeen.
76 Gilbert Gerard's earlier appointment to a regency in 1790 doubtless owed something to his brother William's benefaction to the college in 1788 (£100) and to their father's long service. Gerard got his divinity chair in 1797 after an elaborate competition which was almost certainly 'fixed'. In 1798 he thanked Dundas for allowing him to succeed his father as royal chaplain. This was followed by the assurance 'that, as by the death of my worthy father in law Mr. Duncan & I have succeeded to his vote in the Mearns, you may always command me in that way or any other in my power'. Gerard to Henry Dundas, 26 December 1798, SRO, MS GD 51/6/1307. 'Proceedings of delegates in election and admission of professors of divinity 1795–1887', AUL, MS K 140; the announcement of this comparative trial survives in GUL, MS 58359.
77 No information seems to survive about either Bell or his appointment; the same is true of Bentley.
78 Dundas to Alexander Allardyce, 21 May 1793. On 17 May Allardyce, the

MP for the Aberdeen Burghs, recommended a 'W Turner' for Bell's place but 'the Office had been given to Mr. Macpherson, on the recommendation of the Duke of Gordon'. ATCA, Letter Book 13, 62–3.
79 Gordon to Copland, 19 June 1800, Copland Family Letters, AUL, MS 2999.
80 Thomas Gordon, 'Memorial', AUL, MS K 216; K 269; KCM 31 October 1759.
81 This was not altogether true of Robert Eden Scott who had interests in science and its practical uses. He cannot, however, be compared to someone like Patrick Copland at Marischal. P B Wood, 'Science and the Aberdeen Enlightenment' in *Science and Philosophy in the Scottish Enlightenment*, ed. Peter Jones (Edinburgh, 1989), 48, 57–8; John S Reid, 'Late eighteenth-century adult education in the sciences at Aberdeen: the natural philosophy classes of Professor Patrick Copland' in *Aberdeen and the Enlightenment*, ed. J J Carter and J H Pittock (Aberdeen, 1987), 168–79.
82 Wood, 'Science and the Aberdeen Enlightenment', 50; Humphries, *William Ogilvie*, 3–5; David Erskine, 11th Earl of Buchan, was friendly with Ogilvie and ranked him highly as a naturalist; GUL, Murray MS 502/201/65; Murray MS 336/170.

Conclusion, pp. 102 to 106

1 This has also been noticed by R D Anderson, 'Scottish university professors, 1800–1939: profile of an elite' *Scottish Economic & Social History* (1987), 27–54; see also Anderson's monograph in this series. Appendix IV is meant to take parts of Anderson's statistical account into the eighteenth century. This can be supplemented by reference to R L Emerson, 'Aberdeen professors 1690–1800: two structures, two professoriates, two careers' in *Aberdeen and the Enlightenment*, ed. J J Carter and J H Pittock (Aberdeen, 1987), 155–67.
2 The best account of this is still George Davie, *The Democratic Intellect: Scotland and Her Universities in the Nineteenth Century* (2nd edn., Edinburgh, 1964).
3 David Fate Norton, *David Hume: Common-Sense Moralist, Sceptical Metaphysician* (Princeton, 1982), 55–191; M A Stewart, *Warmth in the Cause of Virtue: Intellectual Controversy in the Age of Hutcheson and Hume* (forthcoming).
4 E G R Taylor, *Mathematical Practitioners of Hanoverian England 1714–1840* (Cambridge, 1966).
5 Richard Sher tends to see the careers of the Moderates as founded on the patronage of Lord Bute, but Robertson, John Home, Blair, Ferguson, John Jardine and others not studied in his recent work had already by 1761 become intimates of Lord Milton and protégés of Argyll. R L Emerson, 'Lord Bute and the Scottish universities 1760–1792' in *Lord Bute: Essays in Reinterpretation*, ed. Karl Schweizer (Leicester, 1988), 151.

Appendices

Appendix I	Population of New Aberdeen, Old Machar, Old Aberdeen: Arts Enrolment Figures for King's and Marischal Colleges and Universities
Appendix II	Offices at King's and Marischal
Table 1	A List of the Professorships and Some of the Offices of King's College and University
Table 2	A List of the Professorships and Some of the Offices of Marischal College and University
Appendix III	King's College Factions 1710–87
Table 1	1710–17
Table 2	1717–42
Table 3	1741–3
Table 4	1760–2
Table 5	1785–7
Appendix IV	Marischal College Factions 1717–45
Appendix V	Scottish University and College Chairs 1690–1800, Noting Legal Patrons of Chairs and the Foundation Dates of Those Established After 1690
Appendix VI	A Statistical Account of Scottish University Professors 1690–1799
Table 1.1	Known Familial Relations Among the Professors at King's College
Table 1.2	Known Familial Relations Among the Professors at Marischal College
Table 2	Relationships between Professors 1629–99/1700–79
Table 3	Father's Occupation and Social Status 1620–99/1700–79
Table 4	Maternal Grandfather's Social Status and Occupation 1620–99/1700–79
Table 5	Apparent Counties of Origin for Professors born 1620–99/1700–79

Table 6	Educational Experiences of the Professoriate 1629–99/1700–79
Table 7	Qualification or First Occupation of University Professors
Table 8	Persistence in One of Father's Principal Roles or Occupations and Status Changes
Table 9	Male Sibling Order of Professors
Table 10	Numbers of Professors Married
Table 11	Ages of Marriage, Entry to Profession, Appointment, Length of Tenure and Age at Death
Table 12	Estimated Minimum Professorial Incomes 1700–99
Table 13	Estimated Total Real Professorial Incomes
Table 14	Average and Median Estimated Real Peak Professorial Incomes
Table 15	Known Publication Record by Category of Men Born 1620–99/1700–79

Appendix I

POPULATION OF NEW ABERDEEN, OLD MACHAR, OLD ABERDEEN: ARTS ENROLMENT FIGURES FOR KING'S AND MARISCHAL COLLEGES AND UNIVERSITIES

Year	Parish of New Aberdeen	Parish of Old Machar	Burgh of Old Aberdeen	Estimated Arts Enrolments at King's	Marischal[7]
1690				c. 100	c. 100
1700				c. 100	c. 90
1707	c. 4,000[1]				
1730				c. 150	132
1750				157	136
1755	10,488[2]	4,945[2]			
1769		15,435[4]		c. 100	c. 140
1775					c. 170
1789	16,386[3]				
1790		8,107[3]	1,713[3]		
1795	16,120[3]				
1800		27,508[4]		c. 100–130[3]	c. 120–140[3]
		33,370[4]			
1801		27,400[5]			
1811	21,639[6]	14,731[4&6]			

SOURCES

1. William Ferguson, *Scotland 1689 to the Present* (Edinburgh and London, 1968), 85.
2. J G Kyd, ed., *Scottish Population Statistics Including Webster's Analysis of Population 1755* (Edinburgh, 1975), 51, 54.
3. *OSA*, 1, 286, 318; 14, 285–6.
4. James Playfair, *A Geographical and Statistical Description of Scotland*, 2 vols (Edinburgh, 1819), 2, 96.
5. T C Smout, *A History of the Scottish People* (London, 1970), 261.
6. Robert Wilson, *An Historical Account and Delineation of Aberdeen* (Aberdeen, 1822), 225. This contains the census figure for New Aberdeen; the figure given here for the parish of Old Machar has been derived by subtracting the census figure for Aberdeen given in Playfair from the one listed here for New Aberdeen. It is almost certainly an inflated one.
7. The figures which follow are based on sources found in R L Emerson, 'Scottish universities in the eighteenth century, 1690–1800', *Studies on Voltaire and the Eighteenth Century*, 167 (1977), 473 and on P J Anderson, ed., *Fasti Academiae Mariscallanae Aberdonensis: Selections from the Records of Marischal College and University*, 3 vols (Aberdeen, 1889–98), New Spalding Club, 2 and 3), *passim*. Some estimate of the relative size of the Aberdeen colleges for the years 1776 to 1830 can be found in Alexander Morgan, *Scottish University Studies* (Oxford and London, 1933), 76–7. The number of divinity students in each college was about half of the enrolment in arts.

Appendix II

Offices at King's and Marischal

TABLE 1 A LIST OF THE PROFESSORSHIPS AND SOME OF THE OFFICES OF KING'S COLLEGE AND UNIVERSITY

Chancellor—the bishop of Aberdeen *ex officio* until 1689; after 1690 elected by rector, principal, subprincipal, professors and masters.
Vice-chancellor—the commissary of Aberdeen *ex officio*.
Rector—elected annually by the principal, subprincipal, professors and masters or by the above with other members of the college.
Assessors to the rector—chosen by the rector from a short list prepared by the principal, subprincipal, professors and masters.
Procurators of the Four Nations [Lothian, Moray, Angus, Mar]—elected by the principal, subprincipal, professors, and masters.
Principal—a doctor of divinity elected by the rector, procurators of the Four Nations, professors, and masters; admitted by the chancellor or his vice.
Professor of divinity—elected by the principal, two members of the college or university, the Moderator and two delegates from each Presbytery in the Synod of Aberdeen (nineteen votes); admitted only after a comparative trial.
Professors of law and medicine—elected in the same manner as the principal; admitted by the chancellor.
Subprincipal—elected in the same manner as the principal; admitted by the chancellor.
Three professors of philosophy (regents in arts)—elected by the principal, subprincipal, professors, humanist and regents supposedly after a comparative trial of candidates; admitted by the principal. In 1799 these chairs were 'fixed' and became the nominal professorships of moral philosophy, natural philosophy, and mathematics.
Humanist—elected by the principal, procurators of the Four Nations, professors, and regents; admitted by the chancellor.
Professor of oriental languages—elected by the principal, subprincipal, professors and masters until 1695, thereafter presented by the crown.
Professor of Greek—elected as were the regents.

TABLE 2   A LIST OF THE PROFESSORSHIPS AND SOME OF THE
OFFICES OF MARISCHAL COLLEGE AND UNIVERSITY

Chancellor—elected by the rector, principal, professors and masters.
Vice-chancellor—appointed by the chancellor.
Rector—elected by the procurators of the Four Nations, often from leets given them by the masters.
Assessors to the rector—chosen by the procurators of the Four Nations.
Procurators of the Four Nations [Mar, Buchan, Moray and Angus]—chosen by all members of the university.
Dean of Faculty—elected by the chancellor, rector, principal, professors, masters and the minister of New Aberdeen (St Nicholas) with a quorum formed by the principal and minister.
Principal—chosen by the Earl Marischal until 1715; by the crown thereafter.
Professor of divinity—chosen by the town council of Aberdeen (supposedly after a comparative trial).
Three professors of philosophy (regents of arts)—chosen by the Earl Marischal until 1715; by the crown thereafter. In 1754 these chairs were 'fixed' and became the professorships of civil and natural history, natural philosophy, and moral philosophy and logic.
Professor of mathematics—chosen by the town council after a comparative trial but with some obligation to pick the founder's descendants.
Professor of medicine—chosen by the Earl Marischal until 1715; thereafter by the crown.
Professor of oriental languages—chosen by the Ramsay Lairds of Balmain, failing whom by the town council of Aberdeen.
Professor of chemistry—chosen initially by the founder, Barbara Blackwell, widow of Principal Thomas Blackwell; thereafter by the senatus.
Professor of Greek—a nominal post held by a regent chosen by the senatus until 1715; thereafter a real place in the gift of the crown.
Professor of law—a nominal post filled by the senatus.

Appendix III

King's College Factions 1710–87

TABLE 1 1710–17*

Principal's Relatives	Whigs and the Gordon Connection
Principal George Middleton, deposed 1717	Subprincipal George Fraser, d. 1711
Regent William Black–1711; subprincipal, 1711–d. 1714	Regent Alexander Fraser I–1714; subprincipal 1714–42
Prof. George Anderson, divinity, d. 1710	Prof. David Anderson, divinity, 1711–d. 1733
Civilist John Gordon, 1697–deposed 1717	Prof. George Gordon, oriental languages, d. 1730
Mediciner Patrick Urquhart, d. 1724	Prof. Thomas Bower, mathematics, 1704–resigned 1717
Regent James Urquhart, 1709–deposed 1717	Humanist Alexander Gordon, 1695–d. 1738
[Regent William Simpson, 1715 illegally elected]	Regent Alexander Burnet, 1711–
Regent Richard Gordon, 1715–deposed 1717	

* Dates of appointment are given only for those placed after 1690.

136

Appendix III

Table 2 1717–42*

Squadrone Men	Argathelians
Principal George Chalmers,† 1717–	Subprincipal Alexander Fraser, d. 1742
Prof. David Anderson,† divinity, 1710– d. 1733	Prof. George Gordon, oriental languages, d. 1730
Civilist Alexander Garden, 1717– resigned 1724	Civilist Alexander Fraser, 1724–d. 1741
Mediciner James Gregory, 1725–d. 1733	Prof. George Gordon, oriental languages, 1730–
Mediciner James Gregory II,† 1732	Prof. John Lumsden, divinity, 1735–
Regent Alexander Burnet, 1711–1742; subprincipal 1742–	Regent Thomas Gordon, 1739–
Prof. John Ker, Greek 1717–resigned 1734	
Regent Alexander Rait, 1734–	

* Dates of appointment are given only for those placed in 1717 or later.
† After 1727 became Argathelians.

Table 3 1741–3 Civilist Election and Appointees to 1751

Squadrone and Opposition	Ilay's Friends	Gordon Faction
Regent Alexander Burnet, subprincipal 1742–	Principal George Chalmers	Subprincipal Alexander Fraser I, d. 1742
Regent Daniel Bradfute	Prof. John Lumsden, divinity	Civilist Alexander Fraser II, d. 1741
Regent Alexander Rait, d. 1751	Mediciner James Gregory II	Prof. George Gordon, oriental languages
Civilist James Catanach, 1743–		Humanist Thomas Gordon

After 1743 the Gordon faction was joined by:

Regent John Chalmers, 1746–

Regent John Gregory, 1746–

Regent Roderick McLeod, 1749–

Regent Thomas Reid, 1751–

TABLE 4   1760–2 CIVILIST ELECTION

Principal's Faction	Gordon Faction
Principal John Chalmers Subprincipal Alexander Burnet Civilist James Catanach, d. 1760 Regent Roderick McLeod Prof. John Leslie, Greek [Civilist William Thom, illegally elected 1761]	Prof. John Lumsden, divinity Mediciner John Gregory Prof. George Gordon, oriental languages Humanist Thomas Gordon Regent Thomas Reid Civilist David Dalrymple, 1761–

TABLE 5   1785–7 UNION OF THE COLLEGES AND UNIVERSITIES

Against Union ('*the Sapient* Septemviri')	For Union (*Deskford's Men*)
Principal John Chalmers Subprincipal Roderick McLeod Prof. Alexander Gerard, divinity Civilist William Thom Mediciner William Chalmers Prof. John Leslie, Greek Regent Thomas Gordon	Prof. John Ross, oriental languages Humanist William Ogilvie Regent James Dunbar

Appendix IV

Marischal College Factions 1717–45

	Squadrone	Ilay	Argyll and the Opposition
Principal Thomas Blackwell	d. 1728		
Prof. Matthew MacKaile,			
medicine, 1717		⟶ *c.* 1725★	
regent, 1729		d. 1734	
Prof. Colin Maclaurin			
mathematics, 1717		⟶ *c.* 1724,★	
		resigned 1727	
Prof. George Cruden			
Greek, 1717	d. 1723		
Regent Patrick Hardie,			
1717	d. 1724		
Regent David Verner, 1717		⟶ *c.* 1725★	*c.* 1739†
Regent John Anderson, 1717	d. 1721		
Regent George Turnbull,			
1721		⟶ *c.* 1725,★	
		resigned 1727	
Prof. Thomas Hadow,			
Greek, 1723	d. 1723		
Prof. Thomas Blackwell,			
Greek, 1723	d. 1758		
Regent Daniel Gordon, 1724	d. 1729		
Regent William Duff		1727 ⟶	*c.* 1729†
		?‡ ⟵	
		resigned 1738	
Prof. John Stewart,			
mathematics, 1727	d. 1766		
Prof. James Chalmers,			
divinity, 1728	1728 →	1728★	
	?§	⟵	
	d. 1744		
Principal John Osborn, 1728		d. 1748	
Prof. James Donaldson,			
oriental langs, 1732		d. 1754	
Prof. James Gordon,			
medicine, 1734		d. 1755	
Regent Francis Skene, 1734		? ⟶	*c.* 1739†
		c. 1746 ⟵	‡
Regent Alexander Innes, 1739		d. 1739	
Prof. Robert Pollock,			
divinity, 1745		d. 1759	

★ Moved to Ilay faction. ‡ Moved back to Ilay faction.
† Moved to Argyll faction. § Moved back to Squadrone.

Appendix V

SCOTTISH UNIVERSITY AND COLLEGE CHAIRS 1690–1800, NOTING LEGAL PATRONS OF CHAIRS AND THE FOUNDATION DATES OF THOSE ESTABLISHED AFTER 1690

	Edinburgh	Glasgow	St Andrews	King's	Marischal
Principal	T	C	C (United College)	S	P, C (1717–), n.11
Principal			C (St Mary's)		
Provost			C (St Salvator's)		
Principal			C (St Leonard's)	S, n.9	
Subprincipal				SA	
Divinity	T (1692)	S (1691)	C	S, C (1695)	T
Oriental languages	C (1702), n.1	S (1692)	C		P (1732)
Ecclesiastical history		C (1716)	C (1707)		
Law		C (1713)			
Public law	C (1707)			S	S (?1766)
Civil law	T/FA (1709)				
Scots law	T/FA (1722)				
Botany [Surgeons Company, 1676]	T (1695)	S (1704), n.7			C (1717)
Anatomy	C (1768)	C (1718)			
Medicine & chemistry	T (1713)	S (1747), n.14			P/S (1793)
Medicine	T (1720)	n.7			
Midwifery	T (1724), n.2	C (1714)	S (1720)	S	P (1700)
Medicine (Institutes)	T (1726)				
Medicine (Practice)	T (1726)				

APPENDIX V

	Edinburgh	Glasgow	St Andrews	King's	Marischal
Materia medica	T (1768)	S (1766)			
Surgery	T (1777), n.3				
Humanist	P (1690), n.4	S (1691)	P P P, n.10	S	S
Regent → Greek	T (1708), n.5	S (1704)	S S	S	S
Regent → logic	T	S	S S	S	P, C (1717)
Regent → moral phil.	T	S	S S S	S	
Regent → nat. phil.	T, n.6	S, n.6	S S S, n.6	S, n.6	P, C (1717)
Regent → nat. hist.					P, C (1717)
Regent → logic, meta. rhetoric			S		P, C (1717)
History	T (1719)				n.6
	T/FA (1720)		P, n.10		
Natural history	C (1767)				n.12
Astronomy	C (1785)	C (1760)		S (1703)	T, n.13
Mathematics	T	S (1691)	C	C (1707), n.13	
Agriculture	P/S (1790)				S, n.15
French			(1792)	S, n.8	
Other languages	n.8	n.8			
Rhetoric & belles lettres	T (1748)				n.6
	C (1762)				

T = Town council
C = Crown
P = Private patron
SA = Synod of Aberdeen
FA = An *ad hoc* body with a majority from the Faculty of Advocates, Edinburgh or the Faculty itself
S = Senatus, college or university body
→ = Post renamed (see *n.*6)
Notes 1 to 15 overleaf

NOTES

1. This is the year in which Professor John Cuming presented his warrant which may have been issued earlier.
2. This chair disappeared in 1726.
3. This was until 1831 associated with the chair of anatomy.
4. Appointments were made by an *ad hoc* committee composed of two Lords of Session, a member of the Faculty of Advocates, one Writer to the Signet and two town councillors. The chair was sometimes called 'Humanity and Roman Antiquities'.
5. The founding of all the Greek chairs has recently been studied by M A Stewart, 'The Origins of the Scottish Greek Chairs', in '*Owls to Athens': Essays on Classical Subjects Presented to Sir Kenneth Dover*, ed. E M Craik (Oxford, 1990), 391–400.
6. The regencies were converted to professorships at Edinburgh in 1708, at Glasgow in 1727, at St Andrews in 1747, at Marischal in 1753 and at King's in 1799. At Marischal the teaching of Latin was a responsibility of the regents, one of whom in 1753 became a professor of natural history and another professor of moral philosophy and logic, a division which included some metaphysics and rhetoric.
7. This chair, until 1818, was a chair of botany and anatomy.
8. Provision for instruction in French, Dutch, German and Italian was often available in the towns, sometimes even in the colleges. But only two schools seem to have assigned language instruction to a teacher paid by the foundation, Glasgow (*c.* 1765) and St Andrews (*c.*1792).
9. The subprincipal was normally the senior regent and held this post with a regency.
10. The three columns here refer to St Salvator's, St Leonard's and the United College formed in 1747. Civil history and natural history were joined in one chair at St Andrews as they were to be at Marischal College after 1753.
11. The town council had some influence upon the selection of principals since it normally gave the incumbent a city church living.
12. Astronomy was also taught by Patrick Copland at Marischal College.
13. This chair lapsed with the resignation of Thomas Bower in 1717. The masters gave the title of professor but little or no salary to Alexander Rait in 1732 but when he succeeded to a regency in 1734 no-one replaced him as professor of mathematics.
14. The Glasgow chair of chemistry and materia medica was split into two lectureships in 1766.
15. A chair of agriculture had been founded at Marischal College in 1790, but, under the terms of the bequest, it was not filled until 1840. At Edinburgh only the initial appointment was made by the private patron and founder, Sir William Johnston Pulteney.

Appendix VI

A Statistical Account of Scottish University Professors 1690–1799

TABLE 1.1 KNOWN FAMILIAL RELATIONS AMONG THE PROFESSORS AT KING'S COLLEGE

Born 1629–99
1. David Anderson		T		
2. George Anderson	★, b-i-l13		A	R
3. William Black				
4. Thomas Bower				
5. Daniel Bradfute	n6, r7, ?r51			
6. Alexander Burnet	u5, r51			
7. James Catanach	r6, 5, 51			R
8. George Chalmers	f-i-l20, gf43, ?r32			
9. Alexander Fraser I	?r24, f10, c11			R
10. Alexander Fraser II	s9, r11, ?r24			R
11. George Fraser	★, c9, r10, 11; f-i-l15			R
12. Alexander Garden				
13. James Garden	★, r23, b-i-l2			R
14. Alexander Gordon	★, s17, b19, 15; r23			R
15. George Gordon I	★, s17, s-i-l11, r23, f40, 41, 42; b14, 19			R
16. John Gordon	★, f18, r23			R
17. Patrick Gordon	★, f14, f15, r23, f19			R
18. Richard Gordon	★, s16, r23, b14, 15			R
19. Thomas Gordon I	★, s17, b14, 15, r23			R
20. James Gregory I	s-i-l8, f43, r20, 37, 44			
21. John Ker				
22. John Lumsden	r34			
23. George Middleton	r13, r14, r15, r16, r17, r18, r19			R
24. John Moir	?r9, ?r10		M,	?R
25. George Skene		T		
26. James Urquhart	s27			R
27. Patrick Urquhart	f26			

143

TABLE 1.1—*continued*

Born 1700–79			
28. Sir Alexander Bannerman	s29		R
29. James Bannerman	f28		R
30. Alexander Bell			
31. James Bentley			
32. John Chalmers	?r8, c19, 40, 41, 42; b-i-l54, r53	M	R
33. William Chalmers		?	R
34. David Dalrymple	r22		R
35. Alexander Dauney	n-i-l54, ?b-i-l32	M	R
36. James Dunbar			
37. Sir William Forbes	★, r20, 43, 44	M	R
38. Alexander Gerard	f39		
39. Gilbert Gerard	s38		R
40. Sir Alexander Gordon	s15, b41, 42; c32, r53		R
41. George Gordon II	s15, b40, 42, c32		R
42. Thomas Gordon II	b40, 41; s15, c32, gf53		R
43. James Gregory II	s20, gs8, r37		R
44. John Gregory	1/2b43, rm41, 42; r37, 51		R
45. William Jack			
46. John Leslie	★ by m		
47. Roderick McLeod	f-i-l48		
48. Hugh MacPherson	s-i-l47		
49. William Ogilvie	C		
50. Alexander Rait	r6, r5, r7, r51		R
51. Thomas Reid	★, r43, 44, 50	A	R
52. John Ross			
53. Robert Eden Scott	r32, 40, 41; gs42		R
54. William Thom	u-i-l35, b-i-l32		R

f = father
s = son
b = brother
i-l = in-law
u = uncle
n = nephew

c = cousin
gf/gs = grandfather, grandson
r = relative
rm = relative by marriage
R = related to a sitting member
C = related to chancellor

Related to professors at Edinburgh (E), Glasgow (G), St Andrews (A), Marischal (M); related to Aberdeen town council member (T).
★ = related to earlier member of King's College.

Several other men were offered professorships but did not choose to serve: Charles Gordon (divinity, 1697), Thomas Hogg (divinity, 1701), Allan Logan (divinity, 1703) and William Smith (regent, 1711). William Simpson (regent, 1711), although he taught for one year, was found by the courts not to have been properly elected. They have not been counted in the tables which follow.

TABLE 1.2 KNOWN FAMILIAL RELATIONS AMONG THE PROFESSORS AT MARISCHAL COLLEGE

Born 1629–99
1. John Anderson   T K
2. Thomas Blackwell I   f27, u34   G
3. James Chalmers   T K
4. Patrick Chalmers
5. George Cruden   T
6. Patrick Hardie   A
7. George Keith   C
8. George Liddell   ★
9. Alexander Litster
10. Matthew MacKaile
11. Colin Maclaurin
12. William Meston
13. Alexander Moir   ?r14   R
14. James Moir   ?r13   K
15. James Osborne   u16   ?K
16. John Osborn   n15   T
17. Robert Paterson   f-i-l20
18. George Peacock
19. Patrick Sibbald   K
20. William Smith   s-i-l17
21. George Turnbull
22. David Verner (or Warner)   G

Born 1700–79
23. James Beattie I   f25, u24, rm38
24. James Beattie II   n23, c25, rm38   K R
25. James Hay Beattie   s23, c24, c35, r38   K R
26. William Laurence Brown   A
27. Thomas Blackwell II   s2, c34, u35   T G R
28. George Campbell   T
29. Patrick Copland
30. Alexander Donaldson   s31, r40
31. James Donaldson   f30, n40   Krm R
32. William Duff
33. William Duncan
34. David Fordyce   c27, n2, r35   T Krm R
35. George French   n27, r34
36. John Garioch
37. Alexander Gerard
38. George Glennie   r23, 24, 25, r51   Rm
39. Daniel Gordon   ?K
40. James Gordon   u31   K
41. Thomas Haddow   A
42. Robert Hamilton   E G
43. Alexander Innes
44. William Kennedy   ?r46
45. James Kidd
46. William Livingstone   ?r44, b-i-l50

TABLE 1.2—*continued*

47. William Morgan			
48. Robert Pollock		K	
49. Francis Skene	f50		
50. George Skene	b-i-l46, s49		R
51. John Stewart		T	
52. John Stuart	rm38		
53. William Trail		G	

f = father
s = son
b = brother
i-l = in-law
u = uncle
n = nephew
c = cousin
gf/gs = grandfather, grandson
r = relative
rm = relative by marriage
R = related to a sitting member
C = related to chancellor
Related to professors at Edinburgh (E), Glasgow (G), St Andrews (A), Marischal (M), King's (K).
★ = related to earlier member of Marischal College.

TABLE 2 RELATIONSHIPS BETWEEN PROFESSORS 1629–99/1700–79

1629–1699 Relation	Edinburgh No.	%	Glasgow No.	%	St Andrews No.	%	King's No.	%	Marischal No.	%
Related to one other	24	51	19	66	21	51	21	75	8	36
R	22	47	11	38	17	41	14	50	?1	5
F or S	11	23	8	29	6	15	10	36	0	
B or B-i-l	2	4	2	7	0		4	14	0	
Total	47	100	28	100	40	100	27	100	22	100
1700–1799										
Related to one other	29	49	13	26	17	50	21	78	13 [?15]	42
R	10	15	5	10	11	32	16	59	7	23
F or S	14	21	6	12	4	12	10	37	6	19
B or B-i-l	3	5	1	2	9	26	5	19	2	6
Total	66	100	50	100	34	100	27	100	31	100
Related 1690–1799	53	47	33	42	38	51	42	78	21	40
No. of Professors 1690–1799	113	100	78	100	74	100	54	100	53	100

R = related to a sitting member
F = Father
S = Son
B = Brother
i-l = in-law

TABLE 3 FATHER'S OCCUPATION AND SOCIAL STATUS, 1620–99/1700–79*

(First line has no. and % for those born 1620–99; second line no. and % for those born 1700–79)

	Edinburgh No.	%	Glasgow No.	%	St Andrews No.	%	King's No.	%	Marischal No.	%	Total
Titled & landed	4	9			1	3					
	3	5			1	3			1	5	
Landed	14	30	2	7	10	25	11	41	4	18	
	16	24	10	20	2	6	9	35	5	16	
Merchants	2	5	2	7	3	8	3	11	4	18	
	4	6	10	20			3	12	2	6	
Artisans	2	5					2	7	2	9	
	2	3	1	4					2	6	
Lawyers	4	9			4	11	1	4	2	6	
	10	15	1	2	1	3	1	4	1	5	
Physicians	3	7	3	11	1	2	1	4			
	7	11	5	10	1	3			1	5	
Surgeons	6	13	1	4					4	13	
	3	5	1	2							
Ministers	15	33	10	34	10	25	3	11	6	27	
	14	22	16	32	19	56	8	31	11	35	

APPENDIX VI

	Edinburgh No.	%	Glasgow No.	%	St Andrews No.	%	King's No.	%	Marischal No.	%	Total
Civil officers	1	2									
	1	2	2	4			1	3			
	1	2	1	4							
Military & naval											
Professors	3	7	3	11	2	5	8	30	6	19	
	12	18	8	16	6	18	8	31			
			1	4	1	3	1	4			
Schoolmasters			2	4			2	6			
Other professions	2	5	1	7	1	3					
			2	4	1	2					
Farmers	2	5									
			2	4	3	7	2	6	6	27	
Unknown	9	20	9	32	13	33	3	22	4	13	
	5	8	5	10	3	9	2	8			
Total 1620–99	47	41	28	36	40	54	27	50	22	42	165
1700–79	66	59	50	64	34	46	27	50	31	58	208
Total 1620–1779	113	100	78	100	74	100	54	100	53	100	†

* These and following tables do not include King's College men born 1620–99 who were either illegally elected or elected but refused to serve or were otherwise prevented from doing so—William Simpson, William Smith, Charles Gordon, Thomas Hogg and Allan Logan, or one at St Andrews—Thomas Black—and one from Glasgow—James Dick.

† These totals cannot be added without counting twice men who served in two universities.

TABLE 4 MATERNAL GRANDFATHER'S SOCIAL STATUS AND OCCUPATION 1620–99/1700–79

	Edinburgh No.	%	Glasgow No.	%	St Andrews No.	%	King's No.	%	Marischal No.	%
(First line has no. and % for those born 1620–99; second line no. and % 1700–79)										
Titled & landed	2	4					2	7		
	4	6			1	3	1	4		
Landed	4	9	2	4	3	8	6	19	4	18
	10	15	8	14			6	23	7	23
Merchants	2	7	2	4			1	3		
					1	3	1	4	1	3
Artisans					1	3	1	3		
Lawyers									2	6
	2	3	1	2			1	4		
Physicians							1	3		
	1	2	1	2						
Surgeons										
			1	2						
Ministers	8	17	3	11	5	13				
	5	8	5	8	10	29	4	16	5	16
Civil officers										
	1	2	1	2						
Military & naval	1	2								
Professors										
	4	6	2	4	9	26	6	23	3	9
Schoolmasters										
									1	3
Other professions										
Farmers										
			1	2	1	3			2	6
Lower Orders										
									1	3
Unknown	32	68	21	75	30	75	14	56	18	82
	44	67	33	66	22	65	10	38	15	48
Total 1620–99	47	42	28	36	40	54	27	50	22	42
1700–79	66	58	50	64	34	46	27	50	31	58
Total 1620–1779	113	100	78	100	74	100	54	100	53	100

APPENDIX VI

Table 5 Apparent Counties of Origin for Professors born 1620–99/1700–79

	Edinburgh No.	No.	Glasgow No.	No.	St Andrews No.	No.	King's No.	No.	Marischal No.	No.
(Defined by father's estate location, residence or other source)										
Aberdeen & Old Aberdeen	1	2			1		11	9	5	10
St Andrews		1		1	3	10			1	1
Edinburgh	4	25		2	1	1		1		1
Glasgow	1	1	5	12	1	1			1	
Aberdeenshire	1	1					9	2	6	9
Argyllshire	3		2						1	
Ayrshire	1	2	2	2					1	
Banffshire	2				1			2		
Berwickshire		1								
Buteshire										
Caithness										
Clackmannanshire		1							1	
Cromartyshire										
Dumfriesshire		2		2		1				
Dunbartonshire	1		1	1						
Midlothian	7	6		1		2		1		
Morayshire	2							1		
Fifeshire	3	4		3	7	9			1	
Forfarshire		1		1	1	1		1		
Haddingtonshire	1	3	1			1				
Inverness-shire							1	1		
Kincardineshire		1		2			1	3		3
Kinross-shire										
Kirkcudbright										
Lanarkshire	5	2		10	3		1		1	
Linlithgowshire	1	1								
Nairnshire							1			
Orkney & Shetland								1		
Peeblesshire										
Perthshire	2	2	1	3	8	3				
Renfrewshire			5	2				1		
Ross-shire				1	1					1
Roxburghshire		2			1					
Selkirkshire	2									
Stirlingshire	1	1	2	2	1	1				
Sutherlandshire								1		
Wigtownshire										
Unknown	9	3	8	3	12	3	3	2	5	2
Foreign			3	1	2		1		1	3
Total	47	65	28	50	41	34	27	27	23	30

TABLE 6 EDUCATIONAL EXPERIENCES OF THE PROFESSORIATE 1629–99/1700–79

6.1 Partially Educated At:

	Edinburgh No.	Edinburgh %	Glasgow No.	Glasgow %	St Andrews No.	St Andrews %	King's No.	King's %	Marischal No.	Marischal %
Edinburgh			7 / 21	25 / 75	19 / 40	38 / 80	11 / 6	28 / 15	14 / 6	41 / 17	3 / 2	11 / 7	8 / 1	30 / 4	2 / 4	9 / 18	4 / 1	13 / 3
Glasgow	29 / 9	62 / 19								
St Andrews	3	7			3 / 2	6 / 4	30 / 1 / 1 / 2	75 / 3 / 3 / 5	19 / 2	54 / 6	16 / 6	59 / 22	13 / 10	48 / 37	3 / 13	14 / 59	3 / 23	10 / 74
King's	1	2								
Marischal	3	7					1 / 1	4 / 4			3	10
Oxford										
Cambridge	2	3								
Leyden	21 / 6	45 / 13	8 / 4	29 / 14	8	16	5 / 1	13 / 3	2	6	3	11	2	7	2	9	3	10
Utrecht	1	2													1	5
Gröningen	4	9					4	10	1		1	4				
Other Dutch										
Paris	3 / 1	7 / 2								
Rheims			1	4											1	5	1	3
Angers					1	2				
Other French										
Eton										
Other English							1	3			1	4	1	5
Uppsala	2	4					2	6										
Padua	1	2			4 / 3	8 / 6				
Other	5	11	2	7	1	2			4	15	2	7
Apprent.	4	9	2	4	1	2	1	3	2	6			4	13
Apprent.-Only										
Unknown	4	9	2	7					1	4	2	9	1	3

6.2 Educated at One or More Colleges and Universities

1629–99	No.	%	No.	%	No.	%	No.	%	No.	%	No.	%	No.	%
Attended 1	17	36	53	35	15	51	27	54	21	53	23	68	21	66	18	67	16	73	23	74
Attended 2	13	28	30	20	7	24	19	38	15	37	6	17	7	25	5	19	4	18	8	26
Attended 3	10	21	8	5	4	14	4	8	4	10	3	9			4	15	1	5		
Attended 4	2	4																		
None													3	1						
Unknown	4	9	8	5									4	1			1	5		
Total	47	100	66	100	28	100	50	100	40	100	34	100	27	100	27	100	22	100	31	100

6.3 Sources of Honorary Degrees or Degrees Not Obtained in a Course of Study or by Examination

	Edinburgh No.	%	Glasgow No.	%	St Andrews No.	%	King's No.	%	Marischal No.	%
Edinburgh	5	11							1	5
Glasgow	1	2	3[a]	11			1	4		
St Andrews							9	33		
King's	2	4			1	3				
Marischal	1	2			2	5	1	4	5	23
Source unknown	1	3	1	4						
Total number of honorary degrees	9	19	4	14	3	8	11	41	6	27
Total holders	8	17	3		3	8	10	37	6	27
Eligible professors	47	100	28	100	41	100	27	100	22	100

[a] = includes one honorary MA degree

6.4 Source of Honorary Degrees or Degrees Not Obtained in a Course of Study or by Examination before 1800

1700–79	Edinburgh No.	%	Glasgow No.	%	St Andrews No.	%	King's No.	%	Marischal No.	%
Edinburgh	15[a,c]	23	2	4	4	12	1	4	2	6
Glasgow	2	3	13[a,b]	26						
St Andrews	3	5	1	2	11	32			1	3
King's	3	5	1	2	2	6	8	30	5	16
Marischal			2	4	2	6	4[a]	15	3	10
Oxford									1	3
Cambridge										
America	1	2					1	4		
Other									1	3
Sources unknown										
Total number of honorary degrees	24	36	19	38	19	56	14[a]	52	12	39
Total holders	22	33	19	38	18	53	13[a]	48	10	32
Eligible professors	66	100	50	100	34	100	27	100	31	100

[a] = includes one honorary MA degree or LLB
[b] = includes one declined
[c] = includes one deprived of his degrees

APPENDIX VI

6.5 Holds (1) a Doctorate and (2) One from an Institution Other than the One in Which He Teaches

1629–99	Edinburgh No.	%	Glasgow No.	%	St Andrews No.	%	King's No.	%	Marischal No.	%
Holds a doctorate	16	34	7	25	4	10	12	44	7	32
Holds a doctorate from another university	10	21	4	14	3	8	3	11	4	18
Holds 1 doctor's degree	13	28	7	25	4	10	11	41	6	27
Holds 2 doctor's degrees	3	6					1	4	2	9
Holds 3 doctor's degrees										
Holds no known doctor's degree	31	66	21	75	36	90	15	56	15	68
Total no. of professors	47	100	28	100	40	100	27	100	22	100

6.6 Holds (1) a Doctorate and (2) One from an Institution Other Than the One in Which He Teaches

1700–79	Edinburgh No.	%	Glasgow No.	%	St Andrews No.	%	King's No.	%	Marischal No.	%
Holds a doctorate	40	61	29	58	23	68	18	67	18	58
Holds a doctorate from another university	17	26	14	28	11	32	7	26	11	35
Holds 1 degree	37	56	29	58	22	65	6	22	16	52
Holds 2 degrees	3	5			1	3	14	52	2	6
Holds 3 degrees										
Holds no known doctor's degree	26	39	21	42	11	32	9	33	13	42
Total no. of professors	66	100	50	100	34	100	27	100	31	100

APPENDIX VI

6.7 Prior to Appointment Travelled Abroad

1629–99	Edinburgh No.	%	Glasgow No.	%	St Andrews No.	%	King's No.	%	Marischal No.	%
England	4	9	2	7	2	5	2	7	1	5
Ireland			1	4						
America			1	4						
Caribbean										
Africa										
Far East										
Holland	1	2	9	32	1	3	5	19	1	5
France			1	4					1	5
Europe			2	7						
Other										
Unknown	42	90	12	43	37	93	20	74	19	86
Travelled	5	11	16	57	4	10	7	26	3	14
Total	47	100	28	100	40	100	27	100	22	100

6.8 Prior to Appointment Travelled Abroad

1700–79	Edinburgh No.	%	Glasgow No.	%	St Andrews No.	%	King's No.	%	Marischal No.	%
England	7	11	16	34	4	11	3	11	2	6
Ireland	1	2	2	4					1	3
America	2	4	2	4			1	4	1	3
Caribbean	2	3	2	4					1	3
Africa										
Far East	2	3								
Holland	8	12	8	16	3	9	4	15	4	13
France	3	5	4	8						
Europe	14	21			3	9	1	4		
Other			1	2						
Unknown	34	52	23	46	27	79	18	67	21	68
Travelled	32	48	27	54	7	21	9	33	10	32
Total	66	100	50	100	34	100	27	100	31	100

APPENDIX VI

6.9 Travelled Abroad After Appointment but While Employed at the Colleges Prior to 1700

1629–99	Edinburgh No.	%	Glasgow No.	%	St Andrews No.	%	King's No.	%	Marischal No.	%
England	4	9			2	5	2	6	1	5
Ireland										
America										
Caribbean										
Africa										
Far East										
Holland	1	2	1	3	1	3	2	6	1	5
France										
Europe									2	9
Other										
Unknown	42	89	27	96	37	93	23	88	18	82
Travelled	5	11	1	4	3	8	4	15	4	18
Total	47	100	28	100	40	100	27	100	22	100

6.10 Travelled Abroad After Appointment but While Employed at the Colleges Prior to 1800

1700–79	Edinburgh No.	%	Glasgow No.	%	St Andrews No.	%	King's No.	%	Marischal No.	%
England	7	11	5	10	2	3	2	7	7	22
Ireland										
America	1	2								
Caribbean										
Africa										
Far East										
Holland										
France	1	2	2	4						
Europe	5	8	4	8	2	6			2	6
Other										
Unknown	56	85	41	82	30	88	27	100	25	87
Travelled	10	15	9	18	4	12			6	20
Total	66	100	50	100	34	100	27	100	31	100

Table 7 Qualification or First Occupation of University Professors (born 1620–99/1700–79)

	Edinburgh No.	%	Glasgow No.	%	St Andrews No.	%	King's No.	%	Marischal No.	%
Titled & landed										
Landed										
Farmers										
Merchants					1	3				
					1	3			1	3
Artisans										
Lawyers	6	13	1	4	1	3	6	22		
	14	21	3	6			4	15	1	3
Physicians	10	21	3	11	1	3	3	11	2	9
	19	29	13	26	5	15	7	26	6	20
Surgeons	2	4	2	7	1	3	1	4		
	4	6	3	6					1	3
Ministers	12	26	4	14	11	28	7	26	8	36
	13	20	12	24	15	44	6	22	9	29
Civil officers										
Military										
Professors	5	11	6	21	8	20	2	7	3	14
	5	8	2	4	2	6	3	11	4	13
Tutors and	6	13	9	32	2	5	5	19	2	9
schoolmasters	9	14	16	32	9	26	4	15	3	10
Other professions			1	2						
Unknown	6	13	3	11	15	38	3	11	7	33
	2	3			2	6	3	11	6	19
Totals	47	100	28	100	40	100	27	100	22	100
	66	100	50	100	34	100	27	100	31	100
Total	113	100	78	100	74	100	54	100	53	100

TABLE 8 PERSISTENCE IN ONE OF FATHER'S PRINCIPAL ROLES OR OCCUPATIONS AND STATUS CHANGES

8.1 Persistence 1620–99

	Edinburgh No.	%	Glasgow No.	%	St Andrews No.	%	King's No.	%	Marischal No.	%
Persisted 1620–99	16	34	13	46	9	23	15	56	4	18
Unknown	19	40	10	36	17	43	2	7	5	23
Changed roles	12	26	5	18	14	35	10	37	13	59

8.2 Status Change 1620–99

	Edinburgh No.	%	Glasgow No.	%	St Andrews No.	%	King's No.	%	Marischal No.	%
Advanced in status	25	53	12	42	15	38	8	30	10	45
Declined in status	11	23	2	7	10	25	7	26	4	18
Same status	1	2	4	14			7	26	2	9
Unknown	10	23	10	36	15	38	5	19	6	27
Total	47	100	28	100	40	100	27	100	22	100

8.3 Persistence 1700–79

	Edinburgh No.	%	Glasgow No.	%	St Andrews No.	%	King's No.	%	Marischal No.	%
Persisted 1700–79	30	50	25	50	19	56	16	59	13	42
Unknown	6	9	3	6	5	15	7	26	3	10
Changed roles	30	45	22	44	10	29	4	15	15	48

8.4 Status Change 1700–79

	Edinburgh No.	%	Glasgow No.	%	St Andrews No.	%	King's No.	%	Marischal No.	%
Advanced in status	50	76	38	76	22	65	16	59	18	58
Declined in status	8	12	2	4	3	9	2	7	5	16
Same status	1	2	8	16	2	6	6	22	5	16
Unknown	7	11	2	4	7	21	3	11	3	10
Total	66	100	50	100	34	100	27	100	31	100

TABLE 9   MALE SIBLING ORDER OF PROFESSORS

1620–99	Edinburgh No.	%	Glasgow No.	%	St Andrews No.	%	King's No.	%	Marischal No.	%
1st/1st SS	15	32	10	36	9	23	7	26	4	18
2nd/2nd SS	7	15	2	7	5	13	4	15	2	9
3rd/3rd SS	10	21			1	3	2	7	2	9
4th/4th SS	1	2	1	4	1	3			1	5
5th & younger									1	5
Younger	3	6			3	8	2	7	2	9
Unknown	11	23	15	54	21	53	12	44	10	45
Total	47	100	28	100	40	100	27	100	22	100
1700–79										
1st/1st SS	20	30	12	24	11	31	9	30	11	35
2nd/2nd SS	11	17	13	26	4	11	4	15	5	16
3rd/3rd SS	3	5	4	8	3	9	1	4	1	3
4th/4th SS	4	6	3	6	1	3	1	4		
5th & younger	4	6	2	2	3	9			2	6
Younger	1	2	1	1	1	3	1	4	1	3
Unknown	23	35	15	30	11	32	11	41	11	35
Total	66	100	50	100	34	100	27	100	31	100

TABLE 10   NUMBERS OF PROFESSORS MARRIED

1620–99	Edinburgh No.	%	Glasgow No.	%	St Andrews No.	%	King's No.	%	Marischal No.	%
Married	35	74	21	76	29	73	22	81	13	59
Single	4	9	1	3	3	8	1	4	5	23
Unknown	8	17	6	21	8	20	4	15	4	18
Total	47	100	28	100	40	100	27	100	22	100
1700–79										
Married	47	72	32	64	27	79	22	81	23	74
Single	5	8	8	16	2	6	3	11	3	10
Unknown	14	21	10	20	5	15	2	7	5	16
Total	66	100	50	100	34	100	27	100	31	100

TABLE 11

11.1 Ages of Marriage, Entry to Profession, Appointment, Length of Tenure

	1690 1† 2† 3†	1690–1716 1 2 3	1717–25 1 2 3	1726–40 1 2 3
Marischal College				
Age at entry into profession	0 7	33 1 5	21 3 9	22 4 9
Age at 1st appointment	30 3	39 2	24 6	33 6
Age at 1st marriage	0	0	41 2	38 2
Length of tenure	29 7	11 4	14 9	19 9
Age at death	60 3	63 2	54 5	57 6
King's				
Age at entry into profession	25 2 9	26 4 10	24 1 6	23 4 5
Age at 1st appointment	28 5	37 5	45 3	27 4
Age at 1st marriage	31 3	35 4	25 1	28 3
Length of tenure	33 9	20	19 6	34 5
Age at death	72 5	68 5	65 3	65 4
St Andrews				
Age at entry into profession	0 1	26 12 34	24 2 2	25 3 8
Age at 1st appointment	0	39 13	25 2	33 3
Age at 1st marriage	0	30 5	0	38 3
Length of tenure	12 1	22 34	25 2	27 8
Age at death	0	69 13	61 2	69 3
Glasgow				
Age at entry into profession	0 3	24 7 19	23 1 2	26 3 5
Age at 1st appointment	0	33 10	36 1	52 3
Age at 1st marriage	0	40 2	0	31 3
Length of tenure	24 3	26 19	27 2	16 5
Age at death	0	63 10	58 1	70 3
Edinburgh				
Age at entry into profession	22 1 4	27 10 24	21 3 5	25 15 22
Age at 1st appointment	29 2	41 13	25 4	37 15
Age at 1st marriage	0	33 7	33 3	32 10
Length of tenure	13 4	20 24	27 5	17 22
Age at death	62 2	69 14	69 4	70 16
Total professors	24	92	24	50

* See note to Table 11.2.
† 1 = average
2 = number known
3 = total number in group

… APPENDIX VI 165

Average Ages*

and Age at Death for Men Teaching in 1690, and Appointed Thereafter

| 1741–46 ||| 1747–61 ||| 1762–65 ||| 1766–79 ||| 1780–99 ||| Total |
1	2	3	1	2	3	1	2	3	1	2	3	1	2	3	
24	1	2	22	4	9			0	23	3	4	22	3	7	52
34	2		26	7					28	3		32	6		
38	1		31	5					32	2		32	4		
11	2		24	9					23	4		35	7		
46	2		57	7					68	4		74	6		
22	2	3	22	4	4	23	1	4	23	2	2	22	7	10	53
33	3		34	4		33	3		40	2		31	10		
28	1		40	4		51	2		29	1		30	8		
24	4		30	4		32	4		23	2		34	10		
59	3		77	4		68	2		67	2		63	10		
	0	1	26	3	7	20	1	4	23	5	8	25	6	9	74
	0		36	5		30	1		37	8		44	9		
	0		32	3				0	30	4		35	7		
6	1		24	7		14	4		29	8		19	9		
	0		61	5		60	1		75	8		65	9		
22	3	6	24	12	16	25	3	3	23	6	8	24	12	16	78
33	6		32	13		33	3		35	8		36	14		
37	1		35	3		27	2		37	2		27	3		
17	6		20	16		31	3		27	8		29	16		
57	5		58	14		68	3		67	8		72	14		
22	2	5	24	13	16	23	4	5	23	8	12	23	17	20	113
34	4		36	13		36	3		33	11		33	18		
49	1		33	8		30	2		36	6		30	9		
24	5		29	16		26	5		23	12		31	20		
52	4		73	13		75	3		69	11		71	19		
		17			52			16			34			62	370

Double counted	17
Professoriate	353
Professors unpurged 1690	24
Appointees 1690–1799	329

11.2 Median Values of the Variables in Table 11.1

	1690	1690–1716	1717–25	1726–40	1741–6	1747–61	1762–5	1766–79	1780–99
Marischal College									
Age at entry	21	33	22	21/23	24	22		23	23
Age at 1st appointment	28	27/51	23	30/38	36	24		27	31/33
Age at marriage	?	?	35/47	36/39	38	32		28/36	30/31
Length of tenure	29	14	7	20	14	24		13/28	40
Age at death	56	57/68	50	58	40/51	61		74/85	75/76
King's College									
Age at entry	22/27	26/28	24	21/24	21/22	21/22	23	22/24	21
Age at 1st appointment	27	30	46	24/25	30/34	32/41	28	37/43	25/30
Age at marriage	30	32/39	25	28	28	33/42	42/61	27/29	27/29
Length of tenure	29	21/13	17	35	20/17	13/36	29/30	23/24	25/40
Age at death	81	73	61	74/55	59	68/87	65	67	63/72
St Andrews									
Age at entry	?	25/26	23/24	26	?	27	20	24	25
Age at 1st appointment	?	32	23/26	34	?	38	30	30/34	45
Age at marriage	?	30	?	31	?	28	?	26/32	37
Length of tenure	12	14	6/44	26	6	25	6/7	20/40	18
Age at death	?	69	53/68	66	?	64	60	69/77	66
Glasgow									
Age at entry	?	24	23	25	24	23/25	25	23	23
Age at 1st appointment	?	31/32	36	35	28/35	28	32	30/34	33
Age at marriage	?	36/43	?	31	37	30	24/30	35/38	25
Length of tenure	27	29	22/31	17	6/15	12	32	20/31	30/31
Age at death	?	63/73	58	74	64	58/65	66	66/70	73/75

APPENDIX VI

	Edinburgh								
Age at entry	22	25/26	21	24	20/23	24	23	23	23
Age at 1st appointment	22/35	40	23/28	31/42	27/39	36	41	31	33
Age at marriage	?	32	35	32/33	49	30/34	30	30/36	27
Length of tenure	8/14	13/17	21	15/18	17	31/33	26	24/29	32/33
Age at death	43/76	63/72	48/70	74/75	39/57	80	72	68	70

* Tables 11.1 and 11.2 deal with appointees in the universities and not with professors as such. Seventeen men who were translated from one university to another have been double counted. For that reason these figures cannot be aggregated to yield an accurate profile of the professoriate 1690–1799. What they do show are the characteristics of the men appointed under different political regimes which have been used to periodise this information. Entry into a profession has been defined by the date at which men were ordained, passed advocate, were granted MDs or medical licences or by the date at which they began to teach as tutors, schoolmasters or professors. The age of first appointment refers only to the first university appointment. Without double counting the average length of tenure would be somewhat longer. Birth dates given in the *Dictionary of National Biography* and other sources as 'c. 1690' etc. have been entered as if they were certain. Tenure counts all years of service including that of the joint appointees who were often virtually retired. This is not unrealistic since the senior members of the conjoint pairs usually retained their senate seats, some income and sometimes continued to teach. Age at first marriage has been calculated by subtracting one year from another. In other cases fractional portions of years have been entered when they were known. All of the universities provide anomalous cases. Charles Gordon, Thomas Hogg, Allan Logan and William Smith have not been included in the King's figures although they were chosen to serve but declined. The first man to teach midwifery in the University of Edinburgh has been excluded here; he was not a full member of the university and could not sit on its senate. The Edinburgh clinical lecturers have also been excluded. At St Andrews and Glasgow similar cases have been excluded. Neither has William Simpson who illegally taught one year, but at Glasgow John Gordon, John Marshall and Robert Carrick have been counted. James Sutherland's tenure at Edinburgh has been dated from 1695. In the completed table all figures are rounded off to the nearest whole number. Elsewhere I shall publish and discuss figures which analyse the changes in the Scottish professoriate over the period covered here. Because there was no movement from other universities to those in Aberdeen and only one person who migrated from Marischal to King's, the Aberdeen figures do present a nearly accurate picture of their professoriates. The dividing line between men born in the seventeenth century and those in the eighteenth comes in 1726. Only three men at Marischal born in the earlier period were appointed after that date; at King's the number is probably two. This was generally true elsewhere with Edinburgh showing a cluster of appointees after 1725 who were born in the 1690s.

TABLE 12 ESTIMATED MINIMUM PROFESSORIAL INCOMES FROM ACADEMIC SALARIES IN £s 1700–99*

12.1 1690–1724/1725–49

	Edinburgh		Glasgow		St Andrews		King's		Marischal	
990–900										
899–800										
799–700										
699–600										
599–500										
499–400										
399–300										
299–200	1		2							
199–150	1		3		2	2	4	2			1	2
149–100	7		8		4	1	10	11		1	2	1
99–50	10		10		4	3	12	7	7	3	1	1
49–25	2		7		13	4	24	3	17	10	20	4
24–0	15		5		7	4			8	2	2	1

12.2 1750–74/1775–99

	Edinburgh	Glasgow	St Andrews	King's	Marischal
2000+–1000					
999–900					
899–800					
799–700					
699–600					
599–500					
499–400					
399–300					
299–200	1	4	1	2	
199–150	3	2	1	3	2	6			4	1
149–100	9	8	3	2	3	4	6	11		
99–50	15	14	15	13	9	6	6	8	2	9
49–25	3	3	10	6			4	1	5	4
24–0	10	9	3	6				2	2	

* These are the values of chairs, not total income figures. They also exclude student fees, perquisites, houses, gratuities, boarders' rent and other normal sources of income which would have increased all the incomes. At Edinburgh these appear to have declined owing to the establishment of unpaid medical chairs. See also note to Table 14.

TABLE 13 ESTIMATED TOTAL REAL PROFESSORIAL INCOMES AT ACADEMIC CAREER PEAKS IN £s 1700–99 INCLUDING ALL KNOWN AND LIKELY SOURCES OF REVENUE*

13.1 1690–1724/1725–49 (Peak Years)

	Edinburgh		Glasgow		St Andrews		King's		Marischal	
1999–1000		2								
999–900										
899–800		2								
799–700										
699–600										
599–500										
499–400										
399–300	2	4								
299–200	2	6	1	1	1	2	1	1	1	
199–150	1	4	2	2	3			2		3
149–100	6	4	5	7	5	9	5	4	2	3
99–50	7	3	6	3	11	7	9	4	10	5
49–25			1				1		1	
24–0										

13.2 1750–74/1775–99 (Peak Years)

1999+–1000	1	2								
999–900		1								
899–800	1	4								
799–700		1								
699–600	1	2								1
599–500	1	4								
499–400	3	10				1				
399–300	4	9		1		2				2
299–200	11	7	6	15	2	12	1	2	2	2
199–150	3	3	5	12	5	3	1	11	1	7
149–100		2	6	4	5	6	4	5	2	3
99–50			1				2	1	5	2
49–25										1
24–0										
Total	113		78		74		54		53	

* See note to Table 14.

TABLE 14   AVERAGE AND MEDIAN ESTIMATED REAL PEAK PROFESSORIAL INCOMES BY FACULTY IN £s
1690–1799*

(Numbers of professors are indicated within the brackets)

	Edinburgh			Glasgow			St Andrews			King's			Marischal		
1690–1724	Av.	Med.	No.	Av.	Med.	No.	Av.	Med.	No.	Av.	Med.	No.	Av.	Med.	No.
Divinity	245	260	(5)	173	175–187	(4)	150	130–140	(4)	63	51–75	(2)	98	120	(3)
Law										188	125–250	(2)			
Medicine	142	140–145	(4)	135	135	(1)				108	100–116	(2)	105	105	(1)
Arts	85	82	(9)	101	98	(7)	94	78	(16)	77	60	(9)	91	70	(13)
1725–49															
Divinity	489	350	(5)	111	90–120	(4)	191	190	(5)	201	170	(3)	190	150–230	(2)
Law	499	295	(5)	195	185–205	(2)				125	125	(2)			
Medicine	296	133–460	(2)	105	105	(3)				100	100	(1)	120	120	(1)
Arts	169	150	(13)	112	114	(7)	98	90–101	(12)	64	60	(7)	81	70	(8)
1750–74															
Divinity	568	318–880	(4)	199	150–247	(2)	165	165	(1)	265	150–380	(2)	220	220	(1)
Law	490	255–425	(4)	185	185	(1)				120	110–130	(2)			
Medicine	373	358	(7)	144	135	(5)	163	153–173	(2)	115	125	(3)	118	110–125	(2)
Arts	234	226–237	(8)	147	140–144	(10)	145	191	(9)				92	75	(5)
1775–99															
Divinity	312	350	(5)	214	200	(7)	264	233–256	(8)	192	191–192	(2)	370	220–520	(2)
Law	625	425	(7)	275	275	(1)				225	210–240	(2)			
Medicine	599	560	(13)	244	250	(9)	212	212	(1)	143	160–185	(4)	145	125	(3)
Arts	353	340–352	(20)	184	170	(15)	210	222	(15)	145	165	(12)	166	161	(13)
Total no. of professors	111			78			73			54			53		

APPENDIX VI

* Eighteenth-century professorial incomes are difficult to establish. Many varied with the yearly fluctuation of grain prices because the salaries were in part stated in terms of rights to fixed amounts of grain or meal; others depended, in part, upon feudal incidents such as kain hens. Most men had other perquisites such as houses or rent money, rights to shares in graduation fees and incidental windfalls coming from the management of college or university properties. Early in the period, regents could expect gratuities from pleased parents; later professors often boarded students for fees ranging from a few pounds to sums over £100. Publishing scholars could also make money on textbooks or even bestsellers. Calculating incomes is an inexact business; generalising on one's findings is also risky. Tables 12, 13 and 14 do not pretend to be more than a beginning to the study of this topic in Scotland. They do, however, provide information which sheds light on recruitment patterns, upon the reasons men had to change chairs, upon the status and social mobility of the professors and upon the levels of cultural expenditure to which they could aspire. And they show some of the clear differences between the faculties and universities. Tables 12.1 and 12.2 try to estimate the incomes which professors drew from their foundation endowments, from the bishops' rents, from Queen Anne's Bounty and various other parliamentary or crown grants. Those figures exclude all students' fees, perquisites, offices and other sources of income. A salary figure has been entered for every teacher in 1690, for every new appointment, for both holders of conjoint appointments but not for men who struck informal retirement deals or for other deputies. Lecturers appointed by the universities and colleges have been counted as professors. Those who served without salaries are entered in the lowest category. At St Andrews those appointed in 1747 to the United College livings have all been entered anew in Tables 13 and 14 even though some were sitting members of the two arts colleges then merged. The principal source for the information given in these tables is the evidence given to the 1826–30 Royal Commission on the Universities of Scotland. This was summarised for me by Sheila Emmerson to whom I am very grateful. Tables 13 and 14 add to this whatever other information I have been able to accumulate. This was somewhat arbitrarily handled but in a manner which does not overstate professional incomes. Many professors owned small estates which added dignity to their names, e.g. George Gordon of Rainieshill. Often these produced very small incomes. All those with estates have had £25 added unless I possessed reliable data on their rents. This has drastically undervalued the incomes of professional men in Edinburgh and Glasgow. Outside professional income has been rated at £100 in Edinburgh and at £75 elsewhere. This, too, biases the figures in a similar way after c. 1750. The emoluments of pensions and offices in the Church or state have been entered at their untaxed values. I have chosen to state peak values because some places were often held for short periods. The peak incomes were what men hoped for and, of course, what many long enjoyed. No attempt has been made to enter the proceeds of publishing. Doing so, however, would increase the figures for some men by hundreds of pounds, e.g. William Robertson. Students' fees have been estimated. Generalisations have been made from known cases. Where this seemed difficult matriculation records and student population estimates have been used to derive a rough formula. That assigns a £1 fee to each student and then assumes that over the period this did not change. Student number multiples have been set as follows:

TABLE 14—*continued*

	1690–	1730s–1750s	1770–99
King's	30	40	50
Marischal	30	40	70
St Andrews	30	30	40
Glasgow	60	70	100
Edinburgh	60	100	100

It has been assumed that each professor gave only one course unless evidence to the contrary has been found. For the professional chairs more careful enrolment figures have been used. This procedure more fairly states incomes early in the century but badly understates income from fees later and particularly at Edinburgh. At all three of these places professors like Patrick Copland and Robert Hamilton had incomes from consulting and commercial activities. These have not been possible to estimate. Table 14 attempts to compare men teaching during the period in different faculties and at different places. It merely presents the data used in Table 13 more precisely and in a different form. Professors of Hebrew or oriental languages are here assigned to the faculty of arts which was their place at Edinburgh. Early in the century some arts students took Hebrew; at the end of the century the professors at Edinburgh and Marischal were teaching Arabic and Persian to boys intending to make secular careers in the Far East as well as Hebrew to a few divinity students. Men who held two chairs have been assigned to the faculty which accounted for their income peaks. The Marischal College chair of law has been ignored. Again, these are rough calculations but they seemed worth making, if only to dispel the illusion that Scottish university men were poverty-stricken, and their places unlikely to attract men of talent and ambition.

TABLE 15   KNOWN PUBLICATION RECORD BY CATEGORY OF MEN BORN 1620–99/1700–79

Publication	Edinburgh		Glasgow		St Andrews		King's		Marischal	
Sermons	11	13	4	3	3	4	1	5	2	5
Religious works	5	6	5	4	5	4	1	6	2	12
Moral philosophy	1	8	2	3	2	1		2	1	2
Law (excludes cases and briefs)	1	5	2	1	1			1		
Politics		1			2	1		1	2	
Political economy		2	1	2		1		1		
Political polemics	6	12	5	2				3	1	7
Natural philosophy	4	8	2	8	1			1	1	
Mathematics	3	4	2	2		1			1	2
Astronomy	2	1	1	3				1		1
Technology	2									
Medicine	9	13	3	8	1	2	2	2		
Surgery	1	5		1		1				1
Anatomy	1	4		5		1				1
Botany	3	4		1		1				1
Chemistry	2	5		5		1				
Zoology		2						1		
Improvements	1	11		2		1				
Agriculture		3		1						
Metaphysics								3		
Logic & phil. of mind		2	2	2	1	2		1	1	3
Rhetoric		4		2	1	1		2		1
Criticism		6	1	5		1		2	1	6
Poetry	1			2		1	1		1	8
Plays				1						
Essays		6		4						
History	2	5	2	4	1	5		1		6
Biography	1	7		2	1	1				1
Antiquities		2	1	1		5				1
Education				1				4		2
Periodicals						2		1		4
Editing	8	13	1	5		3			1	5
Translations	3	3		1		3				4
Dictionaries		4				1				1
Grammars			2	1		3				
Texts	9	8	3	2	2	4				4
Theses and orations	3	1	2			1	9	2	5	
Categories of publications	22	30	18	30	13	26	5	19	12	21
Total publishers	34	50	15	33	9	21	11	11	8	15
% of professors	72	76	52	66	25	62	35	41	36	48

Bibliographical Note

The footnotes to this monograph provide a list of the most useful secondary sources which have been consulted for this study. Additional materials on Aberdeen and its neighbouring towns and counties can be found in Hugh Scott et al., *Fasti Ecclesiae Scoticanae* (Edinburgh, 1928) vol. 7 and in other studies in this series. Two unpublished doctoral theses should also be cited here: Paul B Wood, 'Thomas Reid, Natural Philosopher: A Study of Science and Philosophy in the Scottish Enlightenment' (University of Leeds, 1984) and Stephen A Conrad, 'Citizenship and Common Sense: The Problem of Authority in the Social Background and Social Philosophy of the Wise Club of Aberdeen' (Harvard University, 1980). In addition to the materials held in the town council archives of Aberdeen and at Aberdeen University Library, the following collections of papers have been useful: HM Register Office, Edinburgh, Clerk of Penicuik Papers (GD18), Mar and Kellie Papers (GD124), Melville Castle Muniments (GD51); the National Library of Scotland, Saltoun Correspondence (SC), Yester Papers (MSS 7043–75), Papers of Robert Dundas, Viscount Melville (MSS 1–6), Fettercairn Manuscripts (Acc. 4796); Edinburgh University Library, Laing Manuscripts; 'Papers Illustrative of the History and Constitution of the University of Edinburgh' (DC 1.4); Papers of William Carstares (DK.1.1); Glasgow University Library and Archives, Papers of Principal John Stirling, Professor Charles Morthland and Thomas Reid; St Andrews University, Melville Papers (MSS 4427–923); the Library of the Marquis of Bute at Mount Stuart, Papers of John Stuart, 3rd Earl of Bute and James Stuart-Mackenzie. Other materials relating to the Aberdeen colleges are available in the collections of: the British Library, the Newcastle Papers, the Papers of Thomas Birch; the University of Michigan at Ann Arbor, Papers of Henry Dundas; HM Register Office, the Papers of the Dukes of Montrose; Mitchell Library, Glasgow, the Papers of Ilay Campbell; and Edinburgh University Library, the Papers of Robert Dundas. I regret that I have been unable to make use of these sources in preparing this study. The best recent bibliography of works on eighteenth-century Aberdeen is contained in H Lewis Ulman, ed., *The Minutes of the Aberdeen Philosophical Society 1758–1773* (Aberdeen, 1990), 252–62.

Index of Names

Aberdeen, Earls of (*see* Gordon)
Adam, William, 92
Aikenhead, Thomas, 2
Allardyce, Alexander, 92, 128 n. 57, 129 n. 78
Anderson, David, 5, 23, 24, 25, 26, 32, 39, 40, 43, 53, 54, 55, 58, 62, 111 n. 24, 136, 137, 143
Anderson, George, 22, 24, 136, 143
Anderson, John, 36, 41, 114 n. 8, 139, 145
Anne, Queen of Scotland, 5
Anstruther, John, 24, 25
Anstruther, Sir William, 24
Arbuthnot, Alexander, 5
Arbuthnot, John, 2nd Viscount, 68
Arbuthnot, Robert, 5, 68
Argyll, 2nd and 3rd Dukes of (*see* John and Archibald Campbell)
Atholl, Dukes of (*see* Murray)
Auckland, Baron (*see* William Eden)

Baillie, Robert, 113 n. 56
Bannerman, Sir Alexander Burnet, 97, 129 n. 75, 144
Bannerman, James, 97, 129 n. 75, 144
Batoni, Pompeo, 88
Beattie, James (poet), 71, 72, 74, 76, 89, 90, 91, 92, 93, 101, 145
Beattie, James, 90, 145
Beattie, James Hay, 72, 90, 127 n. 43, 145
Bell, Alexander, 97, 144
Bentley, James, 97, 144
Black, William, 24, 25, 26, 136, 143
Blackwell, Barbara, 135
Blackwell, Charles, 57
Blackwell, George, 57
Blackwell, Thomas I, 5, 31, 32, 33, 34, 35, 36, 47, 48, 50, 51, 53, 55, 56, 57, 135, 139, 145

Blackwell, Thomas II, 6, 12, 36, 38, 45, 53, 54, 55, 58, 65, 66, 69, 70, 72, 76, 104, 118 n. 91, 139, 145
Blair, William, 11, 29
Boston, Thomas, 23
Bower, Thomas, 21, 22, 24, 25, 26, 30, 34, 110 n. 13, 136, 143
Bradfute, Daniel, 40, 60, 62, 63, 64, 66, 137, 143
Brand, John, 115 n. 17
Brown, William Lawrence, 92, 93, 128 n. 60, 145
Buccleuch, 3rd Duke of (*see* Henry Scott)
Buchan, 11th Earl of (*see* David Erskine)
Bulloch, John Malcolm, 22
Burnet (or Burnett), Alexander, 25, 39, 53, 59, 62, 63, 64, 65, 66, 69, 81, 82, 83, 86, 136, 137, 138, 143
Burnet, Alexander of Kemnay, 95, 96, 129 n. 66 and 75
Burnet, Andrew, 11, 30
Burnet, Andrew (merchant), 83
Burnet, George, 82, 83, 84, 86
Burnet, Helen, 62, 64
Burnet, James, 70, 82
Burnet, John, 64
Burnet, Sir Thomas, 20
Bute, 3rd Earl of (*see* John Stuart)

Callender, John, 70
Campbell, Archibald, 1st Earl of Ilay, 3rd Duke of Argyll, 4, 6, 7, 12, 23, 38, 40–89 *passim*, 100, 103, 104, 105, 115 n. 24 and 25
Campbell, Professor Archibald, 47
Campbell, Colin, 45
Campbell, D[aniel of Shawfield?], 45
Campbell, George (mathematician), 52, 145

175

INDEX

Campbell, George (principal), 45, 72, 73, 90, 91, 93, 101
Campbell, John, 2nd Duke of Argyll, 4, 6, 12, 34, 40, 43, 45, 47, 58, 59, 63, 64, 65, 66, 103, 104
Campbell, John, 4th Earl of Loudoun, 72
Campbell, Neil, 47
Carmichael, Frederick, 70, 121 n. 45
Carmichael, Gershom, 36
Carstares, William, 5, 6, 7, 23, 25, 31, 36, 40, 103, 104
Catanach, James, 65, 66, 67, 69, 74, 81, 83, 84, 137, 138, 143
Catanach, Margaret, 66
Chalmers, George (principal), 39, 40, 41, 42, 43, 48, 50, 53, 54, 55, 56, 57, 58, 60, 61, 62, 63, 64, 65, 66, 74, 116 n. 41, 137, 143
Chalmers, George (advocate), 70
Chalmers, James (professor), 48, 65, 66, 70, 139, 145
Chalmers, James, 56, 57
Chalmers, John, 12, 65, 66, 69, 74, 75, 81, 82, 83, 84, 86, 87, 95, 97, 98, 137, 138, 144
Chalmers, Patrick, 30, 144
Chalmers, William (professor), 51, 144
Chalmers, Dr William, 98, 126 n. 30, 138
Chalmers, William (baillie), 56, 65
Charles I, 42
Charles II, 8
Charles, Alexander, 117 n. 66
Charles, George, 117 n. 66
Charles Edward Stuart ('Bonny Prince Charlie'), 12
Clerk, Sir John, 4
Cochrane, Thomas, 6th Earl of Dundonald, 60, 82
Copland, Patrick, 87, 89, 90, 91, 93, 97, 106, 145
Craig, James, 67
Craigie, Robert, 69
Cruden, George, 36, 139
Cruden, William, 51, 52, 56, 114 n. 8, 145
Cruickshank, William, 51, 52, 56, 57, 65, 118 n. 75
Cumberland, William, Duke of, 12, 55, 118 n. 75

Dalrymple, Sir David, 42, 87

Dalrymple, David, 81, 82, 83, 84, 86, 138, 144
Dalrymple, John, 2nd Earl of Stair, 4, 60
Dauney, Alexander, 97, 144
Dempster, George, 90
Deskford, Lord (*see* James Ogilvie)
Donaldson, Alexander, 72, 74, 145
Donaldson, James, 59, 72, 123 n. 61 and 68, 139, 145
Douglas, James, 1st Duke of Hamilton, 4
Douglas, James, 14th Earl of Morton, 82
Douglas, Sholto Charles, Lord Aberdour and 15th Earl of Morton, 75
Douglas, William, 1st Duke of Queensberry, 4, 59
Drew, Joseph, 5
Drummond, Anne, wife of 12th Earl of Erroll, 32, 112 n. 45
Drummond, James, 1st Duke of Perth, 4, 28, 111 n. 38, 112 n. 48
Duff, Hugh, 51
Duff, Patrick, 45, 46, 48, 50, 51, 52, 53, 55, 56, 57, 59, 61, 66, 69, 70, 82, 83, 84, 120 n. 28
Duff, William, 51, 55, 59, 121 n. 44, 139, 145
Duff, William of Braco, 50, 51, 57, 58
Dunbar, James, 9, 86, 87, 95, 100, 101, 126 n. 27, 129 n. 66, 138, 144
Duncan, William, 71, 74, 145
Dundas, Henry, 1st Viscount Melville, 3, 4, 6, 7, 13, 80, 87, 90, 91, 92, 93, 95, 96, 97, 100, 102, 103, 127 n. 43, 129 n. 76
Dundas, Robert, Lord Arniston, 5, 64, 68, 69, 80
Dundas, Robert, 6, 97
Dundonald, Earl of (*see* Thomas Cochrane)
Dunlop, Alexander, 39
Dunlop, William, 39
Dyce, William, 43

Eden, William, 1st Baron Auckland, 92, 93, 128 n. 60
Edinburgh University, xiii, xiv, 2, 3, 5, 6, 7, 10, 32, 36, 39, 40, 47, 58, 62, 67, 104, 105, 106
Elliot, Sir Gilbert, 70
Elphinstone, Bishop William, 42
Erroll, 12th Countess of (*see* Anne Drummond)

INDEX

Erroll, Earls of (*see also* Charles, James and John Hay), 18, 32
Erskine, Charles, 51, 52, 67, 68, 69
Erskine, David, 11th Earl of Buchan, 6, 130 n. 82
Erskine, Henry, 6
Erskine, James, Lord Grange, 5, 6, 54, 59, 61
Erskine, John, 11th Earl of Mar, 5, 11, 18, 21, 22, 25, 30, 32, 105

Farquharson, John, 23, 24
Ferguson, Adam, 105
Ferguson, James, 82, 92, 93, 129 n. 75
Findlater, 4th Earl (*see* James Ogilvy)
Fleming, John, 8th Earl of Wigton, 28
Fletcher, Andrew, Lord Milton, 4, 6, 48, 49, 50, 52, 55, 56, 57, 58, 59, 61, 66, 72, 78
Forbes, family of, 18, 38, 43, 64, 65
Forbes, Alexander, 5th Lord Forbes of Pitsligo, 11
Forbes, Archibald, 23
Forbes, Sir Arthur, 91
Forbes, Arthur of Echt, 31, 36, 43, 48, 50, 113 n. 56
Forbes, Arthur of Craigievar, 56, 63, 64
Forbes, Arthur, 82
Forbes, Baillie, 50
Forbes, Charles, 83
Forbes, David, 23
Forbes, Duncan, 23, 113 n. 56
Forbes, Thomas of Echt, 38, 48, 64
Forbes, Sir William of Craigievar, 21, 23, 38
Forbes, Sir William of Monymusk 63, 64
Forbes, Sir William of Pitsligo, 89, 92, 127 n. 40 and 41
Forbes, Sir William, 5th Baron of Craigievar, 95, 129 n. 67
Fordyce, Alexander, 91, 92
Fordyce, Baillie, 65
Fordyce, David, 65, 69, 70, 72, 74, 76, 92, 145
Fordyce, George, 51, 52, 55, 56, 57
Fordyce, William, 65
Fordyce, Sir William, 92
Fraser, family of, 18, 39
Fraser, Alexander I, 20, 24, 26, 42, 62, 65, 75, 136, 137, 143

Fraser, Alexander II, 62, 63, 116 n. 43, 137, 143
Fraser, Alexander, Lord Strichen, 38, 54, 81
Fraser, Charles, 4th Baron Fraser, 11
Fraser, George, 18, 23, 24, 25, 136, 143
Fraser, Hugh, 75
Fraser, Dr James, 53, 54, 116 n. 43
Frederick, Prince of Wales, 48
French, George, 20, 128 n. 57, 145

Galloway, 5th Earl of (*see* James Stewart)
Garden, Alexander, 39, 52, 137, 143
Garden, Francis, 82, 92
Garden, George, 11, 12, 20
Garden, James, 11, 12, 19, 20, 21, 22, 25, 143
Garrioch, John, 90, 91, 145
Gellie, William, 52
George I, 50, 53, 115 n. 17
George II, 12, 55
George III, 89
Gerard Alexander, 72, 74, 87, 98, 126 n. 30, 138, 144, 145
Gerard, Gilbert, 87, 97, 129 n. 76, 144
Gerard, William, 129 n. 76
Glasgow University, xiii, xiv, 2, 3, 5, 6, 7, 10, 20, 32, 36, 39, 40, 47, 58, 60, 75, 86, 104, 105, 106
Glennie, George, 92, 145
Glennie, William, 126 n. 40
Gordon, family of, 4, 18, 39, 50, 62, 64, 75
Gordon, Sir Adam, 128 n. 57
Gordon, Alexander, 4th Duke of Gordon, 91, 93, 95, 96, 97, 100, 105, 129 n. 75
Gordon, Alexander, 5th Marquis of Huntly, 11
Gordon, Alexander, 20, 24, 32, 42, 62, 136, 143, 144
Gordon, Alexander of Keithocks Mill, 20
Gordon, Alexander, MD, 87, 126 n. 28
Gordon, Arthur, 66
Gordon, Charles 22, 144
Gordon, Charles Hamilton, 66, 67
Gordon, Cosmo, 91, 93, 128 n. 52
Gordon, Daniel, 38, 53, 55, 57, 58, 117 n. 65, 139, 145
Gordon, Duchess of (*see* Jane Maxwell)
Gordon, Earl of Aberdeen (*see* George Gordon)
Gordon, George, 1st Earl of Aberdeen, 22

INDEX

Gordon, George I, 5, 20, 21, 23, 24, 25, 26, 32, 53, 54, 62, 136, 137, 138, 143
Gordon, George II, 12, 60, 62, 64, 66, 81, 82, 83, 86, 144
Gordon, George, 2nd Marquis of Huntly, 42
Gordon, James, MD, 59, 72, 74, 123 n. 60, 139, 145
Gordon, James of Seaton, 19
Gordon, James (minister), 60, 61
Gordon, Janet, 19
Gordon, John of Seaton, 20
Gordon, John (civilist), 19, 24, 25, 26, 32, 34, 111 n. 29, 136, 143
Gordon, John, 23, 24, 25
Gordon, Patrick, 18, 20, 23, 143
Gordon, Richard, 26, 32, 34, 136, 143
Gordon, Theodore, 64, 66, 83
Gordon, Thomas of Keithocks Mill, 19
Gordon, Thomas I, 20, 143
Gordon, Thomas II, 12, 41, 43, 62, 64, 66, 81, 82, 83, 87, 89, 97, 98, 137, 138, 144
Gordon, William, 2nd Earl of Aberdeen, 60, 61
Gordon, Sir William of Dalfolly, 66
Graham, James, 1st Duke of Montrose, 4, 5, 6, 34, 35, 36, 40, 45, 60
Graham, James, 2nd Duke of Montrose, 68, 78
Graham, James (advocate), 67, 68
Graham, Mungo, 4
Grange, Lord (*see* James Erskine)
Grant, Sir Archibald, 38, 45
Grant, Sir Francis, 40, 113 n. 56
Grant, William, 64, 67, 68
Gray, John, 91
Greenfield, Andrew, 90, 126 n. 36
Gregory (or Gregorie), Charles, 53, 112 n. 46
Gregory, James I, 48, 50, 62, 137, 143
Gregory, James II, 60, 62, 64, 66, 137, 144
Gregory, John, 69, 74, 76, 81, 82, 83, 123 n. 61, 137, 138, 144

Hadow (or Haddow), James, 36, 38, 55, 113 n. 56
Hadow (or Haddow), Thomas, 5, 36, 38, 139, 145
Haliburton, Bishop George, 18, 19
Hamilton, James, 5th Duke of, 4, 60

Hamilton, Robert, 89, 90, 91, 145
Hamilton, William, 55
Hardie, Patrick, 139, 145
Harrington, Sir James, 2
Hay, Charles, 12th Earl of Erroll, 11, 20, 23, 24, 26, 28, 30, 34, 43
Hay, George, 8th Earl of Kinnoull, 28, 80, 91, 104
Hay, James, 15th Earl of Erroll, 91
Hay, John, 11th Earl of Erroll, 20, 21, 22, 23, 28
Hay, John, 4th Marquis of Tweeddale, 4, 5, 6, 12, 59, 60, 65, 66, 68, 69, 78
Hay, Thomas of Huntington, 4, 5
Hay, Thomas, 50
Henderson, G D, xiv
Hill, George, 3, 73
Hobbes, Thomas, 2
Hogg, Thomas, 22, 144
Home, Henry, Lord Kames, 90, 105
Home, Patrick, Lord Polwarth, 47
Hope, Sir Thomas, 42
Howie, James, 43
Hume, David, 3
Hume-Campbell, Alexander, 2nd Earl of Marchmont, 36, 47, 60, 67
Hume-Campbell, George, Lord Polwarth, 47
Hume-Campbell, Alexander, 67
Huntly, 2nd Marquis of (*see* George Gordon)
Huntly, 5th Marquis of (*see* Alexander Gordon)
Hutcheson, Francis, 70, 104

Ilay, Earl of (*see* Archibald Campbell)
Innes, Alexander, 59, 72, 74, 121 n. 44, 139, 145
Innes, James, 116 n. 51, 120 n. 24
Irvine (or Irving), Alexander, 25

Jack, William, 97, 144
James II and VII, 8, 29, 30
James III and VIII (The Old Pretender), 11, 12, 20, 22, 25, 28, 32
Jardine, John, 105
Johnston, John, 36
Jopp, James, 90, 126 n. 37

Kames, Lord (*see* Henry Home)
Kay, John, 99

INDEX

Keith, family of, 4, 18, 25, 28
Keith, George, 8th Earl Marischal, 28, 29
Keith, George, 10th Earl Marischal, 11, 12, 16, 28, 32, 35, 42, 82
Keith, George I, 29, 145
Keith, George II, 66
Keith, George, regent, 30, 34, 133 n. 60
Keith, James, 28, 30
Keith, John, 1st Earl of Kintore, 11, 28
Keith of Auquhorsk, 29
Keith, William, 9th Earl Marischal, 21, 22, 28, 29, 30
Keith, Sir William of Ludquhairn, 30
Kennedy, William, 72, 74, 127 n. 42, 145
Ker, John, 9, 40, 62, 76, 137, 143
Kerr (or Ker), John, 1st Duke of Roxburghe, 4, 5, 7, 35, 36, 37, 38, 40, 41, 42, 43, 45, 60, 64, 78, 104, 105
Kerr, William, 2nd Marquis of Lothian, 47
Kerr, William, 45
Kidd, James, 93, 145
Kinnoull, 8th Earl of (see George Hay)
Kintore, family of, 11
Kintore, 1st Earl of (see John Keith)

Leechman, William, 60
Leith, family of, 18
Leslie, John, 75, 81, 82, 83, 86, 98, 138, 144
Leslie, Sir John, 3
Leslie, John, 9th Earl of Rothes, 38
Liddell, George, 21, 29, 30, 32, 34, 145
Litster, Alexander, 28, 145
Livingstone, William, 92, 128 n. 59, 145
Lockhart, Alexander, 69
Logan, Allan, 22, 144
Lothian, 2nd Marquis of (see William Kerr)
Loudoun, Earl of (see John Campbell)
Lumsden (or Lumisden), John, 60, 61, 64, 66, 69, 81, 82, 83, 86, 137, 138, 143

Machiavelli, Niccolo, 2
MacKaile, Matthew, 47, 48, 50, 55, 58, 59, 74, 104, 118 n. 90, 139, 145
Mackay, General Hugh, 10
Mackie, Charles, 38, 114 n. 11
Mackenzie, family of, 4
Maclaurin, Colin, 36, 47, 50, 53, 54, 55, 57, 104, 118 n. 90, 139, 145
Maclaurin, John, 60
McLeod, Roderick, 69, 74, 81, 83, 86, 98, 137, 138, 144

MacPherson, Hugh, 97, 144
MacPherson, Sir John, 96
Maitland, Charles, 67, 68
Mansfield, 1st Earl of (see William Murray)
Mansfield, 2nd Earl of (see David Murray)
Mar, 10th Earl of (see John Erskine)
Marchmont, Earl of (see also Alexander Hume-Campbell), 4
Marischal, Earls (see also George, William, James Keith), 17, 32
Mary II, Queen of Scotland, 8, 10, 20
Maule, John, 63, 65, 70
Maxwell, Jane, 4th Duchess of Gordon, 87, 91, 93, 95, 96
Maxwell, John, 66
Menzies, Sir Robert, 47
Meston, William, 30, 32, 34, 112 n. 45, 145
Middleton, Alexander, 18, 20
Middleton, George, 19, 20, 23, 24, 25, 26, 32, 34, 44, 136, 143
Middleton, George of Seaton, 82, 83, 86, 93
Middleton, Col. John, 45, 55, 56, 61, 62, 63, 82
Milton, Lord (see Andrew Fletcher)
Mitchell, the Rev. Alexander, 2, 6, 43
Mitchell, Alexander, 111 n. 31
Mitchell, Margaret, 56
Mitchell, William, 43, 115 n. 17
Moir, Alexander, 28, 29, 145
Moir, James, 28, 29, 145
Moir, John of Stoneywood, 20
Moir, John, 20, 32, 34, 143
Monro, George, 25, 113 n. 56
Monro, John, 25
Montrose, Duke of (see James Graham)
Morgan, Daniel, 126 n. 40
Morgan, William, 90, 126, n. 40, 146
Morrison, James, 52, 65
Morthland, Charles, 36, 113 n. 56
Morton, 14th Earl of (see James Douglas)
Mossman, Thomas, 83
Muir, family of, 18
Mure, William, 78, 105
Murray, David, 2nd Earl of Mansfield, 92
Murray, John, 64
Murray, William, 1st Earl of Mansfield, 69

Nairne, William, 93, 129 n. 75
Newcastle under Lyme, 1st Duke of (see Thomas Pelham-Holles)

INDEX

Newton, Sir Isaac, 21, 22
North, Frederick, Lord North and 2nd Earl of Guildford, 78

Ogilvie, family of, 18
Ogilvie (or Ogilvy, Ogilby), Sir Alexander, 39
Ogilvie, Sir, Alexander, 113 n. 56
Ogilvie, James, 1st Earl of Seafield, 5, 11
Ogilvie, James, 2nd Earl of Seafield, 84, 125 n. 13 and 18
Ogilvie, James, Lord Deskford, 3rd Earl of Seafield, 13, 80, 84, 86, 87, 88, 93, 100, 104, 105
Ogilvie, Skene, 98
Ogilvie, William, 86, 87, 93, 95, 101, 130 n. 82, 138, 144
Orem, William, 43
Osborn (or Osborne), James, 30, 31, 145
Osborn, John, 56, 57, 58, 139, 145

Paine, Thomas, 8
Paterson, John, 19
Paterson, Principal Robert, 19, 28, 29, 30, 32, 34
Paterson, Robert, 67, 145
Paton, John, 50, 62
Peacock, George, 28, 32, 34, 145
Pelham, Henry, 72
Pelham-Holles, Thomas, 1st Duke of Newcastle under Lyme, 62, 69, 71, 84
Perth, 4th Earl and 1st Duke of (see James Drummond)
Pitcairne, Archibald, 21, 22, 30
Pitt, William, 92, 93
Pollock, Robert, 70, 72, 139, 146
Polwarth, Lord (see Patrick Home)
Pringle, Robert, 38

Queensberry, 1st Duke of (see William Douglas)

Raeburn, Sir Henry, 75
Rait, Alexander, 60, 62, 63, 64, 65, 66, 118 n. 89, 137, 144
Ramsay, Sir Alexander, 59
Ramsay, Allan, 44
Ramsay, Robert, 114 n. 9
Ramsay Irvine, Sir Alexander, 92, 128 n. 57
Ramsay, Lairds of Balmaine, 135

Reid, Thomas, 59, 68, 69, 75, 76, 81, 82, 83, 84, 86, 100, 137, 138, 144
Richardson, Jonathan, 33
Robertson, Alexander, 65
Robertson, John, 83
Robertson, William, 80, 104, 105
Rose, [?Hugh] of Kilravock, 38, 113 n. 56
Ross, John of Arnage, 31
Ross, John, 86, 87, 138, 144
Rothes, 9th Earl of (see John Leslie)
Roxburghe, 1st Duke of (see John Kerr)

St Andrews University, xiii, 2, 3, 5, 6, 8, 10, 32, 36, 47, 53, 58, 73, 93, 104, 105, 106
Scot, David, 97, 122 n. 53
Scott, Henry, 3rd Duke of Buccleuch, 4
Scott, James, 45
Scott, Robert Eden, 97, 126 n. 30, 130 n. 81, 144
Scougal, Henry, 18, 19, 29
Scougal, James, 18, 19
Scougal, John, 19
Scougal, Patrick, 18, 19
Seafield, 1st Earl of (see James Ogilvy)
Seton, Sir Alexander, 30
Sharp, John, 26
Sibbald, Patrick, 29, 145
Sibbald, Sir Robert, 21
Simpson, William, 25, 63, 136, 144
Skene, family of, 18
Skene, David, 90, 123 n. 60
Skene, Francis, 59, 65, 66, 69, 72, 73, 82, 83, 105, 119 n. 23, 122 n. 56, 126 n. 40, 139, 146
Skene, Dr George, 72, 73, 90, 93, 104, 105, 126 n. 40, 122 n. 56, 128 n. 59, 129 n. 75, 143, 146
Skene, George of Skene, 65
Smith, Adam, 30, 105
Smith, William, 25, 29, 30, 32, 34, 113 n. 61, 144, 145
Stair, 2nd Earl of (see John Dalrymple)
Steuart, Sir James, 39
Stewart, family of, 4
Stewart, James, 5th Earl of Galloway, 28
Stewart, John, 51, 52, 53, 55, 65, 69, 72, 139, 146
Stewart, Robert, 51, 52, 54, 56, 57
Stirling, John, 5, 31, 36, 38, 40, 47, 113 n. 56

INDEX

Strachan, Alexander, 64
Stuart, John, 3rd Earl of Bute, 7, 13, 35, 78, 80, 81, 84, 85, 87, 89, 90, 91, 92, 93, 95, 96, 100, 102, 104, 105, 127 n. 43 and 48
Stuart, John, 127 n. 42, 128 n. 57, 146
Stuart-Mackenzie, James, 78, 104
Sydney, 1st Viscount (*see* Thomas Townshend)

Tassie, James, 68
Thom, William, 81, 82, 83, 86, 87, 98, 126 n. 29, 138, 144
Thomson (or Thompson), Alexander, 43
Thomson, Andrew I, 29
Thomson, Andrew II, 64
Thomson, James (poet), 91
Thomson, James of Portlethen, 63, 64, 66, 83
Thomson, Walter, 64
Townshend, Thomas, 1st Viscount Sydney, 95, 127 n. 43
Trail, William, 90, 91, 146
Tullideph, Thomas, 5
Turnbull, George, 38, 47, 51, 76, 104, 139, 145
Turner, George, 66
Turner, W, 129 n. 78

Tweeddale, 4th Marquis of (*see* John Hay)

Udney, James, 65
Urquhart, James, 23, 24, 25, 26, 32, 34, 136, 143
Urquhart, Patrick, 19, 23, 24, 25, 32, 34, 136, 143

Verner (or Warner), David I, 12, 36, 47, 48, 55, 65, 66, 67, 72, 76, 116 n. 51, 120 n. 24 and 32, 139, 145
Verner, David II, 72

Walkinshaw, James, 21
Wallace, Matthew, 122 n. 53
Wallace, Mr, 54
Wallace, Robert, 5, 38, 58
Walpole, Sir Robert, 6, 12, 38, 45, 50, 60, 63, 67, 68
Warner, David (*see* Verner)
Whitfield (or Whitefield), George, 60
Wigton, Earl of (*see* John Fleming)
Wilkes, John, 13
William III, 8, 9, 10, 20, 23, 30
Wilson, Patrick, 83
Wodrow, Alexander, 36
Wodrow, James, 36
Wodrow, Robert, 30, 60